Workers of War and Empire from New France to British America, 1688–1783

McGill-Queen's Studies in Early Canada / Avant le Canada

Series Editors / Directeurs de la collection : Allan Greer and Carolyn Podruchny

This series features studies of the history of the northern half of North America – a vast expanse that would eventually be known as Canada – in the era before extensive European settlement and extending into the nineteenth century. Long neglected, Canada-before-Canada is a fascinating area of study experiencing an intellectual renaissance as researchers in a range of disciplines, including history, geography, archeology, anthropology, literary studies, and law, contribute to a new and enriched understanding of the distant past. The editors welcome manuscripts in English or French on all aspects of the period, including work on Indigenous history, the Atlantic fisheries, the fur trade, exploration, French or British imperial expansion, colonial life, culture, language, law, science, religion, and the environment.

Cette série de monographies est consacrée à l'histoire de la partie septentrionale du continent de l'Amérique du Nord, autrement dit le grand espace qui deviendra le Canada, dans les siècles qui s'étendent jusqu'au début du 19e. Longtemps négligé par les chercheurs, ce Canada-avant-le-Canada suscite beaucoup d'intérêt de la part de spécialistes dans plusieurs disciplines, entre autres, l'histoire, la géographie, l'archéologie, l'anthropologie, les études littéraires et le droit. Nous assistons à une renaissance intellectuelle dans ce champ d'étude axé sur l'interaction de Premières Nations, d'empires européens et de colonies. Les directeurs de cette série sollicitent des manuscrits, en français ou en anglais, qui portent sur tout aspect de cette période, y compris l'histoire des Autochtones, celle des pêcheries de l'Atlantique, de la traite des fourrures, de l'exploration, de l'expansion de l'empire français ou britannique, de la vie coloniale (la Nouvelle-France, l'Acadie, Terre-Neuve, les provinces maritimes, etc.), de la culture, de la langue, du droit, des sciences, de la religion ou de l'environnement.

3 Listening to the Fur Trade
Soundways and Music in the British North American Fur Trade, 1760–1840
Daniel Robert Laxer

4 Heirs of an Ambivalent Empire
French-Indigenous Relations and the Rise of the Métis in the Hudson Bay Watershed
Scott Berthelette

5 The Possession of Barbe Hallay
Diabolical Arts and Daily Life in Early Canada
Mairi Cowan

6 Enthusiasms and Loyalties
The Public History of Private Feelings in the Enlightenment Atlantic
Keith Shepherd Grant

7 Fashioning Acadians
Clothing in the Atlantic World, 1650–1750
Hilary Doda

8 Before Canada
Northern North America in a Connected World
Edited by Allen Greer

9 Regards sur l'âme en Nouvelle-France
Histoire des spiritualités individuelles et collectives en espace colonial
Sous la direction de Joy Palacios et Anne Régent-Susini

10 Workers of War and Empire from New France to British America, 1688–1783
Richard H. Tomczak

Workers of War and Empire from New France to British America, 1688–1783

RICHARD H. TOMCZAK

McGill-Queen's University Press
Montreal & Kingston • London • Chicago

ISBN 978-0-2280-2361-6 (cloth)
ISBN 978-0-2280-2362-3 (paper)
ISBN 978-0-2280-2363-0 (ePDF)
ISBN 978-0-2280-2364-7 (ePUB)

Legal deposit first quarter 2025
Bibliothèque nationale du Québec

Printed in Canada on acid-free paper that is 100% ancient forest free (100% post-consumer recycled), processed chlorine free

This book has been published with the help of a grant from the Federation for the Humanities and Social Sciences, through the Awards to Scholarly Publications Program, using funds provided by the Social Sciences and Humanities Research Council of Canada. Funding was also received from Stony Brook University.

We acknowledge the support of the Canada Council for the Arts.
Nous remercions le Conseil des arts du Canada de son soutien.

McGill-Queen's University Press in Montreal is on land which long served as a site of meeting and exchange amongst Indigenous Peoples, including the Haudenosaunee and Anishinabeg nations. In Kingston it is situated on the territory of the Haudenosaunee and Anishinaabek. We acknowledge and thank the diverse Indigenous Peoples whose footsteps have marked these territories on which peoples of the world now gather.

Library and Archives Canada Cataloguing in Publication

Title: Workers of war and empire from New France to British America, 1688–1783 / Richard H. Tomczak.
Names: Tomczak, Richard H., author.
Series: McGill-Queen's studies in early Canada ; 10.
Description: Series statement: McGill-Queen's studies in early Canada ; 10 | Includes bibliographical references and index.
Identifiers: Canadiana (print) 20240409469 | Canadiana (ebook) 20240409523 | ISBN 9780228023616 (cloth) | ISBN 9780228023623 (paper) | ISBN 9780228023647 (ePUB) | ISBN 9780228023630 (ePDF)
Subjects: LCSH: Labor—Canada—History—17th century. | LCSH: Labor—Canada—History—18th century. | LCSH: Corvée—Canada—History—17th century. | LCSH: Corvée—Canada—History—18th century. | LCSH: French-Canadians—History—17th century. | LCSH: French-Canadians—History—18th century.
Classification: LCC HD8105 .T66 2025 | DDC 331.097109/032—dc23

This book was designed and typeset by studio oneonone in Minion 11/14.
Copyediting by Joanne Richardson.

Contents

Figures

Abbreviations

AC Archives des Colonies

BANQ Bibliothéque et Archives Nationales du Québec

CMD *A History of the Organization, Development, and Services of the Military and Naval Forces of Canada from the Peace of Paris in 1763 to the Present Time*

CO Colonial Office Papers of Quebec

DHC *Debates of the House of Commons in the Year 1774 on the Bill for Making More Provision for the Government of the Province of Quebec*

DST *Documents Relating to the Seigniorial Tenure in Canada, 1598–1854*

HP Haldimand Papers (Sir Frederick Haldimand, unpublished papers)

JMC James Murray Collection

LAC Library and Archives Canada

RCQ Reports of the Councils of Quebec relating to Highways, Roads, and Bridges

Acknowledgments

I have benefitted from the insight and input of a great many people across the United States and Canada. While pursuing my PhD, my advisor Ned Landsman provided more suggestions than I could ever thank him for throughout my time at Stony Brook University. His guidance through research, writing, and many presentations helped me build a broader intellectual framework. Most important, perhaps, he always encouraged me to think about the "big picture" as I too often got stuck in the archives. I would still be articulating what my research is even about if it weren't for Jennifer Anderson, who sat me down and helped me (many times) write to clarify my topic. Kathleen Wilson instructed my cohort's dissertation prospectus, and I have to thank her for the many suggestions over those fifteen weeks that pulled the research into focus. Jean-François Lozier not only brought extremely valuable input for the French and French Canadian side of this project but also supervised my Fulbright Canada Fellowship. He took the time to provide me with a condensed oral examination list of French-language secondary sources that sculpted my research in its early stages.

Many people assisted with the feedback necessary for transforming a dissertation into a monograph. Allan Greer got in touch with me a year after I had finished my dissertation and suggested turning it into a book for this series. He provided helpful guidance at that earliest of stages. Cole Jones, Sean Gallagher, and Jennifer Anderson all presented with me in our panel "Workers of War" (to which this book owes its title) at the inaugural "For 2026: Revolutionary Legacies" conference hosted by William & Mary and the Omohundro Institute for Early American History and Culture. They encouraged me to cast this topic within the much broader context of the Atlantic World, and Paul Mapp, the chair of our panel, offered useful feedback on how corvée fit into the American Revolution. Special thanks to Christian Crouch, Donald Fyson, and Matthew Keagle, who provided critical edits and feedback in the final stages of copy-editing.

I discovered the topic of corvée while working at Fort Ticonderoga on an Edward W. Pell Fellowship. In addition to providing funding for the initial stages of research, the entire "Fort Ti" team deserves credit for encouraging me and pushing me creatively (even re-enacting corvée). Stuart Lilie, vice-president of public history, oversaw the project in these early stages and offered the necessary guidance towards sources. Matthew Keagle and Miranda Peters gave extensive feedback in the Thompson-Pell archives. Rich Strum was committed to the project ever since I arrived in Ticonderoga that summer, and I have to thank him for organizing the conferences to present my research. In addition, thanks to the 2015 Interpretative Team – Nick, Gib, Jana, Zech, and Margaret – for humouring me in my endless musings on Marx and corvée labour.

This book has benefitted from several sources of funding that made my research possible. The Gardiner Foundation on Long Island funded the first year of my doctoral studies at Stony Brook. The International Council of Canadian Studies awarded me a scholarship to pursue preliminary research in Ottawa and Montreal. Jennifer Green at Stony Brook went out of her way to help me receive a Fulbright Canada Fellowship – and for that I am in her debt. While in Ottawa, in addition to Jean-François, many others helped me in my ten-month research excursion in Canada. Michelle Emond, Fulbright Canada's program officer for students, not only offered useful advice for navigating Ottawa but also encouraged me to take up interests in the region. David Thompson shared an office with me and provided great conversation on Canadian labour history. Back in the States, Kathy Ludwig and Meg McSweeney at the David Library of the American Revolution helped me immensely in my one-month stay at the archives in Washington's Crossing. Finally, the last stages of this book were made possible by a Fine Arts, Humanities, and Social Sciences Research Award granted by the College of Arts and Sciences at Stony Brook University.

Two earlier versions of chapters appeared in peer-reviewed journals, and I would like to acknowledge all of the hard work that went into formatting and copy-editing those pieces to bring them up to publication quality. At *Labour/Le Travail*, Kathy Killoh, Joan Sangster, and Charles Smith coordinated the peer-review reports, editing, and image placement. That article would be nowhere near as polished if not for the time they put into helping me. Portions of an article published in the *Journal of Colonialism and Colonial History* are also here in the manuscript, and Clare Anderson and Kellie Moss provided guidance throughout that process. In both cases, I also want to acknowledge the time and effort of the peer reviewers who provided the feedback, revisions, and suggestions that made the publications possible.

At McGill-Queen's University Press, Kyla Madden shepherded this manuscript through each stage and coordinated the review process. I'd like to thank the two anonymous peer reviewers for their close attention to detail, suggestions, and feedback. The readers' immensely helpful critiques enabled me to substantially revise the manuscript's framing materials and to reshape each chapter to ensure that these parts cohere into a compelling whole. Kathleen Fraser, Elena Goranescu, Filomena Falocco, and Paloma Friedman formed part of the editing, production, marketing, and administrative team behind this book and helped to make this book a reality. I want to especially thank my copy-editor, Joanne Richardson, for her close attention to detail and thoughtful suggestions throughout the entire manuscript.

Countless people at Stony Brook provided me with opportunities to engage with a wide range of disciplines, teaching strategies, and professional development. April Masten provided a crash course in writing history during my first year in the doctoral program. Shobana Shankar and Alix Cooper both taught research seminars in which I wrote the earliest of early drafts that would later become important components to this book. Elizabeth Newman offered a workshop on working with archival sources that I ended up utilizing during my time in Canada. Brooke Larson introduced me to an entire genre of labour history in the colonial Andes, which formed the bedrock of how I write history. I can't thank her enough for supervising a directed reading seminar and serving on my oral examinations committee. From Stony Brook to Ottawa, to Oneonta, and back to Stony Brook, the studies from that directed reading are always on my bookshelf.

My friends and family have provided the emotional support necessary to make this project the best it could be. Back home in Western New York, Marc and Becky hosted me plenty of times as I made my way home, and they listened attentively as I filled them in on the progress of the manuscript. Michael and Marissa Deci helped me every step of the way, whether it involved navigating doctoral programs, moving away from Western New York, or finding some good vinyl to put on while working. It goes without saying that I would have never pursued a PhD in history without my mother, father, and brother, who have constantly provided words of encouragement through my undergraduate years, graduate school, and navigating the job market afterwards. Finally, I would be nowhere without my wife, Georgia LaMair, who could probably recite my "elevator pitch" on corvée just as well as I can. Her support pulled me through the most challenging moments to say the least. Her belief in me from the beginning made this entire project possible. This book is dedicated to my son Ren, who I can only hope loves researching corvée as much as I do.

Workers of War and Empire from New France to British America, 1688–1783

Introduction

Throughout the eighteenth century, the French and British Empires mobilized thousands of labourers based on feudal social arrangements in Canada. This understudied form of mandatory labour, referred to as *corvée*, was introduced by the French to Canada but was later exploited by the British. Rooted in the feudal obligations of peasants to aristocratic landowners, corvée was adapted to the American context both to extract labour from colonists and to implement public works, such as building roads and bridges. Following the Seven Years' War, the British took over Quebec and, recognizing the need for labour power in an underpopulated region, co-opted the corvée system for their own imperial ends. While retaining some French statutes, British colonial officials enacted new laws mobilizing the male inhabitants to work in state enterprises (such as iron mining and logging) and to provide support services for the military. During the American Revolution, the British Army's surging demand for workers in Quebec precipitated widespread protests. This crisis forced the royally appointed governor to ratify a new provincial code regulating the use of corvée.

This book chronicles the transformation of corvée over nine decades in French and British North America. Although a major focus of this project is untangling the labour arrangements that propped up the Canadian colonial state, it also sheds light on the evolution of French Canadians' work routines, the rhythms of their agricultural lives, and their responses to corvée policy. While the French experimented with the mass use of corvée on fortifications – policies that mirrored public works in Europe – at the local level seigneurs and habitants exerted autonomy in dictating the proper distribution of the parish's work. Under French rule in Canada, local leaders built in several safety-valves, such as the parish assembly, that mitigated corvée exploitation. Even though habitants sometimes threatened mutiny over working conditions, the custom never evolved into a particularly burdensome institution. The British, on the other hand, needed corvée to become an integral part of their imperial economic strategy in the post–Seven Years' War recession. British colonial officials attempted to centralize authority over corvée and manipulated pre-existing labour relationships to draft habitants into a number of economic enterprises. By the end of the American Revolution, British corvée appeared more as a coerced form of wage labour than as a bothersome public service.

The Canadian corvée custom of labour that the British appropriated in 1759 developed throughout the seventeenth and eighteenth centuries largely through an uneasy amalgamation of royal orders from Versailles and local legislation based on the needs of each individual community. In early eighteenth-century New France, no uniform legal definition of corvée existed. Instead, corvée as a form of statute labour largely differed from parish to parish, and seigneurie to seigneurie. Corvée was first and foremost an obligation required of male tenants based on their title deed or by the needs of the Crown.[1] As a result, the rigours associated with corvée and the responses of habitants also changed based on the demands placed on each community by the unique characteristics of environment, geography, and their seigneur.

Canadian habitants inherited three interconnected obligations of corvée from French legal tradition in the *ancien régime*. The first form, *corvée seigneuriale*, stemmed from the relationship between lord and peasant. Habitants of a seigneur's property negotiated a contract in which the individual provided economic services for a portion of the land. Generally, habitants owed two to three days of labour throughout the year on the lord's demesne as part of this agreement.[2] This corvée consisted of mandatory work performed by the tenant of a seigneur's property.[3] Habitants typically used corvée on the lord's demesne as a substitution for a lack of money or surplus harvest to cover the costs of the title deed.[4]

Second, *corvée général*, or *corvée royal*, required habitants to build public works in the name of the king.[5] In both France and Canada, *corvée général* usually took place on the royal highways (*grand chemins*).[6] *Corvée général* typically consisted of five to six days of work in the form of manual labour or driving horse teams to the project sites. In Canada, this levy constantly evolved in accordance with the demands of settlement in the New World. Civil and royal officials commanded habitants to construct roads and bridges that connected remote parishes to mercantile centres. These orders also tended to include mundane public works required for settling land, such as erecting fences and digging ditches. By 1722, the redistricting of seigneuries into parishes also necessitated the construction of churches by corvée.[7]

Several characteristics differentiated Canadian *corvée général* from its French counterpart. In the absence of a *parlement*, *régie*, or provincial "estates," the civil administration of New France oversaw the distribution of most road building orders.[8] In France, engineers followed royal *instructions*, or recommendations, that Crown officials imposed on highways.[9] These pamphlets often dictated the desired route in addition to the tactics that the engineers should use to construct each road. In Canada, however, road construction was more decentralized and mutable at the parish level. Orders of corvée labour stemmed from the intendant (in charge of the civil administration) and filtered down to the grand voyer (the royal surveyor). The grand voyer employed sous-voyers, engineers who met with local leaders in each parish to ensure that the project met the needs of the community. While royally appointed engineers oversaw labour on the highways, the management of corvée fell to the militia captains, principal residents, and the local churchwardens.

Third, metropolitan and colonial officials requisitioned Canadian habitants on *corvée militaire*.[10] Under this obligation, during wartime or periods of martial emergency, officials expected habitants to work up to fifteen days on the construction of fortifications and supply transportation. This primarily took the form of building stone fortifications in Quebec, Montreal, and Chambly, but it also included the construction of communication roads and auxiliary tasks that the military required. For colonial and metropolitan officials, corvée militaire acted as a subsidized labour force to support chronically underfunded construction projects. Habitants, however, resisted or threatened protest when they deemed that the state had violated their local labour arrangements.

A diverse cast of elites and colonial agents called upon each of these three variations of corvée. In Canada, the seigneurial landowning class consisted of aristocrats descended from the Company of New France, lesser nobles seeking land in the New World, upstart civil administrators, veteran military officers, and even well-to-do, opportunistic habitants.[11] Despite each having a claim to nobility, seigneurs were quite stratified even among their own rank. Wealthy families consolidated the most arable land, positions of authority, and royal titles that passed on to their male heirs.[12] While they owned seigneuries – a privilege impossible for many in France – most of the "nobles" lived comparatively modest provincial lifestyles, relying on their habitants to eke out some modicum of wealth in the New World. The Canadian ecclesiastical authorities, especially the Jesuits, also owned seigneuries and thus had access to corvée labour.[13] All of these individuals were vassals and owned land *en fief*, by the grace of the king.

This book is mostly concerned with the evolution of the methods royal and civil officials used to harness corvée labour. This group consisted of a wide range of officers, bureaucrats, and ministers of the Crown. In some cases, these individuals were seigneurs and administered land of their own in conjunction with their royal duties.[14] The office most associated with Canadian corvée under the French was the intendant, the top civil official in New France and the person charged with running its day-to-day operations. While the governor obviously exerted influence over corvée, especially through directives given by Versailles, the intendant drafted ordinances and relayed them to his lesser officers. The Office of the Grand Voyer (the royal surveyor of roads), in particular, became an important office for mobilizing corvée labour in rural parishes.[15]

The habitant's obligation to his superiors was deeply embedded in the social structure of New France. Metropolitan ministers, governors, intendants, and seigneurs expected obedience. Moreover, in conjunction with the fortifications, roads, and bridges the habitants constructed, corvée was a power-laden act that symbolically reinforced their subordinate position in the king's North American colony. In other words, corvée represented demonstrations of their obedience to authority and the fulfilment of the obligations specified in their titles of concession.[16]

*

In this book I address three themes that shed light on the processes of imperial governance in the eighteenth century. First, I investigate the development of Canadian corvée in the French Atlantic. After the brief siege of Quebec (1690) exposed the colony's weak defences, royal ministers in Versailles embarked on a massive overhaul of the region's fortifications, roads, and bridges using corvée labour.[17] Distance from royal oversight ultimately allowed habitants to challenge authority when they felt administrators had violated their local customs. When annually drafted into forced labour for the construction of Quebec's and Montreal's fortifications, habitants "negotiated" relief from excessive or especially onerous assignments and, failing that, collectively discussed mutiny if conditions did not improve.[18] Canadian corvée protests connected workers to a transatlantic culture of resisting mandatory labour sanctioned by the French Crown.

Second, this study illuminates the architecture of British colonial state formation in Quebec. More than most regions of the North American colonies, Quebec experienced the economic and cultural shocks of the centralized, bureaucratic administrative reforms of the British fiscal-military state.[19] Indeed, the Treaty of Paris, 1763, incorporated approximately seventy thousand Roman Catholic colonists of French descent and numerous sovereign Native American nations into a burgeoning empire that Britons had previously imagined as largely Protestant, anglophone, maritime, and free.[20] In order to govern these foreign populations, Parliament appropriated New France's pre-existing labour arrangements, which had long shaped the lives of its people. The British retained French offices, which traditionally organized corvée labour in the parishes. To make the population more legible for administration from the metropole, Parliament took measures to identify and categorize these subjects, most notably through censuses and surveys that quantified rural parishes' labouring potential.[21] Most important, the investigations into local social relations laid the foundation for a hybrid labour regime that adopted and standardized the corvée system, albeit now in the service of British imperial rule.

Finally, this book investigates the habitants' responses to French and British colonial labour policies. Under both regimes, habitants exercised several effective tactics to minimize exploitation or overwork at the hands of colonial agents. Generally, under the French, habitants petitioned the governmental courts (Montreal, Trois-Rivières, and Quebec) to assert their concerns regarding corvée obligations. This process was typically conducted as a parish, with an "assembly of habitants," represented by three "principal" residents vocalizing their grievances or discontent.[22] During large-scale work projects, such as the construction of fortifications, habitants notably also neglected to show up for corvée, argued with their militia officers over the legality of the labour system, or outright refused to work. Canadian officials referred to these tactics as the "spirit of mutiny" and attempted to avoid conflict by scaling back the amount of time an individual had to work.[23]

The hostile change in regimes brought important changes to habitants' strategies of resistance. Indeed, habitants did not stand idly by as British Parliament and the Crown ratified legislation that affected their working lives. In particular, the British colonial state established a direct link between policy and the appropriation of their labour. Over time, the governor and his officers eliminated the parish assembly as a local source of mitigation and marginalized the seigneur's position as an intermediary of state orders. In response, habitants collectively organized, used the newly established common law courts, and submitted petitions to obtain retribution for their grievances related to corvée.

In French Canada, the turmoil of the American invasion of Quebec (1775) and later the American Revolutionary War (1775–83) led to a surging demand for labour in the province. British officials used the recently ratified Quebec Act as a foundation to conscript Canadians on corvée for military expeditions. Most notably, John Burgoyne's 1777 Northern Campaign required a corvée draft of labourers from all Canadian parishes to aid in the transportation of supplies and fortification construction. Habitant communities violently protested conscription in the military and demanded wages for their time spent serving professional British regiments. By the end of the war, petitions, court cases, and desertion forced the colonial administration to re-evaluate corvée labour policy, implementing restrictions on duration and instituting financial compensation.

Petitions from both habitants and seigneurs over the "extreme abuse of corvée" forced the new governor, Frederick Haldimand, to write a series of ordinances that set a standard duration and payment for habitant labour.[24] Corvée became embedded in the provincial legal code as "second class" work and remained this way until the abolition of seigneurial tenure in 1854.[25] The first two critical decades of British rule in Quebec highlight the fraught social tensions that emerged as Parliament and the Crown integrated the conquered peoples into the empire. Habitants' ability to contest corvée illuminates not only the methods of resistance used by subordinate colonists but also the limits of the fiscal-military state in the eighteenth-century British Empire.[26]

*

The events discussed in this book primarily take place in a region that was appropriated from Indigenous nations, settled by French colonists, conquered by British military personnel, and redistricted by representatives in Parliament who, for the most part, had never set foot in the Americas. The borders of the St Lawrence Valley remained fluid as the territory passed from First Nation Canadians to French and then to British hands. Broadly speaking, this study focuses on the parishes and seigneuries along the St Lawrence River, a region heavily settled by the Company of New France in the early to mid-seventeenth century.[27]

At times, both French and British officials imagined utilizing corvée labour to provide the raw output of energy necessary for colonization in the woodlands of North America. For the French, the Champlain Valley represented a potential extension of their settlements in the St Lawrence and nearby Richelieu. Overlaying seigneurial cadastral maps on this region, Canadian officials viewed this area not only as a buffer against British encroachment but also as populated landholdings contributing to the economic prosperity of the empire.[28] Corvée loomed large over this process, and the French imagined a network of roads and fortifications stretching on either side of Lake Champlain that supplemented the fur trade of the St Lawrence and Pays d'en Haut.[29]

The British also envisioned corvée as a critical component of empire building. In the wake of the Conquest, political officials and diplomats wrote extensively on the potential uses of corvée. In reports to Parliament, each of the newly appointed military governors advocated for maintaining corvée and made explicit connections between the custom and imperial economic enterprise.[30] These ambitions came under threat during the American Revolution, and draughts of labourers served on supply routes stretching from the Gaspésie to the Great Lakes protecting the Upper Posts. They ferried goods to the borderlands of British territory in contested spaces where empires jostled for influence. In these ways, corvée played an important role in both the settled region of the St Lawrence and the parts of empire that extended into the borderlands.

From the earliest days of colonization, New France operated under the seigneurial regime, and thus corvée factored into the labouring capacity of the fledgling North American settlements. Indeed, as Benoît Grenier states, the seigneurie "was at the heart of the colonization process."[31] Canadian labour laws and administration followed the customs of France. By the early seventeenth century, France exhibited a robust legal tradition regarding land ownership and tenancy based on an amalgamation of royal orders, written seigneurial statutes, and unwritten social arrangements ironed out and refined through several centuries of local negotiations. At the seigneurial level, custom operated to transform a "legal norm recognized by a community of inhabitants" into a practised tradition.[32]

The king's orders clarified such local arrangements, standardizing each practice and forming a coherent, kingdom-wide code. The king's orders dealt "with the content of the custom and at the same time with the recognition of the public authority which validate[d] it."[33] As the legal historian Martin Grinberg argues, at the core of custom was "reciprocal consent, between the king and his representatives, and the people."[34] Custom served to bind peasants, seigneurs, and king together in mutually beneficial arrangements of governance and order.

Although customary laws maintained the language of "consent" and "reciprocity," seventeenth-century France was by no means egalitarian and functioned within a strict, rigid hierarchy of duty, honour, and obedience. Peasants owed seigneurs numerous obligations, such as corvée, and seigneurs owed fealty and tribute to the king. Locally, for peasants, the intersection of hierarchy and levies was felt most on the seigneuries, large estates operated by a lord and worked by inhabitants. Dues, in the form of labour (corvée), money (cens), and goods (banalités), were an essential characteristic of rural life in France. Customary civil law functioned to mitigate some of the exploitation an inhabitant could experience at the hands of his seigneur, and it allowed limited opportunities to challenge the elite in court to gain compensation for lost work or crops.[35] As E.P. Thompson states, custom maintains the "unwritten beliefs, sociological norms, and usages asserted in practice but never enrolled in any by-law."[36] On the local level, inhabitants wielded these customs, to the best of their ability, as protective measures against exploitive seigneurs to ensure that they upheld consent and reciprocity.

Following the practice of civil law in France, the Crown imported these seigneurial and royal customs into Canada. Similar to seventeenth-century France, royal surveyors subdivided the St Lawrence Lowland into parcelled seigneuries. Nobles, ecclesiastical authorities, or upstart civil administrators purchased these tracts of land *en fief* – by the grace of the king "or some from another lord in homage and subject to other charges."[37] Indeed, all land in New France was owned by the king. The Crown then partitioned these "distant lands through the delegated sovereignty of a proprietor or company," thus extending the monarchies' authority while allowing subjects "a stake in the property of the land."[38] These vassal landowners, titled seigneurs, further subdivided their land *en censive*. The smallholders, referred to as *censitaires* (or habitants in Canada), owed "a small annual sum," in addition to a mutation fine, "the lods et ventes, and additional rents and other charges."[39]

Habitant obligations in New France were not dictated by a monolithic seigneurial "system" but by a patchwork of customs, practices, and royal statutes that generated the various legal codes of the colony. Upon purchasing land from the seigneur, a habitant negotiated a title deed, which stipulated an agreed upon annual fee and a variety of dues and obligations. Calculated by the amount of occupied *arpents* of land, the habitant paid for rent, or cens, through a portion of his harvest or in coin.[40] This agreement between tenant and landlord derived from a private arrangement.[41] In conjunction with the rent paid directly to the landholder, the tenant also often agreed to a grist-mill banalité. This seigneurial monopoly stipulated that habitants should surrender "one-fourteenth of the grain processed" at the local mill.[42]

In 1664, King Louis XIV codified these arrangements into a colonial legal system, articulated in the Custom of Paris.[43] Importantly, the Custom reaffirmed the seigneur's ability to levy *droits extraordinaire*, those feudal privileges agreed upon by tenant and landholder in each title deed.[44] While comprehensive in compiling the array of local and kingdom-wide edicts of the empire, the Custom did leave significant openings for adaptation. Indeed, Greer highlights that "other tenure conditions and exactions could be added, by contractual agreement, to the baseline conditions legally applicable to all *censive* holdings."[45] While corvée, for example, was not directly mentioned in the articles, custom ensured that future title deeds that contained the labour system under *droits extraordinaire* kept tenants tied to that obligation.

The earliest uses of Canadian corvée were the responsibility of the seigneur. Although documents from the early and mid-seventeenth century are sparse, Marcel Trudel shows that habitants owed up to two days of corvée based on the seigneur's prerogative.[46] Although no strict, uniform legal definition of seigneurial corvée existed in the late seventeenth and early eighteenth centuries, the levy consisted primarily of agricultural labour performed in accordance with each individual title of concession. As a legal contract of landholding, these concessions also stipulated the feudal dues that habitants owed to their seigneur. As a result, corvée often appears in these documents and stipulates the type of agricultural labour that seigneurs expected habitants to perform as well as the number of days each individual habitant was expected to work on the seigneur's demesne.[47]

Seigneurial corvée typically conformed to the rhythm of crop rotation and the seasons. Last frost, usually in April, signalled a critical working period when habitants planted seeds for the year's crops. Habitants tended the crops from May to the end of August until the harvest began in earnest from September until the beginning of November.[48] In the summer months, habitants remained busy clearing land in anticipation of next year's planting, tending livestock, cutting wood for the winter, expanding the family farm with outbuildings, and observing the progress of the currently planted crops.[49]

Several documents provide insight into the experiences of habitants on seigneurial corvée. For example, a legal dispute over ownership of the Bouchard Islands, a series of small islands in the St Lawrence, required the Superior Council's clarification over which habitants owed fealty to each seigneur. Michel Bégon, the current intendant, decided that "the habitants must give their lord, seigneur Desjordy, the days of corvée mentioned in their concession titles" but that the seigneur should request the labour "at different times and separately" throughout the year. Furthermore, he asserted that "the seigneurs of this country make their tenants pay to them, while the seigneur makes them give days of corvée for everyone that sustains a possession" and that the seigneur can oblige "them to give him days on his estate." Bégon specified that each habitant owed the seigneur "three days, one in planting, one in the harvest," and one for the construction of buildings on the property, such as a mill. The titles of concession, duty, and obligation compelled habitants to fulfill these three days of labour, and the seigneur, parish priests, and captains of the militia oversaw the distribution of labour.[50]

Depending on the season or the amount of work that needed execution, the seigneur could request extra days of corvée. This especially occurred during wartime, when the demands of the military placed an extra burden on parishes. The seigneur expected the habitants to fulfill these demands. However, the intendant specified: "those who will have to give more than the three days labour during war shall be allowed to exempt corvée by giving 40 sols for each [day] provided that they pay cash for those who come to work for them." These arrangements between habitants were privately organized and the seigneur largely allowed them to pay others for their corvée as long as the work on the property was executed.[51] Each seigneur dictated different terms of concession, and the amount of time habitants spent performing corvée varied from seigneurie to seigneurie. In Saint Ours, for example, along with the expected agricultural duties, the seigneur required habitants to collect wood on the property.[52]

Several overlapping units of administration were grafted on top of each individual community. Within the seigneurie, clusters of *habitations*, or dwellings, formed a parish.[53] The parish represented the Roman Catholic Church's jurisdiction among the Canadian habitants.[54] Priests collected tithes and exerted limited, but influential, authority over habitants' day-to-day lives. Next, for communication purposes, seigneuries with similar geography were grouped into *côtes*.[55] Each côte contained a militia captain in charge of dispensing royal orders, collecting taxes, mobilizing corvée, and mustering the local forces.[56] The various côtes fell under the jurisdiction of one of the "governments" (i.e., administrative units) of New France. In the St Lawrence Valley, these governments consisted of Montreal, Trois-Rivières, and Quebec. The governor general administered New France and Quebec. He appointed two governors to manage affairs in the other governments.

Habitants also owed obligations to the colonial state and the Crown. In addition to corvée, habitants interacted with the colonial state primarily through the organization of the military. Historians have demonstrated that Louis XIV attempted to reform the French Empire and consolidate the authority of the Crown in overseas territories. As Kenneth J. Banks asserts, Louis XIV introduced "far-reaching administrative and political initiatives that directly recast the French Atlantic."[57] Indeed, he "re-organized his top echelon of administrators in 1661 so that four secretaries of state reported directly to him."[58] Moreover, Louis "insisted that all colonies be brought under direct royal jurisdiction and not remain in the provenance of companies." This reform also created the "Council of the Marine," which oversaw colonial government and policy-making.[59] Louis personally appointed each colonial governor and intendant in New France. As a result, labour, feudal dues, and military participation in Canada stemmed from the decisions made in Versailles. Habitants owed these dues to the Crown not only as a requirement of their land settlement but also as an inherent obligation embedded in a developing transatlantic legal system.[60]

The sum of these "feudal burdens" – cens, banalité, and corvée – weighed quite heavily on a population that primarily engaged in a subsistence-level existence.[61] Most of the crops that habitants harvested they consumed in the household, with any surplus traded to neighbours or sold for a meagre profit in local markets. Throughout the eighteenth century, under both the French and the British, corvée competed with the demands of agricultural life along the St Lawrence. Road building, fortification construction, and seigneurial corvée all competed with habitants' time, which, in Canada, demanded that most of their energy go towards working their farms. While their routines were punctuated by repeated calls of corvée from their superiors, it was mundane chores and agricultural routines that would have dominated the seigneurial calendar.

Depending on the region, habitants would also seek wage work to supplement their earnings, potentially further complicating the pool of labourers necessary for corvée. In Montreal, a young man could often find work in the fur trade as an *engagé* (indentured servant), later referred to as a *voyageur*, participating in the transportation of goods and supplies along the waterways connecting the Great Lakes. As Carolyn Podruchny writes, when surplus crops did not go "beyond their own means and seigneurial dues, they became anxious to find another source of tradeable products or a source of cash income, and they found it in the fur trade."[62] Temporary or seasonal participation in the transportation of supplies to the Great Lakes developed into a viable method of supplementing families that primarily lived at subsistence level.

At the seigneurial level, corvée thus formed a critical axis upon which habitants spent their time. It was, however, just one of many obligations and competing pressures that French Canadian men, and their families, had to contend with to forge a life in the New World. In the late seventeenth and early eighteenth centuries, habitants found themselves navigating a complex web of local interests that often intersected with larger imperial initiatives, such as road building or participation in the fur trade. French and British administrators saw corvée as a potential mechanism to mobilize labour in Canada; however, as both imperial regimes discovered, the success of such enterprises depended on willing habitant participation, which was often at odds with their well-being.

❋

Corvée policy adds considerably to a growing body of scholarship on the "entangled histories" of law and empire in the Atlantic World.[63] The labour customs provide much more than simply filling in what Laurent Dubois calls a "regrettable lacunae within the study of the French Atlantic."[64] The laws crafted by royal ministers, and enforced by Canadian administrators, sheds light on the strategies that Europeans used to coerce their subjects into an imperial workforce. In her comparative study on early modern legal regimes, Lauren Benton asserts, "the colonial state emerged in part out of legal politics engaging both colonizers and the colonized."[65] Corvée labourers, enslaved individuals of African descent, Indigenous nations, and indentured servants all acted within the rigid, exploitive, and often violent laws that Europeans imposed on their Atlantic colonies.

Habitants performed corvée within a spectrum of inequality that existed in the seventeenth- and eighteenth-century Atlantic World. Both the French and British required an enormous amount of labour – with varying degrees of coercion – to make their empires run. In the parishes and seigneuries of New France, corvée operated alongside the enslavement of First Nations communities and individuals of African descent.[66] Recent attention to Indigenous enslavement has shed light on France's efforts to install a racial hierarchy and the challenges that First Nations faced as they navigated increasingly restrictive laws that attempted to commodify them, reducing them to the status of property.[67]

Despite the complexity of obligations attached to migrants, servants, and enslaved individuals in New France, corvée labourers did work on specific projects that would have, in general, differentiated them from others in the community. Habitants eligible for corvée were landholders *en censive* – owing seigneurial and royal dues to their superiors as part of tenure. For this reason, nearly all Canadians performing corvée would have been white, adult males of French descent. Furthermore, corvée levies derived from the parish militia, indicating that men fulfilling corvée would have been between the ages of sixteen and sixty. Additionally, corvée tended to be short term and seasonal, aligning with critical time periods of agricultural routines. After the thaw, roads worn down over winter needed repair, and thus the moment after the completion of sowing came to be an important window for corvée in New France. Other tasks would have blurred the lines of corvée and other forms of labour. Church and mill construction, for example, would have required most people in the community to participate in assembling materials, with skilled craftspeople working alongside a pool of workers to raise the structure.

This book argues that habitants were far from peripheral to the French and British Atlantic. Under the French, they constructed the communication networks that supplied resources to the Crown's colonies in New Orleans and, more important, the sugar plantations of the Caribbean. Highways facilitated the movement of goods, people, and ideas, in addition to the colonial officials sent to North America. If the officials of New France wanted to transform the colony into an interconnected component of their burgeoning Atlantic Empire, the rural parishes of Canada had to connect to one another.

The work that habitants performed on infrastructure in Canada connected to a much larger system of coerced labour in the French Atlantic. Arad Gigi's recent scholarship, for example, shows that French colonizers in the Caribbean forewent seigneurial customs of corvée in favour of mobilizing the enslaved populations to build fortifications. A lack of *censitaires* and wage labourers in the sugar islands required plantation owners and metropolitan officials to agree to provide enslaved men for the construction of military outposts.[68] Military officers mobilized squads of enslaved individuals through the legal mechanism of corvée – the plantation owners pooled their captive workforce together to meet the labour requirements of the Crown. In the Lesser Antilles, enslaved individuals of African descent performed corvée alongside soldiers, indentured servants, and skilled craftspeople to erect the symbols of empires and to defend imperial landholdings from invaders.[69]

Following the Conquest, the British appropriated Canada's pre-existing labour policies, ironed out through decades of custom, protest, and legislation. For the British, the acquisition of Quebec signalled not only an enlarged empire in North America but also the plunder of France's economic enterprises. For newly arrived British officials, corvée held the same potential as the French had imagined through their tenure. They believed habitants could provide the labour to build roads, forts, and bridges to expand the economic influence of the colony. For this reason, the British set about braiding corvée into common law, creating the Committees on Highways, Roads, and Bridges to supervise mandatory labour. They also appropriated the Office of the Grand Voyer, installing a state-appointed surveyor to travel to each parish and ensure that habitants completed orders of corvée. Similar to the French before them, the British believed that the economic success of the colony depended in part on the mobilization of corvée labour for the construction of imperial infrastructure.

Importantly, the British did not impose a racial hierarchy upon white Canadians of French descent in the remnants of New France. Corvée, while mandatory for landowners *en censive*, always stemmed from the appropriation of French civil law, or what Governor Guy Carleton's lawyers defined as the "right of conquest."[70] Nevertheless, the British did target French Canadians for specific types of work and preserved the labour relationships necessary for corvée. Canadian parishes, while not regulated by the rigid racialized codes that dominated the Anglo-American colonies, were legally viewed as a culturally distinct population of people. As Carleton stated in a report to Parliament, Canadians were "not a migration of Britons, who brought with them the laws of England, but a populous and long-established colony."[71] The post-Conquest military governors, in particular, targeted labour laws and customs that they deemed potentially useful for integrating Quebec into their Atlantic empire.

Manipulating corvée customs for new imperial ends highlights many of the contradictions in the British Atlantic. Historians have characterized the eighteenth century as anglophone, maritime, and free from arbitrary authority.[72] The fiction that this cultural community ever existed burst at the seams after the Seven Years' War. Britain's imperial acquisitions in Florida, Quebec, and India, as Kathleen Wilson asserts, generated "commercial and territorial peripheries" that ultimately "fostered increased governmental regulation of the transoceanic economy."[73] British administrators struggled to integrate seigneurial law into a provincial code for Quebec. Corvée and the seigneurial regime provided a sharp contrast with legal arguments circulating around the British Atlantic in the post–Seven Years' War era. Indeed, while anglophone colonists celebrated their freedom from arbitrary authority, the British imposed feudal labour drafts on French Canadians that forced them to work for up to ten days at a time on public works.[74]

The transatlantic conversations between officials, under the British and French regimes, highlights the ambiguities embedded in colonial labour legislation. On one hand, Versailles struggled to import labour customs that depended on hundreds of years of obligation to royal authority; on the other hand, Britain incorporated this feudal holdover into an empire that they themselves believed was Protestant, maritime, and free from such arbitrary authority. Generations of habitants added to the chorus of voices arguing over the characteristics of corvée. The laws put into place by the French and British shed light on colonial experimentation with mandatory labour in North America and the larger Atlantic World.

*

Workers of War and Empire puts French Canadian workers front and centre in the narrative. Corvée labourers often did not have input into how the colonial state viewed their well-being. Decisions made in Paris and London rippled across the Atlantic and played out in the small, rural communities of the St Lawrence Valley. While the colonial officials that penned this legislation may not have taken into consideration the habitants' opinions on corvée, this study places those workers and their families at the centre of the narrative. Ultimately, this approach hopes to capture the workers' interpretation of these law codes, in war and peacetime, and the methods they used to voice their experiences.

Reconstructing power relations among the French royal ministers, British conquerors, Canadian seigneurs, and the rural-dwelling habitants presents the historian with the particular problem of capturing the subaltern voices embedded within official documentation. Indeed, an overwhelming majority of the records that recounted the mobilization of corvée labour derive from the literate elite. While the orders that shaped everyday life under the French and British regimes stemmed from this privileged, primarily urban group, few of them were directly involved with the implementation of policy in the countryside. Seigneurs who pledged fealty to the conquerors obliged the British in their orders, but these documents also succumb to what James C. Scott refers to as the "public transcript," or the "public performance of those subject to elaborate and systematic forms of social subordination."[75] The *foy et homage* (the ceremony of feudal homage), for example, represented the "theatrical imperatives that normally prevail in situations of domination" and produced a sanitized narrative of "how the dominant group would wish to appear" in the records.[76]

Habitant protests were not spontaneous events. Letters to and from Versailles and London attest to the "hidden transcripts" in Canadian parishes. Although authored by the elite, these documents provide evidence of the habitants' "offstage speeches, gestures, and practices that confirm, contradict, or inflect what appears" in official discourse.[77] To that end, I examine correspondence, parliamentary debates, and diaries of seigneurs to illuminate the everyday forms of resistance that occurred during the first two decades of British rule. For example, petitions submitted to the district courts provide a collective voice for Canadian farmers and assert in official language that "their quiescence and loyalty will be assured if only the lord abides by their understanding of the hierarchal social contract."[78] In other words, French and British hegemony in Canada was a "language of contention" in which habitants understood the boundaries of imperial authority and voiced discontent, both publicly and privately, when their subsistence was threatened.[79]

Statistical analyses of nearly six decades of work orders, seigneurial account books, and census records provide supplementary evidence to the causes of Canadian unrest. Detailed census records of the French and British regimes enable a partial reconstruction of the depreciation of wages and agrarian surplus value that occurred after the Seven Years' War. Demographic analysis also highlights the correlation between coercion, economic disruption, and migration in the rural hinterlands. Over the long run, evidence from the papers of the grand voyer attests to a distinctive transition from a bothersome public service under French rule to wage labour under British rule.

This book also consults the *Québec Gazette* to examine military ordinances and to gauge public opinion. Similar to other eighteenth-century colonial presses, the bilingual *Gazette* was designed in part to alert the inhabitants to imperial laws and ordinances. Indeed, during the American Revolution, Guy Carleton frequently issued orders of corvée through the *Gazette*. As a medium of imperial ideological formation, the newspaper "consolidated the political order by giving it rigorously elaborated cultural expression," and it provides critical evidence relating to the formation of the "public transcript" in wartime Canada.[80]

*

Corvée, like many other forms of compulsory labour, adapted to new circumstances as European colonies grew and matured. Warfare, conquest, and revolution shaped and reshaped the types of work that the colonial elite called upon French Canadians to perform. To capture how this labour system changed, and its effects on workers, I subdivide the chronology of corvée into three distinct experiences. Part 1 focuses on the first several generations of migrants and Canadian-born inhabitants who witnessed the initial major adaptations to corvée. In the first two chapters, I examine how corvée labour operated under French rule and the tactics habitants utilized to resist mandatory labour. Following the Nine Years' War, French and Canadian officials mobilized corvée for massive fortification projects. Habitants challenged the execution of these orders and argued that the customs of corvée in France did not apply to Canada. In the second chapter, I survey how the elite refined the mechanisms of labour mobilization in New France. Taking into account habitant social unrest, from 1732 to 1759, corvée operated as a labour force for large-scale, state-sanctioned projects, but it also took into consideration the rhythm of agricultural life that habitants required for subsistence. In sum, corvée under the French generated a delicate bond of consent between the colonial state and habitants.

Next, I tackle the mid-eighteenth-century generations of French Canadians who experienced large-scale colonial projects, the fallout of the Seven Years' War, and the early years of British rule in Quebec. Part 2 covers the first two decades of British rule in Quebec and the increased centralization over corvée labour in North America. Chapter 3 investigates British administrators' first encounters with corvée and their utilization of the labour system for the extraction of natural resources. Chapter 4 focuses on the legislative reform instigated by Governor Guy Carleton and the social unrest caused by the American invasion of Canada. Through imperial law, Parliament generated a direct linkage between the state and habitant, increasingly marginalizing the position of seigneurs as intermediaries.

The final two chapters in Part 3 focus on the political turmoil of the American Revolution and how that conflict shaped corvée for men conscripted into service by the British. Chapter 5 assesses the largest use of corvée in the early British period. During Lieutenant General John Burgoyne's 1777 Campaign, he attached corvée labourers to the military and brought habitants with him on his expedition to Albany. Finally, chapter 6 tackles the closing years of the American Revolution. In the wake of the Northern Campaign, the new governor, Frederick Haldimand, mobilized corvée for labour on the supply lines running west to the Pays d'en Haut. Haldimand's attempts to coerce habitants on corvée resulted in widespread protest and would ultimately form the foundation for labour laws in Canada after the war.

PART 1

The French Atlantic, 1688–1759

I propose that it would be appropriate according to custom in such occasions in this country to order the harnesses and carriages of the city with some tip-carts to transport the soil and carry out the works.

– Louis de La Porte de Louvigny, 21 October 1706, Quebec, AC, C11A, vol. 25, p. 26, LAC (transcript)

Figure 1.1
Claude-Joseph Vernet, *La construction d'un grand chemin* (1774).

The painting masterfully catches the burst of activity that took place during corvée on a bridge and highway in the French countryside. Similar activity would have taken place in Canada on the Chemin du Roy – the hauling of rubble, laying of stones, and clearing of debris from the road. The tools Canadian habitants would have used are represented here as well and include the horse-drawn tipcarts, wheelbarrows, pickaxes, and hammers. This painting captures the social dynamics of corvée: on one hand it was a defined system of hierarchy and subordination, and on the other, it was a community coming together to complete a project.

CHAPTER 1

Fortifications, Roads, and Bridges, 1688–1731

INTRODUCTION

On 6 November 1714, Michel Bégon, the intendant of New France, ordered all habitants of the seigneuries surrounding Montreal to quarry and transport limestone for construction of a wall by corvée. During autumn, habitants were "employed to draw the stone from the quarries and to amass it on the fields" while a second corvée of horse teams hauled the materials to the city.[1] By August 1717, the habitants of Longueuil, a seigneurie on the opposite side of the St Lawrence River from Montreal, had yet to fulfill their obligation. As a result, Philippe de Rigaud, Marquis de Vaudreuil, the governor of New France, decided to travel to Longueuil with several soldiers to personally direct the mobilization of labour.[2]

When Vaudreuil arrived, several habitants armed with their muskets greeted him and refused his order of corvée. To subdue the community, Vaudreuil called a meeting in the seigneur's house of all habitants, where he told them "to imitate the habitants of the other côtes." In a letter recalling the events, he described this attempt as "useless because among them were mutineers who spoiled the spirit of others." Tensions escalated when a group of habitants voluntarily left with the governor's armed guard. The mutineers, believing they would soon be imprisoned, "left the house in a crowd and gathered their weapons." Ten of these mutineers went back to their homes, where they barricaded themselves with their muskets overnight. Vaudreuil, seeing "little submission of this people," returned to Montreal to decide how to prevent outright revolt. The parish priest, Seigneur Longueuil, and four of the principal habitants travelled to Montreal and pleaded leniency for the mutineers, who eventually surrendered and spent two months in the dungeons of Montreal.[3]

Notwithstanding the relatively peaceful end to this protest, the episode illustrates the dramatic forms of habitant contestation of corvée in Canada. This chapter examines the evolution of corvée labour in the early eighteenth-century St Lawrence Valley. The Custom of Paris had articulated the uses of corvée in the New World, and the creation of the grand voyer formalized this obligation on roads and bridges in larger settlements. Still, labour remained primarily agricultural and local to the needs of each seigneurie. Large-scale colonial warfare, however, ushered in a new era of corvée in Canada. From the Nine Years' War (1688) to the construction of the Chemin du Roy (1732), colonial officials experimented with mass corvée labour mobilization. The brief English siege of Quebec (1690) exposed the colony's weak defences and lack of communications infrastructure. As a result, metropolitan royal ministers and colonial officials embarked on a massive overhaul of the region's fortifications, roads, and bridges. They agreed that habitants would provide the majority of this labour by corvée.

Ministers in Versailles mobilized Canadian corvée labour for the construction of fortifications and roads as part of a broader royal scheme to extend the authority of the monarchy in the French Empire. In the late seventeenth century, King Louis XIV ordered the construction of a network of massive fortifications on France's eastern border as a buffer to protect recently acquired territory and to impose his prerogative on his royal subjects. In France, the mobilization of corvée relied heavily on the mechanisms of authority embedded in royal statutes and the strength of the seigneurial system.[4] Politically influential ministers, economically powerful seigneurs, and tax collectors fulfilled Louis XIV's orders and coerced the rural population into corvée for these projects by appealing to the peasants' feudal dues to the Crown.

The construction of fortresses and roads in New France correlated with the king's overhaul of royal authority in the metropole. The onset of the Nine Years' War (1688–97) and the siege of Quebec in 1690 convinced ministers in Versailles that the North American colony was vulnerable to English attack. In the aftermath of the siege, envoys and engineers from Paris arrived fully equipped not only with the plans to refortify the St Lawrence city but also with the understanding that they would mobilize the population according to the terms of corvée. Orders of corvée on this project mostly emulated those of Louis XIV. Indeed, ministers and colonial officials expected to call upon the same obligation habitants owed to the Crown as did peasants in France. Chronically underfunded, their plans for the Quebec fortifications relied upon the willingness of habitants to cease their agricultural work, travel from their dwellings to the city, and work ten- to fifteen-day rotations digging earthwork structures and guiding horse teams to the construction site.

To be sure, royal ministers and Canadian civil officials did not make strategic decisions on corvée policies without considering the mechanisms of authority imposed upon other labouring groups of people. In recent years, research has revealed the diverse nature of colonial labour – the spectrum of inequality – that underpinned the economies of European empires in North America.[5] Enslavement, and other forms of compulsory labour, co-existed alongside corvée in New France.[6] Brett Rushforth's recent watershed study on Indigenous slavery draws into sharp relief the sprawling network of violence and coercion that forced several thousand Native people into bondage.[7] From the Great Lakes to the Caribbean, Rushforth shows that French merchants, royal ministers, and civil administrators reckoned with definitions, and justifications, of Indigenous slavery in North America. Indeed, the same officials that penned corvée legislation, such as Intendant Jacques Raudot, did so in an Atlantic context that reinforced the inequality of Native and African peoples.

Dispersed settlement, distance from royal oversight, poor communication networks, and a short growing season ultimately opened up new possibilities for Canadian labour negotiations between the royal elite and habitants not available in either Europe or the Caribbean. Royal and seigneurial levies met the harsh realities of life in the New World. During the early eighteenth century, habitants developed a disdain for corvée and many proprietors evaded the duty whenever possible. When annually drafted into labour for the construction of Quebec's and Montreal's fortifications, some habitants refused to show up for work, called upon their superiors to protect them from service, or collectively discussed mutiny if conditions did not improve. During the first three decades of the eighteenth century, corvée showed characteristics of a "negotiated" process, with groups of habitants constantly putting forth their own definitions of acceptable labour mobilization.[8]

Contempt for corvée was neither random nor arbitrary. Groups of habitants protested corvée when they determined that the French colonial state had overstepped the obligations their concessions stipulated. Royal officials expected habitants' obedience based on written metropolitan legal codes and subordination to their superiors. To be sure, resistance to seigneurial dues was not unique to corvée labour. Canadians protested grain prices, tithes, and the stringent alcohol regulations imposed by the Crown.[9] Corvée protests, however, highlight the intersection of local and royal grievances. Habitants utilized corvée as a medium to protest unremunerated labour, the intrusion of state intermediaries into their communities, and the customs of a kingdom across the Atlantic.

Many parishes, however, obeyed their orders, and ditch by ditch, road by road, corvée constructed the infrastructure of Canada. On the one hand, the orders of corvée acted as a practical means of extending the communication and commercial networks of the seigneuries; on the other hand, the intendant's orders symbolically reinforced the inherent authority of the king and his representatives in the colony. Orders of corvée and their subsequent execution provided powerful reminders to habitants that their obligations were intertwined with their material existence and were a requirement of their land tenure.

THE QUEBEC AND MONTREAL FORTIFICATIONS, 1690–1720

Inter-imperial competition and warfare challenged the French Crown's rule over habitants in its colonies. In the seventeenth and eighteenth centuries, several large-scale conflicts (the Nine Years' War, 1688–97; the War of Spanish Succession, 1701–14; and the War of Austrian Succession, 1740–48) encouraged French administrators and Canadian officials to reckon with marshalling supplies, ammunition, and men to defend their territories sprawled across the Atlantic. While these military engagements mostly centred on dynastic struggles in Europe, colonies transformed into important strategic objectives to force rivals to the negotiating table.

The realities of European empire building in North America required a massive mobilization of labour across a broad spectrum of inequality embedded in colonial legal regimes. Roads had to be constructed to transport men, cannons, muskets, foodstuffs, and horse-drawn carts.[10] Bridges and ferries had to be erected on waterways of all kinds to prevent lengthy portages.[11] Forests had to be clear cut to provide defensive positions with lines of sight and timber for building.[12] Most important, perhaps, fortifications needed to be established to protect strategic locations, such as the Champlain Valley, or the civilian populations in colonial cities.[13] The hard work of warfare at the turn of the eighteenth century cannot be understated. Success hinged on turning out hundreds of people to build the infrastructure necessary to defeat an opponent.

The Nine Years' War (1688–97) had a profound impact on colonial policy in New France. With the exception of the Anglo-Dutch War in New Amsterdam, wars had been primarily waged in Europe, therefore increasing tension in New France but not directly threatening its posterity. To be sure, borderland disputes challenged European supremacy in southern New France and northern Anglo-America, but the conflicts remained small-scale regional disputes.[14] In 1690, however, an English naval squadron, under the command of Sir William Phips, governor of Massachusetts Bay Colony, sailed into St Lawrence Bay and put the city of Quebec under siege. When the current governor of New France, Louis de Buade de Frontenac, refused English terms of surrender, Phips landed English militiamen north of the city and ordered them to prepare for battle. The French garrison answered with a bombardment directed towards the English ships anchored in the river and a sortie of Canadians who easily repulsed the English militia. After losing two ships, Phips retreated and returned with his force to New England.[15]

Nevertheless, the brief, yet traumatic, English siege of Quebec exposed the colony's military vulnerability and convinced Governor Frontenac and his intendant, Jean Bochart de Champigny, that the St Lawrence Valley required a serious overhaul of the colony's defensive fortifications. The Crown had nearly lost its most valuable city in the north, access to the St Lawrence, and the lucrative fur trade as a result. In the aftermath of the siege, envoys and engineers from Paris arrived fully equipped with the plans to refortify the St Lawrence city.

After this near disaster, the first major construction project consisted of strengthening Quebec's fortifications and creating permanent stone walls surrounding the city. To achieve this, Louis XIV ordered Jacques Levasseur de Neré, a Paris-educated engineer, to travel to New France and assess the defensive fortifications. Upon arrival, Levasseur suggested fortifying the Upper Town with a stone wall, in addition to a number of earthwork redoubts and palisades. He proposed harnessing "the Corvées which the habitants must satisfy" the following spring, in addition to explicit orders to the governor and the intendant to "increase them as much as" they could mobilize for the fortification of the Upper and Lower Town.[16]

In addition to Levasseur and his sub-engineers, the mobilization of corvée was carried out under the orders of two different governors: Frontenac and

Vaudreuil. Their orders then passed onto one of several intendants of New France who served their tenure during the construction period, including Jean Bochart de Champigny, François de Beauharnois, Jacques Raudot, and Michel Bégon. Influential subjects of the government of Quebec also stepped into key roles on the construction project, especially Louis de la Porte de Louvigny, a wealthy noble from France and a major in the *troupes de la Marine.*[17] Finally, the project was overseen in Versailles by Jérôme Phélypeaux, comte de Pontchartrain, the secretary of the marine, who approved and issued all funds related to the construction of the fortifications.[18]

As previously mentioned, these ministers and colonial officials assumed that they would call upon the same corvée obligation habitants owed to the Crown as did their Continental counterparts. Each arrived in New France with the expectation that habitants would perform their duty and work on the site.[19] Indeed, historian Anne Conchon asserts that in France the peasantry was "required for the construction of military roads between forts or fortifications on the front line."[20] The royal elite in Versailles viewed corvée on fortifications as a natural extension of the legal obligations that bound tenants to their noble landholders and the Crown. Despite the pleas from those in the colony, the secretary of the marine chronically underfunded the fortifications of Quebec. As a result, the plans for the Quebec fortifications relied upon the willingness of habitants to work for ten- to fifteen-day rotations on the site to mitigate the lack of surplus cash for full-time wage labourers and craftspeople.

Levasseur expected habitants to contribute to the fortifications as part of their obligation to the Crown. Indeed, he wrote that "it [was] his intention that the habitants should do the works of the land by corvée as they have by custom."[21] For Levasseur, habitants – similar to their Continental counterparts – legally owed labour to the Crown. In 1706, Louvigny stated: "it is absolutely necessary to make [the habitants] obey" and to "execute the Corvée as they were set by the Governor and Intendant."[22] Although customary law dictated obedience on behalf of the habitants to the Crown, the officials overseeing the project also had a responsibility to manage labour appropriately and to alleviate abuse. For example, Louvigny continued that Levasseur, "seeing that the work was going on in length" and did not want to "harm the sowing of the seeds," dismissed the habitants, who were "absolutely necessary for the countryside and the harvest."[23] In order to not disrupt the delicate planting and harvest seasons, officials utilized the "ancien roolles," or "Rolles," drawn up by the seigneur to institute an annual draft of labour from the parishes located within the jurisdictional boundaries of each individual government.[24]

The organization, management, and division of corvée depended on the objectives of each fortification project. For the Quebec City corvée, the division of labour signified what type of tasks each habitant would participate in upon arrival. Based on the rolls, officials subdivided habitants by *journées d'hommes* (days of manual labour) and *journées de harnois* ("harness days," or days providing horse teams to cart raw materials to the site).[25] In Quebec, labour primarily took place on the terraces, but between 1707 and 1715 the work also expanded to include "retrenching the barricades," building communication roads between redoubts, and fortifying the "strong entrenchments" that defended the bluff.[26] In each local parish, the militia captains gathered these habitants together and, collectively, they travelled to Quebec City.[27]

Once habitants serving their corvée arrived in the city, the engineer assigned them to a specific location where they would fulfill their required days of labour. Some squads of habitants worked directly on the site, digging trenches, removing earth for redoubts, erecting wooden palisades, or carrying stone to the wall.[28] Others excavated a six-foot-wide (two-metre-wide) moat around the palace.[29] Engineers, artificers, and stone masons supervised their work.[30] Habitants performing manual labour served ten days if they brought their own food for subsistence or fifteen days if they took rations from the king's stores.[31]

The second contingent of corvée, those habitants serving with horse teams, brought carriages for the transportation of supplies and excavated earth. In Quebec, they were divided into two squads and assigned specific tasks related to building the fortification. Both squads carted "timber which arrived at the harbor" to the construction site. These habitants were only required to serve five days before officials dismissed them.[32]

Each October and November, the Quebec fortification corvée must have been an impressive sight for all involved. Several hundred habitants arrived from the surrounding côtes in fifteen-day rotations with carts, tip-carts, and horse teams.[33] Chilled by the autumn air, the construction site exploded with activity as habitants on *journées d'hommes* carried stone and timber and pushed wheelbarrows filled with excavated earth to the walls.[34] Militia captains put habitants armed with scythes to work clearing the thick underbrush that obstructed the fortifications' lines of sight.[35] The workyard would have resonated with the sounds of hammer on stone breaking boulders into manageable pieces and the low thump of dozens of shovels striking the ground clearing the way for redoubts and other earthwork barriers.[36] In the distance, the echo of axe on timber would have been heard everywhere around the city as men felled trees and split the logs into palisade stakes.[37] Livestock and domestic animals would have added to the noise. Oxen teams would have pulled tree trunks and stumps from the ground, while horses struggled with loads of stone and dirt.[38] Habitants driving their teams would have hollered at their horses as carts, over-packed with construction materials, broke down and required repair.[39]

Below the cliffs of Cap Diamant, a second group of habitants would have been hard at work transporting timber and stone down the St Lawrence in flat-bottomed canoes.[40] Carefully navigating their way based on the metronome shouting of their captain to keep the rowers in order, habitants on the shore would have thrown them rope, looping it through a small hole in the bateaux and yanking the team aground.[41] Idle habitants would have loitered in groups, smoking tobacco in pipes and taking sips of brandy far from the watchful eye of the seigneurs strolling around in the city above. Most probably spoke to one another about the upcoming harvest and winter, while others whispered of mutiny and planned their chance to flee the worksite unnoticed.[42] At night, from the banks of the St Lawrence, the shoreline would have seemed ablaze with scores of campfires, candles, and torches.

Seigneurs, militia captains, Levasseur and his sub-engineers, and Vaudreuil would have paraded routinely around the worksite.[43] Militia captains would be seen making rounds of their squads of labourers, frantically checking their documents to make sure that no habitant had deserted the work camp.[44] Some may have quietly cursed the names of habitants who had escaped to their personal farms, either out of subversion or necessity, to prepare for the harvest. Levasseur and his team of sub-engineers would make their rounds yelling up to masons located high above on the uncompleted walls.[45] Quartermasters would have hollered habitants' names to receive their rations, joining the chorus of noise and activity.[46]

From 1701 to 1715, officials reported to Versailles that habitants "satisfied the corvées" in Quebec City with "much goodwill" and "without difficulty" by annually providing labour for the construction of the fortifications.[47] A lack of funds from the Crown and resistance from the colonial elite of the city, however, hampered the project during the early years of the eighteenth century. An initial call for corvée required all residents of the city, regardless of status, to provide "horse teams and carriages of the city with some tip-carts to charter the land and carry out the works."[48] This call led to an outcry from the religious and civil elite, who claimed exemption from corvée by the "prerogatives that they … [had] in France," saying that it "violate[ed] their rights."[49] Indeed, by 1707, Levasseur reported that all of the "affluent people in Quebec City" had petitioned for officer status in the militia, thereby "exempting them from working on the terraces like any other part of the public." Moreover, the elite used custom to reinforce their status, asserting that "they had the excuse that they [were] coated with a character that dispenses them [from public corvée]."[50]

The exemptions of the city's wealthy colonists angered the workers performing corvée, who utilized several techniques to mitigate their exploitation. Accounts of the unrest state that residents asserted: "it is not Custom in France to utilize them to furnish corvée."[51] Habitants in particular argued that they were "pulled from their plow" and that corvée disrupted the fragile social bonds of reciprocity that secured subsistence in New France. They further claimed that they were "vexed to support orders for public works."[52] These pleas not only allowed workers to voice their grievances to the intermediaries of royal authority but also provided them the opportunity to collectively assert their own concepts of proper and legitimate corvée labour. By appealing to their subsistence and the need to return to their homes to work their fields, habitants successfully forced officials to implement time restraints on corvée.[53]

In one case, two habitants, named Gabriel Rouleau and Jean Mandras, respectively, evaded their militia captain at the initial point of collection and did not show up at the city worksite. Once their militia captain realized Rouleau and Mandras were not there, he filed "a complaint in writing" to Louvigny, who gave him leave to return to the parish and reprimand them. Once they were caught, the militia captain imprisoned Rouleau and Mandras for twenty-four hours, making "known that they would have to come to their duty in a few days."[54]

Additionally, in 1707, after the nobility gained exemptions from corvée, habitants collectively began to "whisper of mutiny."[55] Their unrest, Levasseur explained, derived from "the unfortunate who [would] be responsible for the weight of this work." Although little is known about the scope or size of this potential "mutiny," the mere rumours of discontent prompted Levasseur to write Pontchartrain and suggest that it was important "to prevent what might happen to the people of justice or other people being a militia officer or not contributing to the corvées."[56] Veiled threats of mutiny would become a regular tactic used by habitants to voice their discontent about corvée working conditions.[57] In particular, they found it useful in convincing authorities that they would collectively stop working if new conditions, such as shorter rotations of manual labour, were not implemented.

A concurrent change in New France's administration helped clarify the role of corvée. Officials in Versailles nominated Jacques Raudot, a metropolitan legal authority, to the position of intendent in New France, and, upon his arrival in 1705, he immediately set out to investigate the accusations of gross malfeasance in the highest colonial offices.[58] While his investigation is not the focus of this study, his observations and suggestions regarding seigneurial institutions would have a direct impact on the mobilization of corvée labour for the next two decades. Furthermore, Raudot dramatically increased the presence of the Office of the Intendant and the formal legal powers that this position carried.

One of Raudot's objectives was reform of the Canadian seigneurial regime. More specifically, he sought to reduce the power of seigneurs as economic and political elites. By decreasing the privileges of the seigneurs, he could simultaneously generate a direct linkage between the royal authority and habitants. In 1708, after an extensive investigation into the day-to-day activities of the Canadian nobility, Raudot published his "Memorial on Seigneurial Privileges" for the officials in Versailles. Containing a list of suggestions and policy advice, the "Memorial" provided a scathing review of what Raudot perceived as the regional elite's injustice towards habitants. Along with reform suggestions regarding fixing the rent allocated per title of concession, Raudot also reviewed the *privileges extraordinaire*, including corvée and the seigneur's right to timber on his land grant. For corvée, Raudot asserted that his advice "would be to reduce it or leave it for the habitants to contribute between the planting or after the harvest." He continued, saying: "corvée gives their whole day to the seigneur to the vexation of the habitants" and "it demands their time where they need the work for themselves." His suggestion to limit this privilege strictly to seasonal labour on the lord's demesne established the rhythm of the working season, at least during peacetime, for the next several decades.[59] While adding some clarification to the levy, his opinion did not slow down the use of corvée labour on highways or fortifications.

During the War of Spanish Succession (1702–14), the labour of fortification construction also fell on habitants of the government of Montreal. The colonial officials feared the British might attack the southern corridor of New France on Lake Champlain and the Richelieu River. To defend this region, in 1709 Raudot ordered that, after the harvest, "the habitants of the parishes of the government [of Montreal] ... fairly contribute their work," bringing the "stone and wood necessary" for the construction of a small fort on the rapids of the Richelieu River.[60] Later known as Fort Chambly, the Richelieu was sparsely populated and required that the captains of the militia "make the distribution between the different côtes" in the Montreal area. Reminding the inhabitants of the threat of Conquest, Raudot argued: "the security of the habitants of the government of Montreal request their work." Habitants worked transporting stone, lime, and timber to the worksite. By 1711, the small stone fort was completed and the officials turned their attention to fortifying the Isle of Montreal.[61]

Following the war, colonial officials embarked on the third major fortification project of building a stone wall around the city of Montreal. As early as 1714, Claude de Ramezay, governor of Montreal, wrote to Versailles that he "must seriously take advantage of the internal peace to complete fortifying Quebec and Montreal" and requested funds to begin planning the enclosure.[62] The initial plan called for a series of strongholds on the river and "walls sixteen feet high." He proposed "to divide the government by class and oblige each one according to their abilities to work by corvées."[63] Moreover, he planned to implement a similar division of labour as had been used in building the Quebec City fortifications. Habitants on *journées d'hommes* would "draw stone from the quarries" while an additional subgroup worked onsite at the wall carrying the materials. Similar to the Quebec corvée, a second contingent of habitants on *journées de harnois* would provide carriages and tip-carts to transport the stone to Montreal. Ramezay considered November the best month to accomplish these goals for: "the command of corvée is hard to do at the beginning of October until the month of April to gather all the materials during the winter." Additionally, he did not want to disrupt the habitants' "work from sowing until the cutting of the hay."[64]

The governor agreed with Ramezay's plan, and on 20 September 1714 they sent their preliminary report to Versailles for approval. In this document, they asserted that corvée labour provided the most cost-efficient workforce in the absence of funds sent directly from Versailles to hire masons. Indeed, they stated: "as his Majesty does not want to make funds for these fortifications, and it would not be proper to propose a tax ... the only means which we can put to use at present is to have them work by corvées obliging all habitants of the government of Montreal." Habitants would "do their own corvée" to "extract the stone, to do the excavations, and transport on location

Figure 1.2
Cornelius Krieghoff, *Fort Chambly* (1858).

The fort stands above the Chambly rapids on the Richelieu River. The fort guarded New France's southeastern borderlands and formed a chain of defensive positions along the Richelieu and Lake Champlain.

all materials." Habitants located too far away from the city would pay in cash "the number of days to which they [would] be taxed," in lieu of preforming hard labour. The revenue collected from this tax, Vaudreuil and Bégon hoped, would "be used for the payment of labour and the purchase of lime." They assured the minister: "although these corvées are kind of an imposition, the name is not as odious in this country, the people having been accustomed to it for a long time." To avoid disrupting the agricultural cycles, they set the corvée to begin the following year.[65]

Bégon authorized the official order of corvée on 6 November 1714. Calling upon the habitants' obligation to the Crown, he stated that, "the King wishing to have the city of Montreal surrounded by a wall," the intendant had decided that "the work should start without delay … and that the habitants of the government of Montreal should contribute." He continued: "we have judged that the habitants have at the least the responsibility to provide corvée on the openings of the compound." The militia captains were once again responsible for gathering the labour force and designating "the number of days that each habitant [would] furnish corvée in proportion to his property and faculties." Habitants on *journées d'hommes* would "be employed to draw stone from the quarries and amass it on the fields." The habitants on *journées de harnois* would then "work with the pack animals to load the lime necessary" and transport the materials to Montreal. Bégon ended the order asserting that all habitants "without exception" were to "work on the fortifications until the walls of the city [were] complete."[66] To be excused from the labour requirement, a habitant could now pay a fee (three livres per day for *journées d'hommes* or five livres per day for *journées de harnois*).

At the worksite, another contingent of habitants worked on the ditches and fences surrounding the stone structure as well as earthenwork redoubts that protected a portion of the island. The team of engineers in charge of the operation ordered the habitants to "provide all of the materials," and Ramezay oversaw the organization of work teams putting "the habitants back in the places they had to be in order to make the stone wall."[67]

Corvée muster rolls from 1715 allow a partial reconstruction of the population that participated in the Montreal corvée. Habitants came from Montreal, in addition to seigneuries both north and south of the city.[68] To the northwest, habitants travelled to the building site from the Isle d'Jesus (modern-day Laval) and Lachenaie; and northeast of the city from Rivière-de-Prairies, Varennes, Saint Michel, Saint Theresa, Vercheres, and the Isle Bouchard. Immediately south, workers also came from neighboring Lachine.[69] Directly east, orders went to Longueuil to also mobilize their population for corvée.[70] Militia captains subdivided these workers into the two separate groups noted above – *journées d'hommes* and *journées de harnois*. While the rolls do not specify the gender of the individual, most, if not all, habitants were male. Militia captains penned the "distribution of the number of days that each habitant" would be "required for courvée" across from each name on their list.[71] Those offering horse teams worked between one to four days, while those performing manual labour worked up to five days. For example, Jacques Gariépy from Lachenaie provided three days of manual labour, while his fellow community member Michel Filion worked two days.[72] On the Isle d'Jesus, many habitants provided carriages and horse teams – for example, Charles Aube (one day), Pierre Label (one day), Francois Blanchard (two days), and the militia captain, Charles Dazé (two days).[73]

Despite offering a buy-out option, colonial officials in Montreal still encountered scattered habitant resistance to corvée. The following year, on the scheduled start date of construction, as Ramezay and Bégon said later, the "execution of this project did not seem practicable by the little disposition of the habitants of the government to satisfy [their obligations]."[74] Habitants failed to show up for their working parties and rumours of discontent among the parishes trickled into the city. The lack of workers forced the construction to stop temporarily until officials could mobilize the surrounding parishes for corvée.[75] Habitant opposition prompted Vaudreuil to travel to Montreal in 1717 to oversee the mobilization process and to make personal trips to seigneuries who refused to furnish labour.

A poor harvest in 1717 compounded the problems of labour mobilization and prompted one seigneurie, Longueuil, to refuse corvée duty.[76] As mentioned above, when Vaudreuil arrived in Longueuil, he presided over an assembly of habitants "to offer them their Corvées." During the meeting, the governor's armed guard left with several of the reluctant parishioners. Misinterpreted by the protestors as an impending punishment, this "alarmed the others and all fearing to be charged left the house in a crowd to gather their weapons." Ten eventually rushed to get their muskets, and the governor, seeing "little submission of this people," fled back across the river to Montreal. The mutineers barricaded their homes, with Vaudreuil asserting: "they engaged in a sort of revolt by staying with their weapons the rest of the day, except some reasonable people who retired to their home." Indeed, he further comments: "their intention was to prevent anyone from sending out those whom they foresaw that I might send to take them to prison."[77]

Although the ten "mutineers" were eventually imprisoned, this episode not only highlights the fraught social tensions that existed around the obligation of corvée for labour on the fortifications but also illustrates habitants' demonstration of their own form of communal justice. The outburst, and subsequent punishment, convinced other seigneuries and parishes that they should comply with the order. Vaudreuil stated: "it is true that something bad is good, it has caused several habitants of the other côtes, who have not hastened to satisfy what has been promised for the corvées [to fulfill their obligation]."[78]

Despite the short-term success, Montreal officials remained wary of the social unrest. The poor harvest of 1717 convinced the governor that the corvée should be suspended for 1718. When corvée resumed in 1719, habitants again resisted participating "because they would have [had] to provide themselves with food as a result of the bad harvest of the year of 1717."[79] Although both Vaudreuil and Bégon continued "the levy imposed on the habitants and the communities of [Montreal] for that expense," by 1720, Ramezay introduced a formal monetary tax that Montreal habitants would annually contribute instead of mobilizing corvée. The work during the 1720s continued under the supervision of hired masons and day labourers, with habitants only sporadically providing corvée as part of their obligation to the Crown.[80]

ROADS, BRIDGES, AND CHURCHES, 1706–31

Concurrent with the fortification projects taking place in Quebec, Chambly, and Montreal, the Crown also experimented with the use of a second form of labour, *corvées général*, which consisted of mandatory work on public infrastructure. *Corvées général* primarily repaired or constructed buildings, roads, and bridges. Each seigneurie, parish, or côte was responsible for raising a corvée for road construction that passed through their property. Contemporary authorities did not specify this form of labour as legally distinct from the seigneurial or military variety, and the intendant and other royal officials (such as surveyors) referred to this work collectively as corvée.

The creation of a grand voyer for New France facilitated early uses of *corvée général* on roads and bridges. The first grand voyer, René Robinau de Bécancour, issued several orders in the opening years of his tenure, although they primarily remained local roads to enable travel in more populated areas of the colony.[81] From 1680 to 1685, orders from Intendant Jean Talon and Governor Antoine Lefebvre de La Barre also indicate that roads in New France had captured the interest of the king's officials.[82] Despite growing attention from the political elite, corvée remained confined to local interests, the largest of which connected Montreal to Lachine shortly after the village's construction.[83] Similar to fortifications, however, the colony's involvement in the affairs of the larger French Empire pushed into sharp relief the need for a road system that spanned the St Lawrence Valley.

Habitants participated in more *corvées général*, hereafter referred to simply as corvée, than any other form of statute labour during the first two decades of the eighteenth century. Roads in eighteenth-century New France tended to reflect the labour customs of the Old Regime. Indeed, as Katherine McDonough states, "roads in a hierarchal society like Old Regime France were legally associated with the groups of persons that maintained them, even if they were used by a variety of people."[84] For this reason, the categorization of roads also followed the latest engineering principles devised at royal academies. At the local level, foot paths or mill roads sprang out of necessity, moving goods, supplies, and people around the property. Highways, or *grand chemins*, "identified with royal power" were maintained by corvée in service to the Crown and as part of a habitant's obligation to the royal domain.[85] While highways directly stemmed from the intendant and grand voyer, parishes often consulted royal surveyors on local roads as well.

Canadian highways served as the primary commercial routes of traders, merchants, and fur traders travelling between major cities and villages. They also served as arteries of the colonial administration, allowing justices, soldiers, bureaucrats, and officials to disseminate orders to even the most remote of seigneuries. In an attempt to centralize the emerging smattering of roads, Governor Vaudreuil and the Superior Council announced plans to build one continuous highway that connected the major commercial centres of Montreal and Quebec. Although this project, later known as the Chemin du Roy, was not officially launched until 1731, several preliminary stages of this road building were started earlier to connect the seigneuries.[86] From 1708 to 1730, habitants in the St Lawrence Valley constructed interconnected clusters of highways surrounding Montreal and Quebec. In addition, habitants also built other public works, especially bridges, fences, and ditches that supplemented the growing road system of the colony.

Corvée labour played an integral role in the imperial schemes of the French monarchy during the seventeenth and eighteenth centuries, especially with regard to reforming Canada's road system. As much as the engineering of roads depended upon the Old Regime, the reality of colonizing the New World meant a change in the way corvée operated. In France, elites often utilized old Roman roads for a blueprint, and thus most work stemmed from centuries of pre-existing work.[87] In Canada, the highways and footpaths needed to be carved from the land to accommodate the seigneuries were located on the St Lawrence. For habitants, this meant digging drainage ditches, fencing the side of the road, and clearing brush (*fredoches*) from the intended path of traffic.

Thus, corvée fit like a puzzle piece among a spectrum of labour that Europeans constructed in the Atlantic World. The Canadian administration's dependence on corvée stemmed partially from the relatively small population of migrants from France and, thus, a lack of able-bodied labourers to carry out such public works. As stated, however, the French were not new to mobilizing labour through varying degrees of coercion. For example, within Canada, corvée and its peculiar feudal social arrangements operated alongside Indian and African slavery. In mid-seventeenth-century New France, enslaved Indigenous nations (referred to as *panis* or *esclaves*) played an important role not only as a symbolic demonstration of gift-giving in the Pays d'en Haut fur trade but also as labourers in urban settlements. Both Quebec and Montreal merchants traded in Native American captives and sold them to wealthy seigneurs.[88] Enslaved Indigenous nations fulfilled critical domestic and agricultural tasks on seigneuries. While they most likely worked on similar agricultural tasks as did habitants performing seigneurial corvée, their status as *esclaves* prevented them from obtaining a title deed and, thus, exempted them from feudal dues such as road construction.[89]

Similarly, in theory, corvée also made up for a large working shortage by drawing upon *engagés*, day labourers, and skilled craftspeople needed for public infrastructure. Engagés, or indentured servants, played a crucial role in agricultural labour, but their status prevented them from owning land until their service to the seigneur was complete.[90] While many habitants employed engagés, it is not clear whether servants were sent to fulfill their master's days of service building public infrastructure. Indeed, corvée muster rolls simply mark the name of the habitant and days owed, without distinguishing how many engagés they may have employed.[91] Additionally, court records from habitants who refused to perform their labour on roads and bridges do not specify whether engagés could be sent to meet that obligation. Habitants could pay a substitute to work in their stead. These financial agreements, however, almost always included a wage paid in their absence, something that a master would not have owed an engagé. In sum, corvée filled an important role in the spectrum of inequality that developed in early eighteenth-century New France.

The proposals for the roads, primarily in the form of royal highways, derived from the intendant, who then appointed a grand voyer (the surveyor and inspector of roads) to oversee the execution of the orders. Within the hierarchy of New France, the grand voyer emerged as a critical intermediary of the intendant. With the help of sous-voyers (sub-engineers) they determined the location, path, and dimensions of each road.

Appointed by the king in 1689, Grand Voyer Pierre Robineau Bécancour oversaw the initiative to build Canadian roads and bridges. For each construction project in the colony, Bécancour contacted the local seigneur, militia captains, priests, and churchwardens for approval. On 18 May 1710 in the seigneurie of Sainte-Anne, for example, Bécancour asserted that, based on the "consent of the lord proprietor and the lieutenant of the militia of the seigneurie and six of the oldest and most considerable habitants, the churchwardens ha[d] settled the highway." In such orders, the grand voyer typically specified that the habitants would perform this labour under obligation of corvée, making participation in the process a mandatory community obligation.[92]

In periods of both war and peace, the parish militia captains organized labour based on the composition of the community. After the parish mass, the militia captain read the king's order of corvée, and habitants had eight to ten days to contribute their share of labour to the construction project.[93] Each captain oversaw the construction of his highway in segments, with habitants "required to make the roads that pass[ed] through their land."[94] Based on the route of the road, the intendant sometimes called upon habitants to work on more than just the length of road that passed through their land. For example, on 24 June 1713, Bégon ordered that the habitants of Saint-François and Saint-Johns would "be led to the places marked by the plan … and build through the places in the forest." In this case, the clearing of trees required that: "each habitant by the road or the land do all necessary work to make [the road] practicable along his habitation."[95]

The intendant and grand voyer correlated road construction to the rhythms of habitant agricultural production. Corvée labour on roads occurred "after the planting," usually around April, and lasted until the end of August when they expected to begin the harvest.[96] By early December, however, habitants were expected to "mark winter roads" so heavy snowfall would not obscure their route. Officially enforced in 1709, the marking of winter roads obligated habitants to drive poles into the stretch of highway that passed through their land. Originally, Raudot asserted: "being necessary to make a road in this season between the city of Montreal [and Quebec]" all habitants of the colony should "mark in front of their dwelling a road in the places most convenient." This order, posted on the parish door, specified that the winter road maintained: "the business which happens every day and which establishes a necessary relationship between the two cities."[97] In 1713, Bégon continued his predecessor's orders and issued an order stating: "the roads being unpassable this season because of the great amount of snow that is all over the land and [St Lawrence] river the voyageurs are at risk of getting lost if the roads are not clear." This colony-wide order specified that habitants "whose dwellings [were] located on the highway place markers each according to the extent of their dwelling so that the voyageurs [did] not run the risk of falling."[98]

Habitants could contest the construction of a larger highway and submit a plea to the grand voyer to decrease the size of the project. In Argentenay, for example, the habitants met with the grand voyer to discuss the construction of a highway through their parish. The grand voyer asserted: "between them they believe that the road would be most useful and necessary for them to the mill of the seigneurie." The habitants "argued that the [new] road up and down the older highway [would] continue and that there [would] be made a road [that connected to the mill]. In this case, the habitants successfully petitioned the grand voyer for a smaller, local road that was more useful to them than a new highway.[99]

Along with major construction projects, the colonial administration also expected habitants to perform corvée for the associated auxiliary tasks. This primarily took the form of lining each road with a fence and ditches to ensure that the roads would not flood or deteriorate due to grazing livestock wandering the parish. In most instances, the orders for fences and ditches accompanied the orders for roads and the intendant held communities accountable for making "the fences and ditches in accordance with the Regulations according to the Grand Voyer."[100] Another task associated with construction required habitants to clear lands "covered with brambles and shrubbery."[101] Accordingly, in 1714, habitants of Lachine cleared the land of this vegetation "on the edge of the river Lachine in front of their dwellings in order to make the navigation of the river less dangerous for those who [went] to the mill" on the seigneurie.[102]

Building fences emerged as a major source of vexation between neighbours, some of whom ignored lining the roads and their own property as required. Following a number of reports of roaming livestock damaging property, in 1709 Raudot ordered that each habitant "in all sides of this country" had to "build a good and valid fence along their dwelling" to prevent further court cases between neighbours.[103] Some habitants clearly ignored this order and continued to allow their livestock free range of the seigneurie.

In 1723, for instance, habitants of Saint-Antoine complained "several times" to the intendant that "their neighbors ha[d] to make and keep fences" and that their negligent behaviour had led to "cattle going from one land to the another and causing damage."[104] In this case, Bégon reinforced his order under "title of penalty" for negligence. These types of disputes were not uncommon. For example, in 1723 the habitants of Batiscan also complained that several others "of the seigneurie neglected the adjoining fences between their neighbors and them." In this case, Bégon directed the plaintiffs to "scour the woods and to make the fences [themselves] at the expense of the refusers which [he would] make refund [the time needed for the labour]."

In addition to highways, habitants also constructed bridges as part of corvée duty. In order to connect the côtes along the St Lawrence, the intendant ordered the construction of bridges approximately six feet (two metres) wide "and solid enough to suffer the weight of horses crossing."[105] The grand voyer mobilized this corvée labour in a similar manner to that mobilized for the roads. The militia captain read orders for corvée at Sunday Mass and the intendant designated a time schedule for constructing the bridge. Unlike the roads, the construction and maintenance of bridges fell to the entire community, and the amount of labour they contributed was not limited to the location of their dwelling. Indeed, in the parish of Saint-Joseph, the intendant ordered "that the three bridges be maintained in common by the habitants of the parish."[106] Although the size of the bridges depended on each parish's geography, an order from 25 November 1721 specified "that all the habitants of the Petite-Rivières" were ordered: "to incessantly each make, in right, twelve piles of cedar and spruce, thirteen feet long, to serve to reestablish the bridges and roads along the côte as soon as the planting of next year is finished."[107]

The amount of labour required to collect and transport wood for bridge construction had the potential to disrupt the resources of the community. As early as 1713, a number of disputes within the colony over from where in the parish the necessary timber would derive forced Bégon to standardize the system of collection. He decided that, with regard to "the disputes that ha[d] arisen over the furnishing of wood needed to build the necessary bridges on the rivers that pass the highways" that "all wood needed for the construction of the bridges [would] be taken only from the land nearest the river." In addition, Bégon ordered that the captains of the militia should oversee the distribution of corvée to make sure habitants did not delay in conducting the work necessary for these projects.[108]

Larger seigneuries with two rows of settlement, one on the St Lawrence and one further inland, posed problems in mobilizing labour for the colonial administration. The intendant typically ordered habitants to build roads that stretched through their property, and these almost always correlated with the main highway that ran along the river. As a result, in larger communities with multiple ranks of settlement, the intendant specified the various duties associated with the construction of bridges and roads. In these ordinances, Bégon exerted influence in organizing and distributing labour. In Durantaye, he ordered: "the habitants of the second row of the seigneurie of Durantaye[,] whether resident or non-resident, [are] to make their concessions, and make and maintain the new road of the second row which is to descend to the river." Meanwhile, he ordered the first row of habitants "to help and contribute" the "necessary bridge to make the [new] road practicable." Depending on the amount of time it took to build the new road, the second-row habitants would aid in the bridge once they finished.[109]

Habitants exerted considerable influence in the construction of bridges. Following the establishment of parishes as the central focal point of administration, the intendant increasingly relied on an "assembly of habitants" to determine the specifications of the projects based on their local needs. As Christian Blais argues, this local form of representation existed so that "habitants of rural communities could assemble after requesting this privilege from the Intendant." The assembly functioned "to settle common matters, such as construction or expansion of a church or rectory, or the improvement of a road or bridge, or finally the management of communal property."[110]

These meetings occurred after Sunday Mass, and the seigneur, priest, wardens, and militia captains attended to monitor the discussion. Two primary forms of these meetings emerge from the documents. First, the intendant would specify in his order that the habitants should elect among the assembly four to six "principle habitants" who would then meet with the elite and make decisions of corvée based on what they deemed appropriate.[111] The second form of assembly generated a truly representative institution in which the habitants deliberated among themselves. Once a "plurality of votes" rendered a decision, they appealed directly to the intendant's office.[112]

The most detailed example of the "assembly" negotiating corvée comes from the parish of Saint-Laurent. In April 1722, the bridge in Saint-Laurent fell into disrepair and needed to be replaced immediately. The bridge served as a central artery of the seigneurie and was on the "main road that [led] to the mill on which carts cannot pass over it." Bégon asserted: "it is right to restore the bridge[,] and for greater convenience of the habitants" to move the location of a new bridge to "higher up the river where it is wide which would be less important for construction and maintenance."[113] Ultimately, however, he left the decision whether to reconstruct the old bridge in the same location or move it higher up the river to an assembly of Saint-Laurent habitants. Bégon received his answer just three days later: "all the habitants of the parish of Saint-Laurent having assembled the day after the parish mass have unanimously agreed that it is more convenient for the bridge to reside in the same linkage point [as the old one]." He added that the habitants, having collectively made this decision, should furnish the wood and days necessary for construction.[114]

Habitants also provided labour for the construction of churches and presbyteries. The task represented one of the most-used forms of corvée in the first thirty years of the eighteenth century, with twenty-five orders issued by the Office of the Intendant. Throughout the eighteenth century, the churches and presbyteries were fairly modest structures. They typically consisted of a one-room nave, large enough to seat the community, and a single steeple.[115] Time, money, influence, and labour dictated the aesthetic of each individual presbytery. Most ended up as rough, wooden structures that quickly fell into disrepair. If the parish priest was able both to rally the intendant for funds and to convince the habitants to work, the church could be constructed of stone.

Instead of the civil authorities leading the mobilization of labour, the parish priest petitioned the intendant for permission to organize and distribute labour for the purpose of church construction. Upon receiving approval, the priest, in conjunction with the appointed church wardens, summoned the habitants to an assembly at a central gathering point. Most times, they met at the parish to which they formally belonged, and the new church would be constructed with an eye to the convenience of those habitants who lived far from their designated parish.[116]

Once all habitants arrived the assembly meeting commenced. The parish priest announced that a new church would be constructed and that "each habitant present or absent [would] furnish their labour of the construction of presbytery."[117] The parishioners then appointed four principal habitants as representatives of the community to travel with the militia officers and church wardens to the proposed site.[118] There, they collectively decided if they could just repair the old church or if a new one was needed, and, if the latter, whether the new church should be constructed of wood or stone. In the parish of Champlain, Bégon ordered: "those four habitants and carpenters will previously be taken to examine whether the presbytery cannot be repaired." Moreover: "[if] they judge that it is not in a good state, he will deliberate in the assembly if it is more appropriate to rebuild this pious building." Once the community made a decision, "a distribution of each of the habitants of the seigneurie [would] be obliged to contribute for [the construction] in regard to his faculties."[119]

In several ways, corvée on presbyteries would have been recognizable to habitants summoned to do the construction. Each habitant was responsible for their "proportion to their means and property of their possessions."[120] Similar to bridge building, the felling of trees and processing the wood into timber represented the primary component of corvée with regard to church construction.[121] The militia captains also divided habitants into six- to ten-person squads, being responsible for their portion of days of labour and any tasks related to the collection of wood, stone, or other materials needed for carpenters and masons. In 1710, for example, the militia captain divided the habitants into six squads, although there is no indication whether these teams worked in rotation at separate times or took on different tasks more akin to fortification construction.[122]

Initially, in the first decade of the eighteenth century, the intendant authorized construction projects exclusively on a local scale. Bégon designated which individual parish would participate in corvée, and the local seigneur or captain of the militia would distribute their labour as they deemed fit. By the late 1710s, however, as clusters of roads and bridges emerged from the patchwork of small fiefs dotted on the St Lawrence, he began experimenting with mobilizing corvée in two or more parishes in joint ventures. Indeed, in some cases, an assembly of habitants from both communities met and discussed projects among themselves. The mobilization of combined parishes, however, represented a clear departure from the early years of the century. In an effort to expand the influence of colonial state authority, Bégon implemented a recognizable, but transformed, process of labour mobilization in which groups of habitants contributed corvée for projects that did not necessarily correlate with their individual concession title. In sum, the Office of the Intendant generated a precedent of mobilizing labour across parish lines.[123]

Some habitants chose to evade any form of corvée mobilization. Repeat orders from Bégon to individual parishes suggest that orders for roads and bridges were collectively ignored. In the parish of Charlesbourg, for example, the Office of the Intendant issued seven separate orders addressing the construction of a highway that habitants never built or maintained.[124] Groups of habitants and individuals also ignored orders of corvée. At first, from 1708 to 1715, the intendant simply reissued the order and called upon the necessary intermediaries to compel habitants to complete construction. In 1713, to discourage disobedience, Bégon began issuing a three- to ten-livre fine to the "refusers," those habitants who just simply did not fulfill their individual portion of corvée.[125] This system of penalties expanded in scope over the next decade and transformed into an entire section of each ordinance. Not only did fines reach up to fifty livres, but the intendant also utilized seigneurial law to compel habitants into service.[126] This took the form of writing the refusers' names into the tax roll, a document consisting of each habitant's name and the amount of labour they provided during the year. Seigneurs also presented their tax rolls annually to the governor in the *foy et homage*, which reaffirmed fealty between seigneurs and the Crown. In order to instill obedience in the parishes, the intendant called upon habitants' obligation to colony and Crown. In this sense, their refusal to perform corvée represented much more than insubordination: by placing their names in the tax roll, the intendant assured that the Crown identified the refusers and, if necessary, could intervene and place further sanctions on their titles of concession.

For the "refusers," also labelled "offenders," the penalties for not performing corvée carried social, legal, and financial consequences. Not only did the militia captain label the habitant an "offender" in the tax roll, but the fines levied against these habitants had the potential to disrupt their lives through mandated court appearances. In some cases, such as in 1720 in the parish of Contrecoeur, the churchwardens inspected the tax roll and personally contacted the offenders to pay their fine for not contributing to a ditch and bridge in the community. In the case of Contrecoeur, a refusal to work was equated with neglect of public service, punishable by the appointed churchwardens as representatives of civil and religious authority in the parish.[127]

Further penalties ensued for habitants who continued to refuse corvée. In 1714, Paul Charles Dazé, militia captain of the Isle-Jesus, appeared before the Court of the Royal Jurisdiction of Montreal and submitted a formal complaint that three habitants in his parish refused corvée on a highway and bridge. The court declared that Jacques Foget, Joseph Éthier, and Michel Charbonneau would "be sentenced twenty livres applicable to the parish of said place" for refusing a work order issued on 5 July 1713. According to the court, the crime was that the habitants "refused to work on said bridge." It ruled that if the habitants continued to refuse their corvée, they would be obliged to pay the twenty-livre fine.[128]

THE HABITANT "SPIRIT OF MUTINY"

Despite the fines, court appearances, and disgruntled militia captains, many habitants still refused to perform corvée. By the late 1720s, the fortifications of Montreal and the Chemin du Roy remained unfinished. Statute labour had nearly caused a revolt in Longueuil, and even the tax that replaced corvée proved difficult to collect. Although the grand voyer issued hundreds of orders to the parishes of the St Lawrence Valley, the continuous highway stretching from Montreal to Quebec City was not even close to completion. After many fines and court-mandated corvée, clusters of roads still only existed around the two metropolitan centres.

Contemporaries consistently noted that cold weather hampered any infrastructure construction. All plans to work had to cease from December to March, with the colonial officers noting that "the great amount of snow that [was] all over the land and the Saint Lawrence River" made the roads all but "unpassable in this season."[129] Any projects requiring timber were put on hold "because of the snow on the necessary wood."[130] After the thaw, habitants remained busy farming from April to August, and the harvest occurred in September and October. In vain, the Superior Council ordered corvée "immediately after the harvest and before the first snows by all habitants."[131] With only mid-October to November left, the French engineer Chaussegros de Léry noted that the frost starts early, making projects requiring trenching and digging difficult.[132]

The French colonial state also lacked the mechanisms of authority that promoted efficient, streamlined work orders. Overlapping jurisdictions of the governor, intendant, grand voyer, and local seigneurs produced a diffuse power that lacked the royal credibility found in Europe. For some seigneuries, orders of corvée, especially during wartime, must have appeared chaotic. For example, habitants in the seigneurie of Charlesbourg received from the Crown annual orders for fortification construction in Quebec City, annual orders from their seigneur to work on his demesne, periodic orders from the parish to construct and maintain the presbytery, and, from 1709 to 1729, they received seventeen work orders from the intendant to work on roads and bridges. The chaotic nature of these work orders would only have been amplified by the fact that the grand voyer, militia captains, seigneur, church wardens, and intendant issued each individual order.

Clearly, some habitants collectively refused labour. Despite being labelled "refusers" and "offenders" in the tax roll, entire parishes did not fulfill their orders to build roads. The grand voyer's personal minutes attest to this, with orders in 1731 citing original statues from 1710 that remained uncompleted. While the demands of manual labour undoubtedly convinced some habitants not to fulfill these orders, Governor Vaudreuil offered his own thoughts on the matter. Writing to Versailles on the subject in 1725, he asserted that there would "always be time to punish those who lack[ed] respect and submission to the order of his Majesty."[133] He continued:

> I cannot help on this occasion to inform you that it is not alone the habitants of [Quebec City] that we notice a spirit of mutiny and independence, but that it has already been introduced to all habitants of the countryside who are at their ease, and whose convenient and idle life to which they are accustomed to for a few years has made them less submissive, less ready to execute orders that they receive in the service of his Majesty.[134]

While this scathing report on habitants may contain elements of truth, Vaudreuil encountered a much more systemic challenge than "idle" habitants "who [were] at ease." As colonial officials issued their orders on the customs of France, Canadian habitants developed a separate, unique legal culture that promoted the collective evasion of corvée. If the conditions of work did not suit their interests, they protested by refusing to work, escaping the site, "whispering of mutiny," or revolting against royal authority. In 1732, the new grand voyer, Jean-Eustace Lanoullier Boisclerc, took matters into his own hands, travelling to each parish in the colony and personally overseeing road construction.[135] Under order of the Crown, he established his own tribunal, making punishments easier to enact and fines easier to collect.

Ultimately, however, war forced habitants to finally fulfill their duty. The War of Austrian Succession and the Seven Years' War brought the struggle for New France to habitants' doorsteps. During the last decades of New France, corvée transformed from an easily evaded bothersome tax into labour that meant the defence and survival of the colony. More important, the uneasy relationships forged through evasion, punishment, and law provided a foundation for a corvée labour regime in the New World. Despite the difficulties in mobilizing habitants for work projects, the French colonial administration had established a precedent for utilizing corvée. These relationships became woven into the fabric of habitant life, and, following the Seven Years' War, the British would integrate the civil custom of labour into their conquered North American province.

CHAPTER 2

French Colonialism and Expansion, 1732–59

INTRODUCTION

On 26 July 1746, the colonial officials, merchants, and principal habitants of Quebec held an assembly to discuss the fortifications surrounding the city. The community had good reasons to be concerned. One year prior, the British had sailed to Cape Breton Island, laid siege, and successfully captured the Louisburg fortress. After taking the Atlantic fortification, the British now threatened sailing down the St Lawrence River to Quebec. Moreover, the wall around the city desperately required repair. Engineered by Jacques Levasseur using corvée labour in the early decades of the century, the walls had started to deteriorate. In 1745, Governor Charles Beauharnois wrote to Jean Frédéric Maurepas, *ministère de la Marine*, asserting that "it would be of infinite consequence for the safety of this city and the whole colony" to build "at the expense of his Majesty with all possible diligence a fortification." The project, however, would require taxation and draughts of corvée from the neighbouring parishes.[1]

Not wanting to incite protest from the peasant population by compelling them to perform corvée, the governor invited a representative group of habitants to a July assembly where they met with the governor, intendant, and some of the wealthiest merchants in the colony in the Chateau de Saint-Louis.[2] For two hours, the group debated the necessity of a new wall and whether "it [were] not more suitable and more advantageous to demolish what ha[d] been done" and start fresh. The habitants "asked for some days to deliberate" their position.[3] On 30 July, after more debate over taxation to fund the enclosure, the assembly made its decision. The merchants and the habitants decided the wall must be repaired and must enclose the entire city.[4] The northern côtes would provide annual drafts of corvée along with all the necessary carts and carriages.[5]

By the mid-eighteenth century, administrators in New France embarked on a new strategy to harness corvée from the king's Canadian subjects. Learning from the previous decades of social unrest, they refined the techniques of mobilizing corvée to meet the needs of the empire and the military. From 1732 to 1744, officials only issued orders of corvée during breaks in the agricultural cycle and included an assembly of habitants to represent their parishes' interests. Administrative reform in the Office of the Grand Voyer and in the Office of the Intendant led to the completion of the Chemin du Roy (the highway from Montreal to Quebec City) and the Chambly Road, stretching from Longueuil to Fort Chambly. In peacetime, the Superior Council offered incentives to habitants to move to regions of New France where corvée labour was much needed for infrastructure. Inter-imperial competition and two large-scale colonial wars, however, ultimately tied habitants to taxation, corvée, and full-time service in the militia. For example, during the War of Austrian Succession (1740–48), the Superior Council began issuing orders of corvée that solely aligned with military interests, such as the construction of ships, fortifications, and signal fires. By the time of the Seven Years' War, the French use of civilian corvée labour dwindled as service in the militia, and defence of the colony, overwhelmed the need for building projects.

This chapter utilizes official correspondence from New France and Versailles, court records, orders of the intendant, and the minutes of the grand voyer to trace the deployment of corvée in the mid-eighteenth century. Records from the Archives des Colonies include all reports sent to Versailles for approval, such as expenses for construction projects. Hidden in the bookkeeping and supply lists, habitants performing corvée emerge in most major projects authorized by the king. Additionally, the minutes of Grand Voyer Jean-Eustace Lanoullier Boisclerc allow a reconstruction of the Chemin du Roy and the other major colonial highways branching off from it. Habitants built the continuous highway from Montreal to Quebec in segments, with each parish completing the section of the road that passed through its property.[6] As a result, surveyors kept detailed reports that catalogued the progress and hindrances of construction from each parish. These records shed light on the communication networks that corvée produced throughout the colony.

The Chemin du Roy, hereafter referred to as the King's Highway, was just one road within a network of larger roads and riverine passages that connected the dispersed settlements of New France. Boisclerc prompted construction of the Longueuil-Chambly Road and the Fort Saint Jean-Chambly Road.[7] He also completed clusters of roads on the northern shores of the St Lawrence and the Gaspésie that connected remote seigneuries to the commercial centre of Quebec. While these highways served a functional purpose for habitants who lived in these regions – connecting them to markets in New France's urban seaports – colonial officials imagined a wide range of uses for these roads, the most important being the extraction of resources. Roads in the Richelieu, for example, linked the government of Montreal to the Champlain Valley and forests of hardwood timber that the Crown coveted for ship construction in the transatlantic trade. The governor and his appointees projected cadastral maps onto these largely unoccupied areas and offered incentives to habitants to take concessions there. They imagined a populated defensive buffer between the ever-encroaching British colonists and a communication network that could alert the St Lawrence settlements to approaching enemies.[8]

The challenges of mobilizing habitants for corvée during the opening decades of the eighteenth century had a profound effect on how state-sanctioned labour continued under French rule. During construction of the Quebec City fortifications and the Montreal enclosure, habitants developed several tactics either to mitigate the amount of labour that they performed or to evade the system entirely. In particular, they argued that *corvée militaire*, the ten- to fifteen-day rotation of work on Crown military projects, did not fall under the "customs" of the Canadian seigneurial regime.[9] The metropolitan officials sent from Versailles to Canada obviously protested this assertion and utilized a rhetoric of obligation to the Crown and, when necessary, coercive force.

Mobilizing corvée during peacetime, however, generated new challenges for the colonial elite. The Nine Years' War (1688–97) and the War of Spanish Succession (1702–13) had legitimized corvée as a necessary component of extracting labour from habitants for state projects during war, especially after the English had sailed down the St Lawrence and laid siege to Quebec City in 1690. The French Crown recognized the inadequacies of the military fortifications in the colony and ordered corvée to provide the labour to improve the defences of the two major commercial cities in Canada. Although they met resistance from some habitants, many parishes begrudgingly fulfilled their duty and constructed the enclosures. The governor and intendant expected habitants to continue this custom, providing corvée without the extant threat of an English invasion. Projects like roads and bridges, however, lacked the gravity or immediacy of a looming military invasion.

Canadian officials carefully considered the necessity of peacetime corvée. As we saw in chapter 1, the colonial states' increasing dependency on corvée for most forms of construction had provoked groups of habitants to riot, protest, or simply ignore orders. By 1730, the labour custom, and the distribution of those orders, was just as unclear as it had been when Jacques Raudot initially authorized the construction of the King's Highway twenty-four years earlier.

The solution for the governor, intendant, and other bureaucratic officials lay in the appropriation of habitant labour power for major state-run projects. By reframing local infrastructure as an expansion of empire, they could call on corvée as an obligation exercised by the Crown that benefitted all those involved. Local roads, for example, transformed into the "King's Highway" and provided habitants access to various regions of the colony. Moreover, administrators often offered additional incentives for fulfilling corvée, such as relief from paying the cens, land, or privileges to use certain resources. These mechanisms of authority differed from the coercion of the previous decades and generated a distinctive colonial variety of corvée in New France.

THE COLONIAL BUREAUCRACY OF NEW FRANCE, 1726–31

The mid-eighteenth-century corvée labour reforms derived from a new generation of administrators that sought to increase the economic productivity of France's North American colonies. In Canada, the new governor, Charles de Beauharnois, and his intendant, Gilles Hocquart, implemented a series of economic reforms.[10] As David J. Horton asserts, "the capitalistic market mechanisms of demand and price replaced state paternalism," and both the governor and the intendant set out to streamline the extraction and transport of natural resources.[11] The renewed interest in corvée, natural resources, and the infrastructure required to facilitate trade stemmed from a larger initiative on behalf of the French Crown to transform its North American colonies into profitable ventures to rival its European competitors, especially Britain and Spain.[12]

In the colonial imagination, stockpiling Canadian resources not only benefitted the domestic economy but also a broader vision for the expanding transatlantic French Empire. Between 1717 and 1731, the French Crown settled, conquered, and appropriated land in North America for the establishment of new colonies. In the Midwest, the Illinois Country (renamed Upper Louisiana) emerged as a focal point of agriculture to supply a modest number of French colonists migrating to New Orleans (Lower Louisiana) and to trade posts in the Mississippi Valley. In the Illinois villages, French settlers, Indigenous Americans, and enslaved individuals of African descent formed what Robert Michael Morrisey calls an "empire by collaboration."[13] These borderland families became "indispensable suppliers of food for Louisiana," and thus provided the sustenance upon which the Mississippi communities relied.[14] Through kinship, marriage, and negotiation, they also generated, and maintained, the incredibly valuable interpersonal alliances with western Algonquin-speaking people that formed the backbone of the fur trade.

Looking south down the Mississippi from the Illinois Country, French schemes of imperial expansion included the large-scale forced transportation of thousands of enslaved West Africans to the Americas to work on cotton, tobacco, and indigo plantations established in the southernmost portions of Lower Louisiana.[15] Although slow population growth ultimately hindered the expansion of a French market economy in the South, administrators continued to hope that the importation of West African slave labour to the fledgling region would produce a plantation economy to rival that in the Caribbean. As Leslie Choquette states, "tobacco and indigo were produced for export quantities, but as in the French Caribbean of the previous century, large-scale plantation agriculture emerged only gradually."[16]

Beauharnois and Hocquart intended to connect Canada – and corvée workers – to this enlarged French Empire.[17] They believed that the raw materials from New France, especially timber, could stimulate an imperial shipbuilding industry that would supply the Caribbean Islands with vessels for trade. But first those resources had to be extracted, which necessitated the development of highways and ferries constructed by habitants to facilitate commercial activity. For newly appointed colonial bureaucrats and royal ministers alike, corvée held the potential to achieve this.[18] Lacking enslaved individuals of African descent, Indigenous slavery, or a large population of readily available engagés, the French often turned to habitants, whom they decided would provide the necessary labour for restructuring the colony's domestic communication networks, trade depots, and fortifications.

After taking office in 1726, Beauharnois quickly set out to overhaul the Canadian economy to fit with France's transatlantic expansion. Before habitants could construct roads and dredge ditches, the first step in his plan required stabilizing New France's existing borders and trade alliances. In addition to securing diplomatic relationships with the Algonquin-speaking communities critical to the fur trade, Beauharnois encouraged commerce between other parts of North America, such as the Illinois Country, and Quebec.[19] This expansion relied heavily on coercing Indigenous nations to increase the reach of the fur trade through intimidation, raids, and elaborate gift-giving ceremonies orchestrated by the French.[20] Furthermore, Beauharnois grew concerned about British encroachment on New France.[21] As Anglo-American settlers moved inland away from the coast, the British put pressure on French-allied Native American communities and undermined the potential profit of France's monopoly over the fur trade in the New World. To protect these alliances, Beauharnois ordered the securing of New France's borders, especially on Lake Ontario to the west and, in the 1740s, Lake Champlain to the south.

While Beauharnois occupied his time shoring up New France's borders, his intendant, Gilles Hocquart, sought a massive overhaul in the St Lawrence Valley's communication network. In order to connect Canadian communities to imperial markets, they first had to be linked to one another. Indeed, as Horton states, "roads, he [Beauharnois] realized, were important for the development of internal commerce."[22] As a result, he undertook the uncompleted project of the King's Highway to connect Montreal and Quebec City. This endeavour included the overhaul of all local roads so that habitants could bring their goods to nearby markets and purchase supplies from around the empire.[23] In addition to aiding habitants, the roads would provide a system of transportation for the hardwood timber that colonial officials desired for ship-building in the Caribbean.[24]

Hocquart's scheme to extract resources from New France relied on willing and enthusiastic subordinates (*subdélégués*) to translate his policies into achievable orders.[25] Perhaps most important, he required a grand voyer to mobilize the rural population for corvée labour on the highways. In 1729, after the death of Pierre Robineau de Bécancour, Hocquart nominated Jean-Eustace de Lanoullier Boisclerc to the position of grand voyer. Hocquart's ambition of economic reformation in Canada required the Office of the Grand Voyer to efficiently achieve the construction of the King's Highway and to improve the clusters of roads that already existed. To this end, Hocquart empowered the Office of the Grand Voyer, largely allowing Boisclerc to independently survey roads in the rural communities while he focused on large-scale projects, such as the timber industry. This included granting the grand voyer his own court system to effectively punish disobedience related to corvée and appointing a number of subordinates to aid Boisclerc in each of the three St Lawrence governments.[26]

Many commissioned intermediaries filled out the lower echelons of the Canadian colonial administration as it related to corvée labour.[27] They reported directly to the intendant of New France and other top-ranking civil administrators. The grand voyer, for example, employed several sous-voyer, lower-ranking surveyors, to implement direct orders. They "organized the assemblies" and "intervened when the habitants did not get along."[28] In addition, militia captains also came to hold a specific place in this social order. They worked with the surveyors to manage the implementation of corvée and ensured that the project was completed.[29]

The creation of a bureaucratic colonial state in New France should be engaged in dialogue with scholarship that addresses the centralization of authority in early modern European civil administration. Scholarship on the British Empire, for example, has exposed the relationship between taxation, warfare, and state building. As John Brewer argues, in eighteenth-century Britain, Parliament and the Crown generated a "fiscal-military state" constructed upon enduring military engagements, the collection of taxes to fund imperial expansion, and the civil administrative institutions associated with the production of revenue.[30] Kathleen Wilson asserts, however, that "historians have been less interested in the thinking about 'the colonial state' as such, which has been conceptualized by default … as *un état manqué* of weak institutional forms and limited coercive powers."[31] As she illuminates, colonial state power was "performative rather than institutional and … focused on the organization of social life and national affiliation among colonizers and colonized alike."[32]

During the mid-eighteenth century, corvée came to function as what James C. Scott refers to as a "regulation of individual and collective behavior that polity depended upon, rendering 'domestic order' within and without the state possible."[33] For the habitants performing corvée on roads, ditches, and fortifications, the labour was not only pragmatic but also symbolic. As a community, habitants agreed that the allocation of their work towards a given project aligned with their own objectives. In response, the French regime increasingly turned to corvée as a strategy to mobilize labour for its own ambitions, such as constructing a continuous highway that connected its largest seaport in the north, Quebec, to its most profitable ventures in the southern portions of New France.

THE CONSTRUCTION OF THE KING'S HIGHWAY, 1730–40

For the habitants coming of age in the 1730s, the most striking difference between corvée for them and that for their fathers or grandfathers would have been the centralization of work orders through the Crown's officials. In particular, the reforms of Charles de Beauharnois and his intendant, Giles Hocquart, streamlined corvée mobilization. Empowering the grand voyer and his sous-voyers with a legal mechanism to enforce corvée in the parishes transformed the road construction initiative at the local level. For the first time, the Crown installed observable accountability to ensure that parishes would build and maintain roads. Militia captains, those local intermediaries previously responsible for mobilizing corvée, had subdélégués of the king in their communities to aid them in this endeavour. This ambitious new cohort of subordinates eventually completed a series of highways that sprawled across the St Lawrence and Champlain Valleys.

The various appointments to positions in the civil and military bureaucracy occurred during a three-decade period of peace that provided the time these individuals needed to undertake public infrastructure projects not possible during war. While Governor Beauharnois occupied his time fortifying the posts on Lake Ontario, Hocquart focused his efforts on improving the communication and defensive networks of Canada. His plan included a multifaceted approach that involved securing resources and surveying territory not yet settled by habitants.

First, under the direction of Boisclerc, the road system of New France desperately required an overhaul. The patchwork of roads that surrounded Montreal and Quebec City needed repair and, more important, had to link at Trois-Rivières to form one continuous highway.[34] This highway would then connect with several new fortified posts planned for construction on the Richelieu, thus forming a web of roads that knit the region together.[35]

Finally, Hocquart planned to survey and settle the Champlain Valley.[36] This area would include two forts on Lake Champlain – Fort Saint-Frédéric and Fort Carillon (with the latter defending a portage point at Lake George to buffer against a British invasion).[37]

In order to execute these state-sponsored public works, the governor and intendant fell back on utilizing corvée labour. By 1730, colonial officials had generated a delicate but legally competent strategy of mobilizing corvée for public works. Over the first three decades of the eighteenth century, habitants begrudgingly provided corvée for the fortifications at Quebec and Montreal.[38] Although they often refused to show up for work and whispered of mutiny when they did, French engineers and administrators had learned several strategies to ensure that habitants would comply with orders of corvée.[39] The system of fines and branding those who did not participate in construction projects as "refusers" on the tax roll also served to stymie large-scale disobedience among the parishes.[40]

Although inefficient and prone to provoking unrest among the local population, the previous intendants had established a general legal framework and "custom" of mobilizing corvée for road construction.[41] Militia captains and the parish assembly appointed "principal habitants" to organize labour and the number of days that each individual would contribute.[42] Habitants typically constructed the portion of the road that passed through their "dwellings."[43] Militia captains could, in special cases, reorganize squads of workers based on the layout of the parish and assign special tasks to those inhabitants who lived in the second, third, and fourth ranks of dwellings.[44] With regard to those habitants who disobeyed, the seigneur or parish priest could impose fines and legal recourse. Nothing, however, reinforced the power relationships attached to corvée more than the actual performance of the labour. French civil law relied on repetition to fortify "customs," those unwritten social arrangements that bound habitants, seigneurs, and the Crown together.

In this sense, every road, ditch, and bridge constructed by habitants set a precedent for utilizing the agrarian population for mandatory work. As James C. Scott suggests, "every visible, outward use of power [provides a] symbolic gesture of domination that serves to manifest and reinforce the hierarchal order."[45] On one hand, the routine associated with corvée on roads became normalized by the 1730s. This routine fostered the production of a Canadian custom of corvée that integrated into its legal traditions not only French influences but also the realities of the New World. On the other hand, punishment and public sentencing in the government courts dissuaded habitants from violating custom. Indeed, legal enforcement coerced the "refuser" to publicly acquiesce to "the judgement of his superior" and "implicitly the punishment that follow[ed] from it."[46]

The punishment of refusers was more symbolic than disciplinary. Habitants who evaded corvée could expect a day in prison, but, more likely than not, the intendant or the government court would impose a heavy fine and send the individual to fulfill his obligation.[47] This sentencing represented both a dramatic demonstration of state authority and a form of intimidation that re-established the power relationships in the parish or seigneurie. With the full weight of royal authority, the punishment of refusers most likely functioned to make an example of disobedient habitants and to dissuade others from being similarly negligent.

Building on the precedent of using corvée for road building, as discussed in chapter 1, by 1732, several concurrent changes stemming from the Crown rekindled plans for the construction of the King's Highway. In France, King Louis XV and his administrators in Versailles undertook a calculated program of improving the land communication networks of the empire.[48] Indeed, as Kenneth Banks asserts, the king and his ministers "demanded not merely to understand the extent of the kingdom but to grasp its potential and fully impose royal order in every corner."[49] Philibert Orry, controller general, ordered a new road system that connected the provinces and territories of the kingdom. These relied on the mobilization of mass corvée labour, in which French peasants worked up to fourteen days on the sections of roads that passed through their seigneuries.[50]

Hocquart and his new grand voyer echoed the Continental initiatives in North America. First, he ordered habitants of the southern parishes in the Montreal government to construct a road that connected the city to Fort Chambly.[51] The new road would provide a critical communication line for the city of Montreal, not only facilitating supply routes to the St Lawrence from the Champlain Valley but also accelerating troop movement to rebuff any attempted British invasion from the south should it occur. Boisclerc designed the road to pass through Longueuil – the site of the corvée riot in 1717 – and the village centre was to function as a primary depot for goods transported to Montreal.[52]

This time habitants from several parishes contributed corvée for the Chambly road. Hocquart ordered all "habitants who ha[d] land on both sides of the Saint-Antoine Creek together with those who established on the

Côteau Rouge" and all "those of the Barony of Longueuil who [were] holding [land] along the Chambly road" to participate in a joint operation to complete the project. In an effort to alleviate the corvée duty of Longueuil habitants, he proclaimed that, "in order not to prejudice the lands of the other habitants of the seigneurie and to avoid the multiplicity of King's roads," all parishes in the region would contribute. Between "forty to sixty habitants" worked on the highway "to make the Chambly road practicable," also adding "two ditches and dykes." Hocquart ordered all habitants "to maintain it thereafter being of their common good and useful to all." To execute these orders, the clerk of the grand voyer, Languetan, and the captains of the militia surveyed the road and organized corvée for construction.[53]

The Chambly road represented the first step in a larger scheme to connect the regions of Canada. With Chambly under construction, Hocquart and Boisclerc turned their attention to the King's Highway. Determined to complete the unfinished project that had been under way since 1706, Boisclerc relied on several innovative tactics to do so.[54] Starting in Quebec City, Boisclerc travelled to every parish and seigneurie on the northern côte of the St Lawrence River. In each, he met with the seigneur, captains of the militia, and principal habitants. After collectively discussing the best route, he ordered them to repair or construct the road that ran through their jurisdiction. Boisclerc then moved onto the next parish, eventually making his way south to Montreal.[55] Hocquart seems to have given Boisclerc full responsibility and autonomy to set the roads in order.[56] This shift is evidenced by a sharp decrease in road construction orders from the intendant and an increase in minutes appearing in the papers of the grand voyer.[57] This strategy also reduced the problem of conflicting work orders that had plagued the first several decades of the eighteenth century.

The increased responsibility of the grand voyer for harnessing corvée was met with approval in both Quebec and Versailles. In October 1732, Hocquart praised Boisclerc for putting "in order all the habitants for the repair and maintenance of the highways, service which had been neglected until now."[58] In another letter, he emphasized Boisclerc's efficiency, stating: "[the king] can not, Monseigneur, choose for this country a better grand voyer then sieur Boisclerc, he is tireless in his courses ... puts all his satisfaction to fulfill his duty with the application and the activities that one can desire." Hocquart continued: "[the] colony is now enjoying the advantages he affords, and it would have felt it for a long time if his predecessors had exercised their office with the same zeal." Writing on the lacklustre performance of the previous grand voyer and his inability to complete the King's Highway, Hocquart envisioned a communication network stretching across that colony that would "remedy their negligence and [the] abandonment in which befell the maintenance and the establishment of the public roads."[59] In 1734, Hocquart granted Boisclerc jurisdiction over a grand voyer court that could settle habitant disputes over labour and punish individuals who neglected their share of corvée.

Habitants had worked on roads surrounding Quebec City and Montreal for the past several decades, most of which only required repair and maintenance. Between 1706 and 1729, habitants in the parishes of Quebec worked on clusters of roads in the immediate area of the city, such as Charlesbourg, Cap-Rogue, Beauport, Ancienne Lorette, and the surrounding environs.[60] These included parishes directly on the St Lawrence, such as Neuville to the southwest of Quebec City and Ange-Gardien to the northeast.[61] Across the river on the Côte Sud, the seigneuries of La Durantaye, Lauzon, and Saint-Nicolas contained a developed system of roads.[62] Similarly, habitants on corvée had also worked the roads for the government of Montreal. These ran throughout the Isle of Montreal, La Prairie, Longueuil, Boucherville, and Varennes.[63] Bégon, the previous intendant, had monitored the construction of many of these projects during his tenure, with the result that the patchwork of roads required only annual maintenance.

The underdeveloped portions of the King's Highway lay in the segment of road that ran through the government of Trois-Rivières. By the mid-eighteenth century, the region contained mostly rural parishes on the north and south côtes of the St Lawrence. The city of Trois-Rivières – roughly halfway between Quebec City and Montreal – served as the administrative centre of the government. Trois-Rivières posed several challenges for the construction of the King's Highway. First, it was the least populated of the three governments.[64] Since custom dictated that habitants only built the stretch of road that passed through their land, underpopulated regions, such as Trois-Rivières, lacked the workers needed to complete the highway. This was especially true in the section that connected Montreal to the city of Trois-Rivières, which contained marshes, streams, islands, and hills that flooded in the spring and dissuaded habitants from taking concessions directly on the St Lawrence River.[65] Furthermore, the St Lawrence widened considerably at the seigneurie of Sorel, forming Lake Saint-Pierre. The lake's unpredictable flooding had previously dissuaded habitants from settling on it, and, thus, the region lacked the personnel to build the elongated section that wrapped around the shoreline.

Between 1733 and 1734 Boisclerc focused his attention on the critical stretch of road that connected Montreal and Trois-Rivières. In January 1733, he surveyed a road around Lake Saint-Pierre that ran over "a hill on the land" and was "covered from floods" that had discouraged settlement in the area. Moreover, this new route "engaged more habitants to take concessions on this côte" and provided an incentive for them to move to the area.[66] His plan proved successful, and twelve habitants and their families took up concession on the lake.[67] By October, Hocquart noted that the Lake Saint-Pierre section of the road "ha[d] engaged a number of habitants to settle there" and that more "hasten[ed] to ask for concessions on the front of the road." Indeed, this also solved the labour shortage, with habitants able to provide corvée for clearing the area of forest and road construction.[68] In a letter to Versailles, Hocquart proudly boasted: "there is reason to believe that in a few years the communication to Montreal will be as free by land as it is now by water."[69]

Boisclerc relied on corvée from the newcomers on Lake Saint-Pierre and the neighbouring parishes of the district. Labour on the highway took place from March until October, with habitants performing a variety of duties. The Saint-Pierre segment of the highway passed through previously uninhabited stretches of the colony and required clearing the roads of trees and the "old stumps" left behind.[70] In addition to the construction of the actual road, habitants worked on ten bridges "from 40 up to 60 feet long."[71] These bridges connected sections of road that passed through the region described by Boisclerc as a "marshy space," subject to flooding in the spring "because of the waters of the lake."[72] For this reason, he chose to build "a league and a half in the depths of land that [was] not conceded," where many "habitants of this place believe[d] it would be easy to pass" with their carts. Building in the interior also eased auxiliary tasks associated with corvée, such as bridge construction. The higher altitude contained only narrow rivers, where Boisclerc insisted "it would be easy to build bridges" over the small gaps.[73]

For segments of the road that needed to pass over larger rivers and rapids, Boisclerc ordered the construction of a system of ferries to transport habitants, their carts, and livestock. In 1733, for example, he ordered the construction of "a ferry to the grande Rivière du Loup."[74] Locals residents collected the timber "necessary for construction" of the bridges and ferries that connected these sections of the road.[75] Habitants performing corvée constructed

Figure 2.1
James Peachy, *A N.E. View of the Bridge at Maskinongé* (1778).

Painter James Peachy not only captures the bridge, typical of Canadian design and construction, but also the fence lining the road in the lower right-hand corner of the painting. Bridges in New France ranged in size but were typically six feet wide to accommodate the size of horse-drawn carts. Most work orders for roads included digging drainage ditches and fences, and the intendant required that the community maintain them.

several additional ferries that augmented the King's Highway communication network. One ferry in the seigneurie of L'Assomption passed over the river of the same name. An additional ferry in the city of Trois-Rivières traversed the St Lawrence to the Côte Sud on the opposite side. These ferries provided the region with a functioning network of roads and bridges that formed the backbone of the King's Highway and eased transportation for travellers between Quebec City and Montreal.[76]

Corvée was essential to building the King's Highway and took place under the customs developed in the New World.[77] As with other roadwork, habitants were responsible for gathering materials, constructing, and maintaining the sections that passed through their seigneurie or parish.[78] In contrast to the haphazard dissemination of orders under Intendant Bégon, all corvée organization was personally directed by Boisclerc. Indeed, he "put in order all habitants for the repair and maintenance of the highways," a service that Beauharnois held "had been neglected" under the previous administration.[79] Moreover, Boisclerc offered several incentives to habitants to settle the area and improve the conditions of the King's Highway in those areas. By 1736, fifty habitants and their families had taken up concession on the Trois-Rivières-Montreal section of the road.[80]

Learning from the previous administration's shortcomings, however, Boisclerc was careful not to overextend the habitants performing corvée on the roads. He ensured that road building did not conflict with the rhythms of agricultural life by timing the work so that it would take place after the spring planting and before the harvest season. After a poor harvest one year, Boisclerc even dismissed corvée workers at Trois-Rivières early so they could "go elsewhere to seek subsistence not having harvested enough in 1732." He also favoured sites that contained enough timber and building materials on location to spare "the poor habitants" from burdensome transportation.[81] In sum, by allowing habitants to take breaks during key points in the agricultural cycle, these policies avoided the social unrest typical of the early eighteenth century.

Governor Beauharnois praised Boisclerc's efforts. In a letter to the minister regarding the progress of the King's Highway, the intendant claimed: "[I could not] choose for this country a better Grand Voyer then sieur Boisclerc, he is tireless in his courses." Furthermore, he commented that the grand voyer "put all his satisfaction to fulfill his duty with the application and the activities that one [could] desire." Indeed, Beauharnois believed that long anticipated completion of the King's road would provide New France with an abundance of opportunities, including ease of travel, the transportation of goods, the communication of orders, and the extraction of resources. He summed up these characteristics, stating: "the colony is now enjoying the advantages that [Boisclerc] affords and it would have felt it for a very long time if his predecessors had exercised their office with the same zeal."[82] In August 1735, Boisclerc successfully completed the journey from Quebec City to Montreal on the King's Highway in just four days. The clusters of local roads surrounding the two cities had been transformed into one continuous highway, uniform in dimensions, with a system of ferries that spanned the watersheds of the St Lawrence.

Habitants living in the vicinity of the King's Highway were responsible for the upkeep and repair of the highway – a custom that was upheld in some places but ignored in others. In Montreal, for example, habitants of the surrounding environs provided corvée on roads and bridges that connected their parishes. In Longue Point, Point-aux-Trembles, and Saint-Laurent, groups of habitants disregarded this obligation, noting that the public suffered from "their negligence and disobedience." Hocquart ordered "all habitants of the côtes on both the north and south côtes of [the Montreal] government to work by law" repairing public works. Jean-Baptise Hervieux, clerk to Boisclerc, spearheaded the initiative to ensure that habitants maintained their roads. Hocquart ordered Hervieux to mark roads and bridges "for the convenience and the utility of the habitants of said côtes" and to collect fines "on offenders of twelve livres payable without further conviction." The churchwardens of the parishes collected these fines and placed the refusers in the tax roll. Hocquart authorized Hervieux to nominate "in place of the refusers other habitants to make the roads and bridges" – men who would receive a certified refund for their additional work.[83]

THE EXPANSION OF NEW FRANCE: THE CHAMPLAIN AND RICHELIEU VALLEYS, 1740–48

Along with the St Lawrence highways, colonial officials also embarked on an ambitious imperial scheme to settle the areas along the Richelieu River and the Champlain Valley. Peacetime allowed the Beauharnois administration time to organize, develop, and cultivate these two regions, which had received little attention since the end of the War of Spanish Succession. Referred to by the governor as a "project of colonization," Hocquart and Beauharnois imagined a series of thriving agricultural series of settlements on the banks of Lake Champlain.[84] Scouts and merchants reported on the quality of hardwood oak trees that the Crown could use for ship construction and the fertility of the soil. In addition, Lake George, the portage on the La Chute River, and Lake Champlain provided a waterway to the British colonies. They hoped these settlements would provide resources for the Crown and serve as a defensive buffer against the encroaching British colonies to the south of New France. The new settlement was to be located adjacent to a proposed fortification called Fort Saint-Frédéric, which was located on a peninsula in Lake Champlain.

The colonization of Lake Champlain hinged on three interrelated objectives in the imagination of the colonial administration. First, the fort would

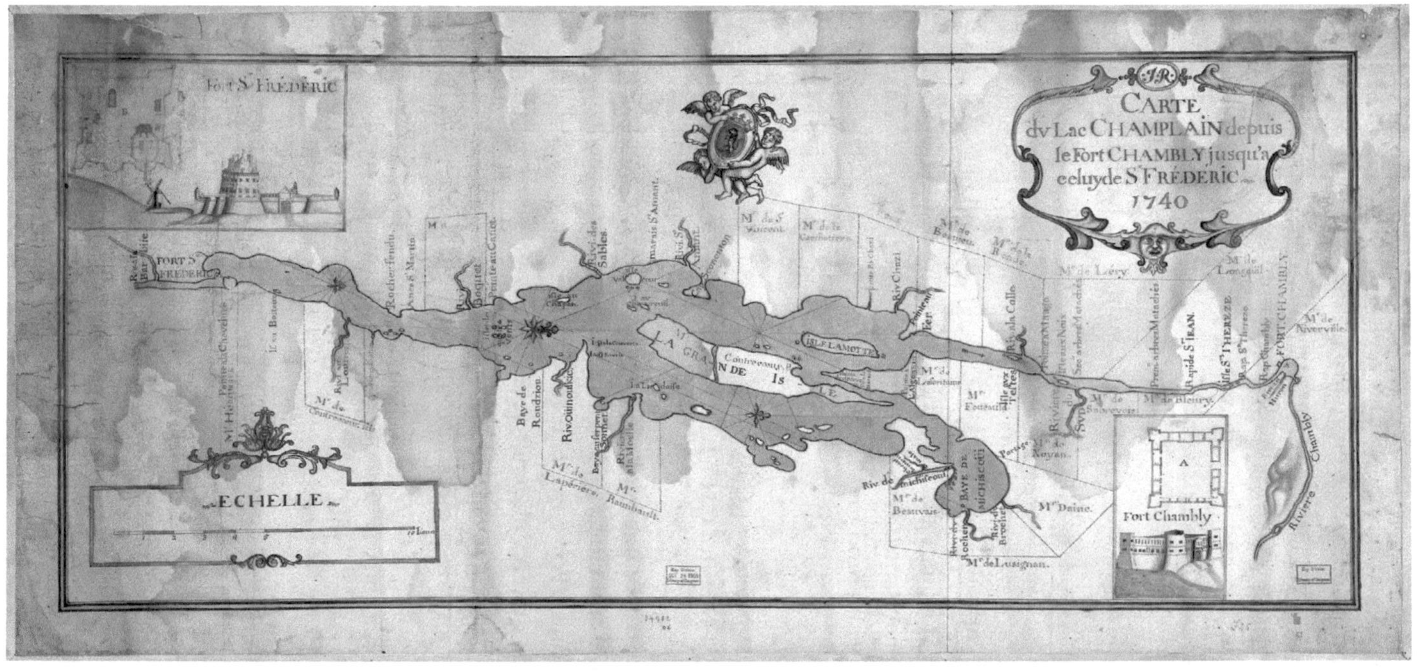

Figure 2.2
Carte du Lac Champlain depuis le Fort Chambly jusqu'a celuyde St. Frederic (1740).

During the mid-eighteenth century, French Canadian administrators hoped to settle the Champlain Valley with seigneuries. This map exhibits the subdivision of seigneuries and land grants along the lake. The insert of Fort Saint Fréderic also includes the mill that was constructed to support the soldiers garrisoning the defensive position.

provide a front-line defence against the British if they chose to invade New France. Fort Saint-Frédéric overlooked a narrow section of Lake Champlain, which made any naval advance impossible without first neutralizing its defensive capabilities.[85] Second, habitants who settled the region could provide corvée to build future roads that Boisclerc mapped in the area and to link them with the newly constructed King's Highway.[86] Third, and most lucratively, the hardwood oak in the region could offer timber for the construction of ships, and habitants could cultivate much needed cash crops, such as tobacco, to bolster Canada's domestic agriculture.[87]

Beauharnois planned an ambitious project of social engineering in the woodlands of southeastern New France. From the beginning of the "project of colonization," seigneurial customs and corvée factored into the decision making of colonial officials.[88] First, surveyors travelled to the region, projecting cadastral maps and subdividing land into seigneuries.[89] Second, the governor then administered titles to seigneurs speculating on the area. The final step required seigneurs to subdivide their landholdings into concessions and to relocate habitants so that they could bring their families and labour to the Champlain Valley.[90] In theory, these new parishes would not only produce self-sustaining communities akin to those on the St Lawrence but also provide the corvée necessary for harvesting timber and wheat for the fort's garrison.[91] The initial plans called for several outbuildings, such as a mill that soldiers and habitants would erect on the King's Domaine.[92]

Plans for the construction of Fort Saint-Frédéric and its seigneurial environs began in 1738 when the governor officially authorized the settlement of the Lake Champlain region. By May, Beauharnois received approval from Versailles and ordered Hocquart to expediently make "concessions to those who wish[ed] to settle on these lands." The prospective habitants would take up concessions "three arpents frontage on forty of depth, at the expense of a cens per acre of frontage and twenty shillings per acres of surface." Each habitant would contribute to the effort providing a "half minot of wheat for forty arpents in area" for the "maintenance of the fort." Furthermore, Beauharnois ordered that surveyors "reserve for his Majesty all the isle of the new fort up to forty arpents of frontage" in addition to a King's Domaine "up to 120 arpents," on which habitants would provide corvée planting, cultivating, and harvesting.[93]

To encourage rapid settlement, the governor offered habitants special privileges if they relocated to the Lake Champlain seigneuries. Indeed, he stated: "to accelerate this establishment his Majesty will find it good that the habitants who will make concessions there are discharged during the first three years of the payments of cens and annuities which his Majesty is willing to hand over." According to this plan, habitants who moved to the region would gain exemptions from burdensome obligations of seigneurial New France, such as land taxes and the grist-mill banalité. As a further incentive, the Crown would provide monetary aid to the first six habitants relocating to Lake Champlain, as long as the assistance did "not exceed the sum of 150 livres for each of these habitants."[94]

After finishing work on the King's Highway in autumn 1738, Boisclerc travelled to Fort Saint-Frédéric to survey Lake Champlain and map a potential route for a road. Hocquart ordered that "two to three good working habitants" from the government of Montreal accompany him to examine "the quality of the lands around the fort and those which [were] vis-à-vis in the extent of five or six leagues." Boisclerc and his companions met with the fort's storekeeper, Merdard Vallette de Chévigny, and together they toured the region. In a letter to Versailles, Chévigny commented that Boisclerc "visited four places around the fort to find out if it was good" and to survey the best locations to build the new communities. He suggested further developing a forty-arpent stretch of land already under cultivation by farmers with wheat and other grains. Indeed, Chévigny proclaimed that he could not "see any more beautiful grains than what he produced" and that there were "in the environs of the Fort enough to make meadows to raise two hundred cows." Boisclerc echoed these sentiments and said that, upon his arrival, he "marked and measured on the King's Domaine in the vicinity of the fort ninety lands to be distributed to habitants who [would] settle there."[95]

The seigneuries in the Champlain Valley connected to a much larger communication network as envisioned by Beauharnois, Hocquart, and Boisclerc. The second stage of the colonization project included the reinforcement of the Richelieu River and consisted of improving Fort Chambly, building a second supply depot further south on the river, and constructing a series of roads that connected these two defensive works to the city of Montreal. As they did with the Champlain construction projects, colonial officials planned on harnessing corvée labour to build the new fortifications, roads, and supply depots along the Richelieu.[96]

As the colony's southern border, the Richelieu required a network of defensive fortifications. By the mid-eighteenth century Fort Chambly remained the only garrison in the area, and the military primarily utilized the structure as an outpost to warn of a British invasion. The fort provided a formidable defensive system, situated on the only riverine passageway into the colony from Lake Champlain and Lake George. Moreover, the fort overlooked a series of rapids that forced any ships or canoes to portage around the post. Built with limestone hauled to the site by corvée workers, the fort itself, while modest, exhibited strategic and tactical value based upon its location on the rapids.[97]

Prior to 1740, the region contained the seigneurie of Chambly with primarily dispersed habitant concessions. Located southeast of Montreal, the seigneurie was connected to the remainder of the region via the Longueuil road built by corvée in 1730. While underdeveloped in comparison to the Isle of Montreal, the Beauharnois administration in Canada envisioned the region as a stronghold of defensive fortifications and a critical supply depot for timber in the Champlain Valley.[98] In order to defend the Richelieu, Beauharnois ordered the construction of a fortified supply depot that was to be located further south on the river than Chambly.[99]

Construction on the supply depot built at Saint-Jean began in 1740. Like Fort Chambly, Saint-Jean sat on a section of the river that had rapids and so required careful navigation.[100] Furthermore, Beauharnois authorized the construction of a flat-bottomed boat that "would sail into Lake Champlain" from the "warehouse or storage area at the top of the Saint-Jean rapids."[101] He intended the Saint-Jean depot to act as a storage facility for supplies heading south to Fort Saint-Frédéric and for timber coming from the Champlain Valley. Additionally, the storehouse would quickly provide resources "to the habitants who establish[ed] it and who settle[ed] following their needs."[102]

While the storage warehouse served the function of docking the Lake Champlain boat, in 1748 the new governor, La Galissoniére, ordered the construction of a true fort at the Saint-Jean rapids. Construction on the new project, renamed Fort Saint-Jean, began in summer 1748, with squads of habitants from the surrounding parishes mobilized for corvée to clear debris and transport earth cleared from the site. Habitants providing corvée brought their carts, described as "small-half tip-carts," to the site.[103] After filling the carts with debris from the warehouse or dirt from the earthworks, the habitants hauled the material away. As an additional incentive to clear the site, the officers and engineers paid the habitants two shillings per trip.[104]

The engineer, Chaussegros de Léry, however, rarely attended the construction site, and the labour for the fort was unorganized. Galissonière's intendant François Bigot commented that the habitants were inefficient and could have made fewer trips to drive down expenses if the site had been "faithfully planned." Half-full carts meant more trips could be squeezed into a day, and the expenses for "the tip-carts of the countryside" reached 2,106 livres and thirteen shillings.[105]

Habitants on corvée also constructed a road that stretched from Saint-Jean to Fort Chambly. Built in July 1748, Boisclerc arrived at the site and organized habitants from the neighbouring parishes to provide corvée on the road. This labour included clearing the forest and covering the road, in addition to building "ditches on either side" that drained into "the small river of Montréal which discharge[d] into the Chambly basin." Boisclerc ensured that the roadwork schedule did not interfere with the agricultural rhythms of habitant life. On 28 July, for example, Boisclerc dismissed habitants on corvée "to do their harvest and hay." After completing the harvest, they returned to the site in September "to complete the rest of the ditches so that they were complete in the beginning of October." He commented that the road "[would] be good and practicable for Fort Saint-Frédéric" and that "it [would] exempt a lot of the expenses to his Majesty for the transport of the effects that [were] led there in that the boat [would] freight them to Fort Saint-Jean."[106]

Corvée played an important role in the construction of highways across Canada. Within two decades, from 1730 to 1750, habitants constructed the Longueuil road, connecting Montreal to Fort Chambly; the King's Highway, connecting Quebec City to Montreal; a number of roads on the Côte Nord; and the Fort Saint-Jean and Chambly road. In order to muster the labour necessary for these projects, colonial officials took a broad approach, only mobilizing corvée for these large state-sanctioned construction projects. Furthermore, they also offered habitants incentives for working, in the form of land concessions, tax-breaks, or payment. Indeed, this differed from the opening decades of the eighteenth century, which witnessed habitants primarily working on local projects or the haphazard communication paths that passed through their parish. In these orders, each parish only worked on its section of a road, compared to what happened in the mid-eighteenth century, when joint-parish operations called upon habitants to complete genuine inter-colony highways.

THE WAR OF AUSTRIAN SUCCESSION, 1744–48

The expansion efforts of the Beauharnois administration were ultimately delayed by a colonial war that required the full mobilization of the habitant labouring population. In May 1744, the War of Austrian Succession reached North America. Initially started in 1740 over Hapsburg claims to the provinces of Silesian and Bohemia, the war eventually erupted into a pan-European conflict. France supported Frederick II's efforts to annex the provinces for an increasingly centralized German state, while Britain, fearing France's influence in Europe, provided aid to the Austrian Hapsburgs. This complex geopolitical engagement eventually spilled into the colonies. Known as King George's War in the Anglo-American colonies, the four-year conflict primarily centred around border disputes. In particular, Britain aimed to challenge French settlement in Acadia and the Ohio Valley, while France sought to defend those areas and to stop the encroachment of American colonists into New England and New York.

The declaration of war in New France required the mobilization of supplies, ammunition, and corvée to ensure that the colony was capable of defending itself against a British invasion. The brief 1690 siege of Quebec loomed large over the conflict, with colonial officials immediately embarking upon improving the fortifications of Quebec City and Montreal. Preparations in Montreal began in 1744, with Josué Dubois Berthelot de Beaucours ordering the re-establishment of the enclosure.[107] Concerning the defences of Montreal, Beaucours lamented that the small parish militias were "so busy that they [were] not of great services" for corvée on the wall. Furthermore, he stated that the habitants of the "countryside ha[d] so much work to do on their own lands that it [was] difficult for them to leave." He added: "the winters are long that is the time that [the habitants] make their seeds and wood for their buildings."[108] Construction on the Montreal enclosure stalled as habitants scrambled to join the militia or picked up the agricultural tasks of those deployed in military service.

Most corvée on fortifications took place in Quebec City. The city's strategic position on the St Lawrence made its inhabitants concerned that the British could invade their colony from the east.[109] These concerns were exacerbated by the successful 1745 British siege and capture of Louisburg. Not only did the capture of Louisburg demoralize French forces but the strategic position on Cape Breton Island afforded the British a launching point for an invasion via the Gulf of St Lawrence.

In response, the military forces deployed to New France (the *troupes de la Marine*) convened a meeting with the civil administration and the "citizens and habitants of Quebec."[110] They argued that the safety of the colony required improving the fortifications surrounding the city. Indeed, the assembly judged that the British meant "to make conquest" of the colony "as judged by the fleet they ha[d] in Louisburg."[111] The initial proposal for the fortification recommended "bastions six feet thick in the ground and eighteenth feet in height under the cord, with rampart, parapet, and buttresses."[112] A provisional committee placed Chaussegros de Léry in charge of the project following a meeting of the residents of Quebec. The committee specifically targeted the corvée, stating that it would be used: "only on the necessity and usefulness of the works represented, to also give the citizens and habitants of this colony our attention on what can equally tend to the maintenance of the government."[113]

The first assembly convened on 26 July 1746 in the Chateau de Saint-Louis. Composed of the colonial administration and the engineers working on the fortifications, the group decided that, based "on representations of the of the Syndic and Corps of merchants as well as by all the citizens and habitants of this city," a second assembly should be organized to include their opinions.[114] The second assembly, which gathered on 30 July, included principal officers of the colony and a select group of principal habitants. During the session, all in attendance contemplated whether to "demolish what ha[d] been done" on the walls or to "continue the enterprise ... if it were decided that the fort [should] be continued." More important, perhaps, they debated who should pay for the wall, and they "deliberated on whether taxation should be done to make it happen."[115] In sum, the assembly consulted the habitant population in an effort to avoid a potentially burdensome taxation.

After several days, the various factions could not arrive at a decision. The military personnel "opted for the continuation of the works" while the "bourgeois" and "the general opinion of all the habitants" called for demolition.[116] As a result, Hocquart left the decision to Versailles. Maurepas decided to "continue the fortifications begun in Quebec," with the habitants of neighbouring parishes providing corvée to aid in the construction. Work on the Quebec fortifications began in July 1747, with "habitants of the côtes" arriving on site with "Banneuax for the transport of land for the ramparts."[117] Careful not to disrupt their agricultural routine, Léry, chief engineer on the fort, dismissed habitants "for the harvest" with the work continuing in late autumn. Despite the habitants' cooperation, Léry reported that "the numbers of workers were not enough for the work he had to do [that] year." Work resumed in the autumn of the following year, with "the habitants of the parishes around Quebec" travelling to the city "with Baneuax to work." They primarily worked on the ramparts of the wall, and Léry commented that, by the end of 1748, "two-thirds of the Ramparts [were] filled with soil and half of the counterscarp [was] finished."[118]

Preparation for an invasion also took place in the countryside. Indeed, habitants primarily performed *corvée de harnois*, providing horses, sleds, and carts "for the service and occasion of war."[119] French High Command believed the British would sail into the Gulf of St Lawrence as they had during the Nine Years' War, and corvée worked to bolster the coastal defences. As a result, most of the corvée labour occurred northeast of Quebec City on the coast of the river leading up to the gulf.

Hocquart ordered the construction of a series of signal fires from the Gulf of St Lawrence to Quebec City on the Côte Sud as a preliminary system of alarm. On 21 July 1744, shortly after the declaration of war in the colonies, he commanded that the signal fires should "pass from côte to côte[] from Pointe Levy to l'Îsle Saint Barnabé to establish fires at night" as the militia captains deemed appropriate.[120] In addition to the clearing, cutting, and transportation of wood necessary to make the signal fires, Hocquart further instructed that "the captains of the militia and officers of the militia of the côtes" raise a "guard day and night of two habitants" to stand guard for two to three hour rotations.[121] He sanctioned *corvée de harnois* for any transportation of materials necessary to the site.[122]

To prevent the British Navy from entering, Hocquart authorized the construction of *cajeux d'artifice*, log rafts with ammunition and black powder on board. If the British fleet entered the gulf, sailors would guide these rafts towards the enemy ships, light them, and ram them into the vessels, thus causing an explosion. At the very least, the cajeux would provide a fiery curtain that would prevent the British ships from advancing.[123]

Habitants provided corvée for the construction of these rafts.[124] Work took place on the Isle d'Coudres. To fortify the small St Lawrence island, habitants constructed a road and fastened together several *cajeux d'artifice*.[125] Although the expense lists from the operation do not mention how many habitants participated in the building of the fire rafts, Hocquart does specify that the cajeux took five months and eighteen days to complete.[126] No habitants lived on the island, and records indicate that militia captains brought them there from the surrounding parishes. Moreover, the intendant compensated these habitants for the time they spent building the rafts. Although the war ended before the British actually invaded, the French did use these types of fire rafts again during the Seven Years' War.

On 24 April 1748, Britain and France signed the Treaty of Aix-la-Chapelle ending hostilities between the two warring empires. In New France, as per conditions of the treaty, the British restored Louisburg to the French. While on a map the war seemed to have affected the colonies very little, on the ground the processes of corvée labour had changed. The defeat of Louisburg had alarmed the entire colony. In particular, corvée became increasingly tied to militia duty, with armed service and defence taking precedent over infrastructure projects. In other words, colonial officials expected habitants to provide militia service first and foremost, with corvée becoming a component of that service. As Louise Dechêne asserts in her watershed study on the Canadian militia, by the War of Austrian Succession, militia duty, war, and the state had become inextricably linked. After this conflict, habitants had as their primary objective an obligation to defend king and country. Orders of corvée would filter through the armed forces and take on more militaristic characteristics.

THE SEVEN YEARS' WAR AND THE FALL OF NEW FRANCE, 1754–59

Peace in North America lasted six years, until a young colonel in the Virginia militia, George Washington, stumbled upon a French sortie in the Ohio Valley borderlands. Originally sent by the governor of Virginia on a surveying expedition in the territory, not far from the French Fort Duquesne, Washington, his Virginia militiamen and a group of British-allied Mingo scouts encountered a French patrol. The two opposing forces collided in the forest and a skirmish erupted, leaving much of the French patrol dead.[127] While the "battle" involved relatively few men, tensions rippled across the Atlantic between the French and British Empires.

Known in Quebec as "the Conquest," or "la Cession," the Seven Years' War led to the demise of New France and the installation of a British colonial administration in the region. From the beginning of the conflict, Canadians played an active role in scouting, combat, and performing labour-intensive tasks. In the opening years of the war (1754–57), *marchél de camp* Louis-Joseph de Marquis de Montcalm mobilized a formidable body of Canadian *milice* as scouts, rangers, and auxiliaries for *la petite guerre* (frontier or guerilla warfare), harassing British troops and their supply lines.[128] In 1756, for example, an estimated nineteen hundred militiamen served in ranks destined for combat in France's western and southern outposts in Ontario, Niagara, and Carillon.[129]

The Canadian militia provided an essential front-line duty in engaging the enemy. Often paired with Indigenous scouts, habitants serving in the ranks of the militia disrupted British supply transports, ambushed enemy patrols, and provided invaluable local knowledge for reconnaissance. Historians have established that these methods of fighting primarily derived from generations of close cultural contact with First Nations Canadians and stood in stark contrast to the rigid rank-and-file discipline of the *troupes de terre* and *troupes de la Marine*. Indeed, according to Martin Nicolai, "constant contact with Indian allies in wartime and the success of their tactics resulted in Canadians adopting not only Indian methods of fighting, but also their attitudes towards war."[130] Christian Crouch has also recently illuminated French officers' observations of Canadians' skill in fighting alongside Indigenous nations in the woodlands of North America.[131] In sum, the vanguard of the Canadian militia contributed to the war effort, prodding the supply routes and front lines of the British Army.

Nearly half of the Canadians mobilized for warfare served in squads of work teams that aided the French professional soldiers with supply and ammunition transportation. Montcalm conscripted over one thousand Canadians each year for labour on supply routes and building fortifications. These men worked ferrying raw materials, ammunition, and weapons to the fortifications that were to provide a buffer against a British invasion. According to François-Gaston de Lévis, the French mobilized fifteen hundred Canadians to operate the supply routes to the west.[132] This group of workers played an especially critical role in securing the western borderlands of the Great Lakes.

Significantly, this labour propped up the communication networks vital to the military operations of the early years of the war. Canadian civilian corvée on bridges and highways connected to the militiamen serving on the western routes and facilitated the supply of information, supplies, and soldiers to the front lines in the woodlands of North America. The militia hauling supplies for the professional French soldiers carried the symbols of empire and weapons of war into the borderlands of New France.

Furthermore, this infrastructure facilitated the maintenance of diplomatic relationships essential for trade with the Iroquois- and Algonquin-speaking people of Canada.[133] The war effort relied on Indigenous alliances both on offensive and defensive campaigns, and French leadership recognized the essential functions that they provided its army in colonial warfare. As Christian Crouch points out, in the woodlands of the Great Lakes and Ohio borderlands "Iroquoians and Algonquians from Kahawake, Kanesatake, or Odanak" navigated the French army through the early stages of the Oswego campaign.[134] They scouted British positions and surveyed the best routes for Canadian militiamen who were transporting supplies, ammunition, livestock, and firearms along the waterways and footpaths.

Despite the larger imperial conflict taking place across North America, many habitants also remained at home – armed and ready to fight, but carrying on day-to-day activities during the bulk of the campaigning season. Archival documentation supports the continuation of mundane corvée routines during the opening years of the war. In 1754, for example, when a bridge fell into disrepair in the seigneurie of Deschambault, the last French-appointed grand voyer, Pierre de Lino, ordered that habitants "immediately repair the bridge over the Portneuf River" as accidents "could happen on this bridge."[135] Similar orders echoed through these early wartime years. Lino ordered the construction of a road in a newly settled fourth concession of Saint-Michel in 1755, and in 1757 a pathway for the fifth and sixth concession in Saint-Charles.[136]

Presumably, maintenance in the parishes and seigneuries also allowed front-line Canadian militia to return from campaigns to functioning homesteads. Even as France's troops in North America prepared for battle in the contested borderlands of empire, many Canadian men carried on their civilian work routines and obligations of corvée. The mundane routines stand in stark contrast to the dramatic confrontations taking place several hundred kilometres to the south. For example, in late July, while Montcalm's army advanced on Fort William Henry, squads of habitants in Cap Santé built a twenty-four-foot (seven-metre) road and dredged two large ditches that connected their community to the King's Highway.[137] Just four days before French artillery fired on the walls of the fort, residents of Saint-Joseph de

Deschambault marked a road that connected the second rank of concession to the parish church and mill.[138]

Habitants who remained at home also assisted the army in providing horse teams and transporting supplies. In his *Mémoire*, Louis Antoine de Bougainville reported that Canadians provided corvée, albeit not without compensation. Bougainville noted that the unique features of corvée in North America, especially its negotiated characteristics, were similar to those used by Parisian-educated engineers who built fortifications in the early eighteenth century. Indeed, he wrote that for Canadian corvée "the habitant [was] paid for his work, either by [the provision of] carriages, journeys [on supply routes], transports, [or] horse teams, sent expressly to carry orders." He continued: "the traveling expenses are paid" to the men performing corvée and "traveling in the King's service."[139] His close attention to compensation reflects how North American corvée diverged from the royal obligations of France.

Scholarship on Canadian participation during the early Seven Years' War has primarily focused on tactics or on the militia's complex interactions with its French counterparts rather than on the full import of corvée that was taking place in the parishes. To be sure, not only did the cross-cultural encounters of Indigenous and Canadian tactics differentiate habitants from professional soldiers stationed in New France, but High Command also deployed them in unique circumstances, often with Indigenous scouts in the woodlands of North America.[140] A vast number of male habitants, however, remained stationed in their parishes, toiling in their fields, preparing for the harvest, and maintaining roads. Tales of muskets, cannons, and fighting in snowshoes have dominated the popular historical memory of Canadian participation in the war. From 1754 to 1757, many habitants spent more time driving horse teams than using a musket, or pushing wheelbarrows and building roads than snow-shoeing in the lower Adirondacks.

Once British High Command mobilized Anglo-American provincial companies that threatened to overwhelm New France, service in the Canadian militia superseded the demand for civilian corvée labour. The loss of Louisburg in particular once again provided the British with a strategic position from which to launch an invasion through the Gulf of St Lawrence. The French suffered losses elsewhere as well. Fort Duquesne in the Ohio River Valley fell into British hands, and the French retreated after a brief skirmish at Carillon in early 1759.[141]

In response, the Crown conscripted all able-bodied men, ages sixteen to sixty, into service for the defence of the colony.[142] During the latter half of the Seven Years' War, especially during the invasion of New France, French colonial officers expected the militia to perform labour as part of its martial duty to the king. Rather than as a separate civil or seigneurial obligation, conscripted Canadians fulfilled work orders as a component of their military service. Commands for labour on earthwork structures and fortifications, for example, appear in relation to Fort Carillon, Fort Saint-Frédéric, and a series of bunkers constructed on the Île-aux-Noix.[143] First and foremost, the French colonial state required all men eligible for militia duty to defend the colony, with any military labour associated with the army integrated into that obligation.[144]

Corvée became a part of soldiers' (both French and Canadian) work routines. In October 1758, for example, François-Gaston, Duc de Lévis oversaw the deployment of Canadian militia "numbering two-thousand men" from the governments of Montreal and Trois-Rivières sent to Fort Saint-Frédéric to build a defensive network in the region. Starting on 18 October, the Canadian militia built a ditch with stakes at the bottom that surrounded the fort. They also constructed a road and palisade enclosure "from the corner of the bastion to the lake." The Canadians completed this work on 1 November, and the "habitants were ordered to return home."[145]

Before their retreat from Carillon, Canadian militia and French professional soldiers also helped to build earthwork defences, such as redoubts. Despite a subdivision of corvée among the *troupes de la Marine* and the militia, Canadians bore a greater burden than did French soldiers. Indeed, as Governor Vaudreuil stated, "the suffering of the Canadians continually charged with degrading corvée and positioning in the most exposed places" made them vulnerable during skirmishes and exhausted the squadrons.[146] In a letter describing corvée to Versailles, Vaudreuil commented: "our officers are responsible for all corvée [and thus should receive] the same compensation as those of the *troupes de Terres*."[147]

In addition to mandatory service in the militia, the safety-valves that the French regime and Canadian parishes had ironed out during the eighteenth century failed to mitigate the burdens related to military labour. The assembly of habitants, for example, seems to have disappeared, instead replaced by the strict and rigid hierarchy of the military.[148] Other agreed-upon customs, such as dismissing habitants for their harvest, also seem to have diminished as the British invasion made service in the military mandatory. As a result, one French solider commented: "the people of Canada must be naturally irritated by the war, many have perished, they are burdened by the most painful work, they have no time to increase their property and even restore their houses [and] some of their livelihoods have been taken away."[149]

As in previoius wars, habitants bore the brunt of corvée required by the military. Their duty to provide this labour and military service was only complicated by the surrender of Quebec City in 1759, which left a third of the St Lawrence Valley in British hands. The British, like the French, sought to use habitant labour and attempted to harness it through a combination of military rule and French custom. In the remaining years of the war, torn between the conquerors and their oaths to the French king, habitants had to make difficult decisions regarding who was to benefit from their labour. The British, ultimately victorious in the conflict, immediately set out to build upon the pre-existing system of corvée that the French had ironed out over the past six decades in the New World. Similar to the French, Parliament and new colonial officials sent to Quebec from around the British Empire also saw corvée as a subsidized labour force that could meet the demands of an expanding imperial market economy.

PART 2

Colonialism and Conquest, 1759–76

The ground I propose for this Citadel commands the whole Town and is commanded no where from the Country; in short it possess every advantage to be wished for, and at a small expense may be fortified, as the Inhabitants of the Country and the Troops in the time of peace may contribute their labour towards it gratis, this the former can have no objection as they were on all occasions formerly liable to Military services, and were all allow'd only provisions.

– James Murray, "Report of the State of the Government of Quebec in Canada," 5 June 1762, mss. 21667, the unpublished papers of Sir Frederick Haldimand, p. 7.

Figure 3.1
Richard Short, *A View of the Jesuits College and Church* (1760).

Richard Short drew a series of sketches after the 1759 British naval bombardment of Quebec City. Buildings exhibit the signs of the cannonade with roof tiles blown off and rubble scattering the ground. Amidst the wreckage, a large cart drawn by three horses passes by carrying barrels. Later in the American Revolution, these same types of carts were commissioned by corvée to transport supplies for the army.

CHAPTER 3

British Conquest and Common Law Corvée, 1759–68

INTRODUCTION

Between September 1759 and December 1767 habitants witnessed the demise of French royal rule and the institution of a new imperial superpower in their colony. In between the battles that ravaged the countryside, political debates in distant London, and treaty signings in Paris, the conquest upended many characteristics of day-to-day life. War, and the consequent fallout of raids, ruined their crops.[1] New English-speaking colonial officials arrived in their seigneuries practising the Protestant faith, which threatened the Roman Catholic customs of New France. The habitants in the seigneuries surrounding Quebec City would have witnessed this all first hand: the battle of the Plains of Abraham, the influx of British soldiers they were forced to quarter, and the pillaging of their hard-worked farms. They most likely believed that the British would replace their Catholic priests as the spiritual leaders of their communities with Anglican ministers and that the conquerors would eliminate all the symbols of the French monarchy, replacing them with that of a Protestant king.[2]

Amidst the uncertainty, an important characteristic of seigneurial life remained constant: corvée. In the immediate aftermath of the war, the new British administration needed habitants to work ploughing fields, collecting timber, building roads, and repairing bridges. For the average habitant, the routine of corvée remained largely unchanged and strikingly familiar. Their superiors still posted work orders to the door of the local parish. They still worked on similar tasks, for a similar number of days, and for similar compensation. Their captains of the militia oversaw and managed the projects.

They petitioned when the labour didn't suit them, and "refusers" received the same monetary punishment for their infractions.[3]

British colonial administrators and military personnel, however, had a problem. Originally derived from French civil custom, corvée did not exist in British common law.[4] Moreover, British ministers overwhelmingly detested French feudal practices and branded these principles as antiquated and despotic compared to their elected Parliament.[5] On one hand, they needed habitants to work, and work for cheap; on the other hand, officials remained hesitant to incorporate French custom into their own Protestant, "free" empire.[6]

To achieve this, behind the scenes – in the offices of colonial bureaucrats and parliamentary ministers – corvée witnessed a transformation. The British desired resources from their new province, and corvée labour factored into that economic equation. Gradually, they formalized and articulated a new law code that integrated corvée into the British imperial system. The profits of habitant labour supported the new endeavours of the Crown and Parliament. To the habitants digging up drainage ditches on their local parish road these changes might not have been readily apparent. Their work, however, was generating a new imperial vision of the province, one that would be challenged and contested in the decade leading up to the American Revolution.

This chapter examines corvée in each of the new "districts" of the province of Quebec (Quebec, Trois-Rivières, and Montreal) to show how the British appropriated pre-existing labour arrangements to support an imperial market economy and to rebuild public infrastructure. In order to harness and standardize the corvée, political officials embarked on an ambitious project to determine the demographics of the population, political hierarchy of the colony, customs of the habitants, and the methods by which Parliament would proceed to mobilize labour in the territory. After the Treaty of Paris, the British experimented with corvée on public works, such as roads, bridges, and ferries. Administrators decided to leave local French customs in place but appointed British magistrates to oversee the deployment of labour. Furthermore, the British actively sought to mobilize corvée for the extraction of natural resources, such as iron and timber. By 1767, inflation and corvée had overextended the habitants of the province, prompting Parliament to initiate debate over reforming the colonial law code of Canada.

Writing about the consequences of the Seven Years' War, Colin Calloway states: "historians have long recognized the significance of 1763 in setting

America on a course to revolution a dozen years later."[7] Eliga Gould echoes this sentiment, asserting that Parliament's protection of Atlantic shipping and access to European markets obligated the colonies to pay taxes based on the "assumption that the colonists were subject to Parliament by virtue of a common nationality."[8] While both historians highlight "the schism between metropolitan and provincial definitions" of empire in the English-speaking Atlantic, most anglophone historians do not take into account seventy thousand of the king's new North American colonists or how those individuals processed the political centralization of the mid-1760s.[9] Whitehall's political reform in the newly created province of Quebec appropriated pre-existing corvée labour arrangements to help bolster an enlarged North American imperial economy. Habitants' adjustments to their new colonial masters deserves to be studied in conjunction with the larger British Empire in North America.

THE BRITISH CONQUEST OF CANADA, 1759–61

During the eighteenth century, Great Britain participated in a number of large-scale, imperial conflicts that dramatically increased the resources devoted to military activities, augmented the number of personnel required to operate civil administration, and inflated the national debt. During the sixteenth century the House of Commons developed a centralized system of tax collection,[10] which was largely a derivative of medieval patterns of landholding. More specifically, the island nation's obligation for a large navy required the production of efficient bureaucratic offices to oversee daily commercial enterprises and military engagements.[11] As Britain conducted warfare against Continental European nations to obtain new colonies and to defend previously established settlements, ministers augmented the number of civil administration offices and standardized these departments through the distribution of annual salaries, government pensions, a fixed time schedule, and the installation of an ethos of public duty.[12] In sum, Parliament and the Crown generated a political entity – a "fiscal-military state" – constructed upon enduring military engagements, the collection of taxes to fund imperial expansion, and the civil administrative institutions associated with the production of revenue.

The British fiscal-military state required an exceptional number of workers to help the armed forces run. During most of the eighteenth century, imperial wars, the demand for soldiers, sailors, and labourers far surpassed the empire's regularly available professionals. The reality of eighteenth-century military engagements meant that supplies, ammunition, equipment, and personnel needed to be ferried long distances, sometimes oceans apart, to meet strategic objectives. More often than not, the actual work of hauling around people, materials, and supplies fell upon the rank-and-file in the military – either by professional soldiers and sailors or through conscription. Indeed, John Brewer asserts that "in every major eighteenth century war the government used conscription to swell the army's ranks."[13]

British military officers stationed in the colonies were no strangers to harnessing a spectrum of inequality and redeploying workers for imperial gain. In the Seven Years' War, planters in the Caribbean, for example, hired out enslaved individuals of African descent to the British military to build defensive fortifications and to ferry supplies during periods of war.[14] In that same conflict, Parliament authorized Anglo-American colonial assemblies to enlist indentured servants into the ranks of the provincial militias (much to the chagrin of the servants' masters).[15] Each provided a building block in constructing a British Empire that increasingly relied on its colonies to produce revenue for the treasury.

Often described as "the great war for empire," the Seven Years' War included military campaigns in the North American colonies, Europe, the Caribbean, Africa, and India. During the North American campaigns of 1755–57, British High Command required provincial legislatures to recruit, fund, and provision its forces.[16] Lacking sufficient financial support, legislatures failed to meet enlistment quotas and often held those who did enlist past their official release date. In the summer of 1758, William Pitt, secretary of state for the Southern Department, drastically reorganized the strategy of the British Army. Rather than defeat France in Continental Europe, Pitt emphasized stripping the French Army of its resources through strategic attacks on French colonies in North America.[17] Beginning in 1759, the British Army embarked on several campaigns to eliminate the French Army in Canada.

On 13 September 1759, the British, aided by New York and New England provincial soldiers, sailed into the Gulf of St Lawrence and invaded New France. After landing his troops north of Quebec, James Wolfe ordered the redcoats and provincials to surround the city. The short battle that ensued forced the city's commander, Jean-Baptise Ramezay, to surrender. Deciding not to overextend the army during the winter months, Brigadier General

James Murray took leadership over the British garrison and the subjugated population of Quebec.[18]

For habitants across the colony, the loss of Quebec City led to a period of exploitation at the hands of both the British and the French militaries. As Murray noted in a letter to Parliament, "the Canadians under [the French] subjection are plundered and oppressed by them."[19] He added: "the little succors or reinforcements they may be able to smuggle by landing near the mouth of the River cannot avail them."[20] Moreover, the conscription of Canadians into the militia and the amount of resources required by the *troupes de la Marine* had expended the year's harvest and left habitants in dire straits for the winter.[21] Disease spread through the countryside, only increasing the privation of habitants.

Despite these hardships, the British invaders conscripted habitants into forced labour. While not explicitly recognized as corvée, forced labour in November 1759 mirrored many of the tasks the French had required of habitants. Indeed, Murray ordered the captains of the militia to "employ people to thresh [corn]" and to transport the crops "to Quebec for the use of the Poor who submitted to His Majesty's arms."[22] Furthermore, the British appropriated all carriages and carts (*corvée de harnois*) necessary for the British garrison.[23] Emulating orders of corvée under the French Regime, Murray put the parish priests and militia captains in charge of reading these orders to the habitants and executing the necessary mobilization of labour.[24] Habitants who disobeyed, or remained loyal to the French, had their crops and livestock seized by British soldiers and their dwellings burned to the ground.[25]

Habitants in the countryside fared little better during the oncoming winter months. In an effort to force the French to surrender, Murray instructed his soldiers to "disarm all Inhabitants, drive before him from thence their Oxen, Horses, Sheep, and carry off or destroy all the Grain or Forage, which they are possessed of."[26] For those habitants who remained in their parishes, the British raids on their wintertime supplies pushed the government of Montreal towards famine.

The war compelled habitants to make difficult decisions over which army would reap the benefits of their labour. A majority of men ages sixteen to sixty were still under royal obligation of the king of France to serve in the militia.[27] Despite the defeat at Quebec City, Vaudreuil decided to continue the war effort. The habitants who remained loyal to the French Crown in the government of Montreal were relocated to the Île aux Noix in the Richelieu

River. Over winter, Vaudreuil and Ramezay utilized corvée to construct a sophisticated network of fortifications to defend against a riverine invasion in the south of New France.

French senior personnel also expected habitants to continue providing corvée for the war effort after the fall of Quebec. At the start of the 1760 campaigning season, with the colony on the brink of falling into enemy hands, François-Gaston, Duc de Lévis, prepared a counterattack on the British to retake the St Lawrence city. As in the previous year of the war, senior officers conscripted habitants to form part of the militia and to provide corvée when needed. To this end, militia captains gathered the necessary Canadians from the government of Trois Rivières and those parishes in Quebec not yet occupied by the British to operate in tandem with the remaining French forces.[28] In his instructions for the impending battle, Lévis wrote: "militia companies will provide service and corvées in proportion to their strength; their detachments will be assembled separately and then led by the side of those of the battalion with which they will have to march, by the officer charged with making the details."[29] During the engagement, known as the Battle of Saint-Foy, Canadians split into three companies and facilitated the assault by providing corvée.[30] While Lévis's initial assault proved successful, the French Army failed to retake the city.[31]

On 8 September 1760, Governor Vaudreuil surrendered Montreal to Major General Jeffery Amherst, ending armed conflict in Canada. In the immediate aftermath of the Conquest, Amherst and British High Command emphasized retaining the social structure of Canadian communities. The Articles of Capitulation of Montreal specifically addressed the seigneurial regime, asserting: "all the communities and all the priests shall preserve their moveables" as well as the "properties and revenues of the seigniories and other estates."[32] Moreover, the British preserved the "privileges, rights, honours, and exemptions" of the seigneurs, such as the cens, the grist mill banalité, and the custom of raising a corvée of labour to work on the lord's demesne.[33] The agreement of surrender also made provision for all Canadians to retain their "entire peaceable property and possession of their goods, noble and ignoble, moveable and immoveable, merchandises, furs, and other effects, even their ships."[34] The British allowed French Canadians to retain their property and did not disrupt the social fabric of peasant communities.

REDISTRICTING CANADA AND IMPERIAL EXPANSION, 1760–65

Although war continued in Europe until the Treaty of Paris, 1763, Parliament ordered Murray to establish military rule in Canada. First, Murray authorized a census of each parish in the British-occupied area of Quebec.[35] Completed in August 1761, the "Survey of Canada" represented the fiscal-military state's penetration into local communities.[36] Indeed, the primary reason Murray chose to gather the data was so that the British would "never again be at a loss how to attack, and conquer this Country in one Campaign."[37] Along with the ages of men eligible for militia service and corvée, the census included the number of women, children, and male and female servants living within each parish. In sum, the "Survey" allowed the state to evaluate the labouring capacity of the communities, establish an understanding of the economic condition of each individual parish, and, most important, produce a supervised, legible population.[38]

In an effort to organize the territory, the British subdivided Canada into several new administrative units, creating three "districts" over the former French courts and population centres. The northernmost district, Quebec, contained the highest population, the seat of the British colonial government, and the largest settlement in the province in Quebec City.[39] Adjacent to Quebec, the district of Trois-Rivières exhibited a primarily rural, dispersed population with several large seigneuries and a French iron mine in the village of Saint-Maurice.[40] The final district, Montreal, included the Island of Montreal and the Richelieu River.[41] At the local level, the British retained the municipal jurisdiction of parishes and seigneuries.

In their reports to Whitehall, each of the district military governors highlighted the importance of maintaining corvée. Parliament appointed James Murray as the military governor of the newly created district of Quebec. This district incorporated the borders of the French "Government of Quebec," stretching from the Gulf of St Lawrence to the environs of Trois-Rivières. This included the most important settlement in the colony, Quebec City, which Murray and the British Army occupied in 1759 following the Battle of the Plains of Abraham. The district of Quebec also contained the highest concentration of population. Based on a 1761 census, 30,261 people resided in the district, approximately half of Canada's total population.[42] In particular, 7,336 of these habitants were males, with 627 of those immediately fit for militia and corvée duty.[43]

In his letters to the Lords of Trade and Plantations, Murray drew attention to corvée and the potential benefits that harnessing labour could provide the British Crown.[44] Appalled by the condition of the Quebec fortifications, Murray proposed the construction of a wall on *Cap Diamond* and a citadel to house a division of professional soldiers. Indeed, Murray asserted: "the Ground I propose for this Citadel commands the whole Town and is commanded no where from this Country."[45] He continued: "in short it possesses every advantage we wished for," especially for imposing rule on the Canadian population, "whose fidelity in case of an attack we cannot for some years rely on."[46] To construct the Citadel, Murray proposed utilizing drafts of corvée. He reported: "the Inhabitants of the Country and the Troops in the time of peace may contribute their labour towards it;" adding that habitants "ha[d] no objection as they were on all occasions formerly liable to military services."[47] A corvée, Murray argued, would provide a "small expense" of the fortifying of the St Lawrence city.[48]

In addition to fortifying the city, Murray also submitted observations on the interworking of the seigneurial regime in Canada. His report on preexisting labour arrangements provided a foundation for the British colonial state to better understand the king's newest subjects. Indeed, he commented that, although seigneurs "of these fiefs enter[] into all the privileges and immunities" associated with the nobility, "by law the seigneur is restricted from selling any part of his land that is not cleared, and is likewise obliged (reserving a sufficiency for his own private domain) to concede the remainder to such of the inhabitants."[49] Habitants owned their land, which "they [could] sell as they please[d]" and the rent "they pa[id could] never be raised upon them."[50] In times of emergency, seigneurs organized militias within their parish for the posterity and protection of the community. Composed "in proportion to [the parish's] extent and number of inhabitants," the seigneur formed "one, two, or more companies, who ha[d] their proper officers, captains, lieutenants, ensigns, aide-majors, serjeants & c.," and delegated orders to the commanding officers.[51] Furthermore, Murray observed: "from these companies detachments are formed and sent to any distance," regardless of their parish affiliation or jurisdictional boundary.[52]

Like Quebec, the new district of Montreal encompassed the borders of the French Regime's "Government of Montreal." This included several diverse and distinct regions of the former French colony: Lake Champlain to the La Chute River, the Richelieu Valley, the city and Island of Montreal, the suburbs of Montreal, and a series of agriculturally based rural parishes that stretched to the southern end of Lake Saint-Pierre.[53] The settled area around Montreal included thirty-six parishes with 30,365 people.[54] Thomas Gage, the military governor of the district of Montreal, commented that all of these landholdings were "held on feudal tenure" that the king of France issued on the basis of "fealty and homage of accustomed dues and acknowledgements agreeable to the Customs of Paris."[55] Seigneurs subdivided their lands to habitants who lived on "farms of about three acres in front upon thirty in depth."[56]

Gage echoed the potential of preserving corvée. In his report, he commented on the possible uses of corvée for the British Crown. In addition to the French requirement that habitants clear their land, he also observed that the rural dwellers were responsible for leaving space "sufficient for the King's High road, or other private roads, judged necessary for private use."[57] This labour, he added, formed additional "conditions in their grants." Moreover, Gage remarked that the French king reserved "a right to build forts, batteries, magazines, etc." in their parish. This included the right of the king to order habitants "to cut timber necessary for such buildings and firewood for the garrisons of such forts." He added that this encompassed a responsibility for all timber "proper for Masts or ship building, without indemnification."[58]

Gage identified Lake Champlain as a potential location for a British-Canadian timber industry. Indeed, he stated: "there are great quantities of Wood Lands unsettled reported to contain Masts and Ship Timber upon the borders of Lake Champlain." Following the Seven Years' War, this region grew into an especially lucrative enterprise, with the provinces of New York and Massachusetts competing over portions of the "unsettled" land. In any case, France's exit from Canada provided the British Crown with an uninterrupted empire from the Hudson River to the Gulf of St Lawrence. Gage encouraged the Crown "[to] reserve the best parts of these unsettled lands for His Majesty's use" and to refortify the king's "Right to the Oak Timber," which formed a portion of seigneurial dues owed by habitants.[59]

A statistical analysis of the 1765 census of the district of Montreal reveals incredibly cohesive, nucleated communities based on kinship. For example, a large seigneurie in the district, Sorel, contained a population of 677 residents who lived in 148 households. Each family owned an average of sixty-eight arpents of land. More surprising, perhaps, the census lists just twenty-eight people as hired servants, and just one person in the category of *estranger*, or a mobile, rural worker who contracted his or her labour for residence in a family dwelling. In other words, 96 per cent of the people living in Sorel were connected, or belonged, to a family household. Similar findings also apply to smaller seigneuries in the Lower Richelieu. The parish of Saint Ours, located across the St Lawrence River, contained 547 people, living in 105 households at an average of 101 arpents of land per family. Moreover, 97 per cent of the population of Saint Ours was associated with a specific family group. In sum, the seigneuries of Montreal exhibited a tight-knit nucleated structure, with each family owning a modest plot of land that met subsistence-level existence.[60]

The scant documentation available allows for a partial reconstruction of seigneurial corvée in the Montreal countryside after the Conquest. Evidence suggests that the obligation of corvée directly for the benefit of the seigneur continued after the establishment of British rule and before the signing of the Treaty of Paris.[61] The best evidence derives from a seigneurial account book kept by Jean-Baptiste Nicolas de Ramezay. In the 1761–63 tax lists, Ramezay noted that habitants were "obliged to furnish to the seigneur one day of corvée each year."[62] Habitants living in Sorel would have executed agricultural work for their seigneur. Indeed, the Capitulation of Montreal legally protected this relationship among seigneur, habitant, and feudal dues. This afforded seigneurs the ability to exercise their authority over their tenants to collect taxes such as corvée.[63] While the account book does not have records of the number of days served, clearly the custom of seigneurial corvée continued – even if in a limited fashion – under the British military government.

The military governor of Trois-Rivières, Frederick Haldimand, also highlighted the economic benefits of maintaining corvée. Indeed, he observed the pre-existing labour arrangements in practice and recorded his description of seigneurial privileges in a letter to the Lords of Trade and Plantations. He commented that corvée consisted of "one to two days labour in the year for the benefits of the seigneur" and up to eight days on public works.[64] In his opinion Parliament should reserve "to the Crown the rights of Cutting timber for building of Ships or erecting fortifications" as well as appropriating all mines in Trois-Rivières as the king's property.[65] By law, he continued, the seigneurs would "bind themselves to the King loyally and faithfully when called upon" and would use their customs for corvée collection of timber and iron mining.[66] In the immediate postwar environment, Haldimand advocated utilizing corvée to subsidize the construction of ships for the Royal Navy.

Located on the St Lawrence River between the governments of Montreal and Quebec, Trois-Rivières exhibited a primarily agrarian economy. In 1760, the government of Trois-Rivières primarily consisted of mid- to large-scale seigneuries and a dispersed population. Indeed, Haldimand noted: "all the lands in this Government as well as through all Canada are divided into seigneuries," with Trois-Rivières having less than "17,000 [acres] under cultivation," of which "hardly 5,000 have been employed hitherto for the sowing of wheat."[67] He estimated that 6,816 people resided in the region.[68] The centre of population, the town of Trois-Rivières, represented a trade depot on the St Lawrence connecting goods going from Montreal to Quebec City. Haldimand described the habitants of Trois-Rivières as "robust and strong" and emphasized the agricultural industry of the region.

The British inherited other mechanisms of free and unfree labour in each district, each of which operated alongside corvée as a part of their conquest. Indeed, estimates suggest that around two thousand enslaved individuals of Indigenous and African descent lived in Canada throughout the eighteenth century.[69] As they did with the preservation of seigneurial dues, the British retained the regulations and customs of slavery in Canada that had been enshrined in Raudot's 1709 ordinance.[70] According to the Capitulation of Montreal: "Negroes and Panis of both sexes shall remain, in their quality of slaves, in possession of the French and Canadians to whom they belong." The Capitulation reaffirmed the institution of chattel slavery that had taken root in both the French and British Empires, relegating the enslaved person to the status of property whose livelihood was at the discretion of the owner. The Capitulation stated that the king's conquered subjects: "shall be at liberty to keep [slaves] in their service the colony or sell them; and they may continue to bring them up in the Roman religion."[71]

Day labourers, indentured servants, and domestiques made up the remaining workforce in the parishes and seigneuries. Despite a second wave of engagés migration in the mid-eighteenth century, scholarship suggests that the population of contracted servants most likely had a limited impact on British plans to mobilize labour in the territory.[72] To be sure, engagés, domestiques, and day labourers continued to work local jobs, primarily assisting with the maintenance of individual estates and homesteads. Depending on the region, these various forms of servitude did factor into the immediate postwar imperial machinations of the British, and, as we shall see, day labourers served alongside habitants performing corvée in Trois-Rivierès.

Overall, however, evidence suggests that servants and labourers continued their role as a supplementary base of local agricultural and domestic work.[73]

Prior to instituting official colonial rule over the former French colony, British officials highlighted the advantages of maintaining corvée. In letters to Parliament, they emphasized the benefits of preserving the pre-existing seigneurial social arrangements that dictated the mobilization of habitant labour. After establishing a civil government in the "Province of Quebec," the British continued to refine these customs, redirecting corvée for public works and the collection of natural resources.

IRON-MINING IN SAINT-MAURICE AND EXPERIMENTS WITH CORVÉE

The reports from Murray and the other military governors in each newly created district arrived at a contradictory moment of collective confidence and uncertainty in the British Empire. The land acquisitions from the Seven Years' War had given Britain unprecedented control over North America's diverse peoples, but it had also thrust to the forefront of Parliament's agenda a tangled series of issues that revolved around empire, law, and revenue.[74] Prior to the war, Parliament had, for the most part, allowed the king's North American colonies to govern internal affairs and rarely meddled in long-standing customary trading practices that had developed while their markets matured. To be sure, Quebec would require more dynamic interventions from British legislating bodies to knit the new province into a broader North American empire, and decisions would need to be made on which local customs might remain in place.

Importantly, however, the province did not exist in isolation and now shared borders with Anglo-American colonies that had, in the words of Jack P. Green, "exercised full legislative authority over their respective jurisdictions."[75] Indeed, throughout the eighteenth century, the thirteen Anglo-American colonies had gravitated "towards increasing limitations on prerogative of power and greater security for individual and corporate rights."[76] By requiring an overwhelming amount of external intervention in local law codes, the reforms suggested by Murray and the military governors stood in direct juxtaposition to how British imperial policy had operated in North America for six decades. In the immediate short term, at least in

Quebec, the British decided to uphold the customs enshrined in the Articles of Capitulation of Montreal and turn their focus to generating revenue for the Crown.

Following the Treaty of Paris, Parliament ordered Murray to enact sweeping economic reforms within the province. These policies specifically targeted natural resources deemed "profitable" by Parliament.[77] Murray and his subordinates wasted no time organizing and establishing economic policies that would knit the new province of Quebec into the empire. First, they planned to open unoccupied lands for British migrants to harvest grains and flax.[78] Second, they sought to identify all forests that could potentially yield timber for the Royal Navy.[79] Third, the ministers ordered the reconstruction of the iron mines at Saint-Maurice to stimulate a domestic economy around raw materials.[80] Fourth, colonial officials were to appropriate habitant labour for cultivation and transportation of these goods.[81]

Along with the St Lawrence Valley and Acadia, the British claimed all land in southwestern New France, or modern-day southeastern Ontario and the Great Lakes region. Ministers schemed to move anglophone settlers to these regions and construct English-style towns in areas deemed "unsettled."[82] To achieve this, the ministers ordered Murray to appoint a surveyor in each district who would evaluate the geography and resources of any "unsettled" land. Following those reports, Parliament planned to parcel that territory into townships, which would receive a church, school, and municipal building. In areas that surveyors identified as "particularly adapted to the growth and culture of hemp and flax," Parliament required each new colonist "to sow a proportionable part of his grant with hemp or flax seed," which the settler would surrender in tribute once every year.[83]

Canadian timber represented an even more lucrative resource for the maritime empire. Indeed, specific instructions from Parliament to Murray state: "[Canada] abounds with woods producing trees fit for masting for our royal navy, and other useful and necessary timber for naval construction." Furthermore, the ministers authorized Murray to appropriate any land "that [should] appear upon a survey to abound with such trees, and [should] lie convenient for water carriage" for use of the colonial state. Anyone caught wasting or destroying timber within the state-designated areas was to be severely punished "in due course of law." Through the appropriation of land, the state intended to subsidize the Canadian timber industry for the use of the Royal Navy.[84]

Finally, Parliament demonstrated an acute interest in the extraction of iron from Quebec. The ministers specifically targeted the ironworks of Saint-Maurice as a potentially profitable venture. Originally owned by François Poulin de Francheville, seigneur of Saint-Maurice, the French had also viewed the mines as a possible source of raw materials for their North American colonies and as a way to supplement the still-lucrative fur trade.[85] Poor planning and the mid-eighteenth-century colonial wars, however, stymied the initial iron-mining venture at Saint-Maurice. The onset of the War of Austrian Succession bankrupted the mine and forced investors to abandon the enterprise. Hocquart and Vaudreuil both recognized the failure as an opportunity to seize the land as the king's domain and to cultivate iron for the war effort.

While limited to nearby seigneuries, the French did experiment with using corvée in the environs of Saint-Maurice to fuel the mines. As part of the Crown's landholdings, the governor ordered habitants near the mines to contribute corvée for wood-cutting and charcoal production.[86] In a summary of the activity at the forges, Vaudreuil wrote that it was often necessary to "draw the habitants of the countryside" and to "employ them [to] travel to the enterprises of the forges construction."[87] He listed "the exploitation of wood" as a primary focal point of their work.[88] The governor's experimentation in mobilizing corvée for an imperial iron industry, and the mining operation in general, ultimately fell by the wayside as, during the Seven Years' War, attention shifted towards protecting the economic enterprises of the Pays d'en Haut.[89]

Whitehall exhibited a similar interest in the mine's potential and ordered Murray to seize all land associated with the production and refinement of iron in conjunction with surrounding land for auxiliary services. None of the land would "be granted to any private person."[90] It then directed Murray to subsidize any industry in the village "upon which the said ironworks were carried on, or from which the ore using such works was procured." Additionally, the governor incorporated all means of transporting iron "in respect to a free passage to the river Saint Lawrence, or for producing a necessary supply of wood, corn, hay, or for pasture for cattle" into the Crown's property. The ministers urged Murray to annex a piece of state-owned land "adjacent to and lying around the ironworks" for the cultivation of grains and livestock.[91]

At the time of the Conquest, the fief of Saint-Maurice contained the largest ironworks in New France. Consisting of an iron mine, forges, and transportation depots on the St Lawrence, French political officials had primarily neglected the mines over the past decade, and, by the end of the Seven Years' War, the ironworks had fallen into disrepair. During his survey of the territory, Haldimand urged the Lords of Trade and Plantations to put the mines into working order. In order to repair the mines and connect them with British Headquarters in Quebec City, Haldimand tapped into the French precedent of harnessing corvée labour from the surrounding seigneuries. As the mine developed into a profitable economic venture, the British instituted a network of labour in the region consisting of corvée, seasonal wage labour, and a skilled trades industry. Under the direct supervision of the military, the use of corvée represented an early attempt of the state to harness pre-existing local labour relationships to subsidize raw materials on the imperial market.

Located "seven or eight miles behind the Town of 3 Rivers," by the end of the war the works consisted of "one furnace and two forges" on a tributary of the St Lawrence River "where water never freezes."[92] Several outbuildings consisting of "a large Stone house for the manager and wooden Houses for the people employed at the forges or other necessary works" also surrounded the property.[93] Originally opened in 1732, the ironworks yielded high-quality iron ore and quickly developed into the largest mine in the colony. In 1741, the French Crown incorporated the mine as royal property as well as several fiefs adjacent to the ironworks to supply a steady supply of timber. The mines, however, failed to meet expectations despite a modest trades industry and over one hundred wage labourers. As the king's property, shortages in timber for charcoal production led to the periodic impressment of habitants into corvée for wood-cutting.[94] In addition, corvée labour repaired a number of roads that connected the ironworks to neighbouring parishes. During the 1750s, shortages in labour and poor management led to a deterioration of the mines' overall output.

Seeking to revive the iron-mining enterprise, the British rebuilt the industry and supplemented the demand for labour with corvée rotations from neighbouring seigneuries. Annual account listings drawn up for the governor illuminate the spectrum of labour performed in the repair of the mines. The British instituted a managerial staff consisting of inspectors, founders, and master craftspeople. Each group then employed skilled and semi-skilled workers, such as blacksmiths, coal makers, joiners, and carpenters, in various tasks related to the refinement of iron ore. Auxiliary "battoe men" transported raw materials, especially timber, from the adjacent seigneuries across the St Lawrence River.[95] The bateaux men also shipped lime brought down the river from quarries in Trois-Rivières. Once across the river, cartmen worked in rotations between twenty-six days and three months bringing the timber to the forges. Day labourers completed the actual task of mining the iron ore.[96]

By 1764, the forges operated on a combination of wage labour and corvée from the nearby seigneuries.[97] On one hand, the forges clearly employed a number of full-time craftspeople and wage labourers in addition to managers who oversaw the day-to-day operations;[98] on the other hand, account books kept by the managers convey that most habitants who worked at the forges did so in short-term rotations and participated in specific tasks.

Carting materials and building roads represented the most common type of work performed by habitants serving in the labour rotations at the mines.[99] Habitants employed carting materials, especially charcoal produced from burnt wood, typically worked eight to twenty days.[100] For example, Pierre Anyer worked eight days carting coal with horses, while Charles Dejarlais carted materials for seventeen days. Some habitants worked longer rotations: for example, Pierre Milot worked thirty-seven days and Jacques Aubry spent thirty-six days carting coal. These workers received cash payments for their labour at a fixed price of three livres per day. Most habitants accumulated between thirty-four to 108 livres during their tenure at Saint-Maurice.[101]

Wage labourers also aided with transportation via the Saint-Maurice River. In addition to carting coal by land, they also worked as bateaux men moving materials by canoe.[102] The wage lists specified that these habitants were responsible for removing the coal and charcoal that the forges had expended. The workers assigned to this task usually worked twenty to twenty-five days and earned cash as payment for their labour. Several habitants took up more than one task, an example being Jacques Aubry, who worked carting coal by land and building roads "in the woods" that connected the forges to the fief of Saint-Maurice.[103]

The British state continued to harness pre-existing labour arrangements in order to repair the mines. In an effort to mobilize the agrarian labour force of Trois-Rivières, the British targeted the relationships among seigneurs, parish militia captains, and habitants. From October 1760 until May 1764, a network of seigneuries provided corvée labour for the repair of the Saint-Maurice ironworks.[104] Under the supervision of the parish militia captains, habitants from ten of the seigneuries adjacent to Saint-Maurice cut, prepared, and transported wood to the mines. Indeed, within the first several years of British rule, corvée labour provided 4,865 cords of wood to the ironworks.[105] Corvée labour also constructed two roads around the mine and a ferry that "attempted to bring over the charcoals from the other side of the River St. Maurice."[106] In sum, British political officials in Trois-Rivières utilized seigneurial privileges to subsidize military industry by conscripting a corvée labour force.

Elsewhere in the province, another form of mandatory labour combined traditional elements of corvée with the objectives of the military. In 1765, Murray accused Ralph Burton, brigadier general of the Northern Department, of exploiting habitants through the use of impressment and press warrants. Supposedly issued by Burton to his deputy-quarter-master Lieutenant Colonel Gabriel Christie in 1765, the press warrants in question had forced habitants in the seigneurie of Lachine to work transporting materials by bateaux to the Upper Posts.[107] The press warrants caught the attention of John Fraser, a Montreal justice of the peace who informed Murray of the indiscretions. The impressment of Canadians precipitated a year-long legal dispute that ultimately decided the course of mandatory labour for the next decade.[108]

As Murray admits in a series of letters condoning Burton's actions, the use of Canadian labour in the immediate post-Conquest years was common. Until 1763, the British remained at war with France and impressment fell under "the services specified in the Mutiny Act," which allowed British officers to mobilize habitants in specific circumstances.[109] Prior to the treaty the use of habitant labour – which had transported materials by cart and bateaux – created an extension of British jurisprudence under the military regime of Quebec. Murray utilized press warrants for the collection of firewood during the winters of 1760 through 1763 and commandeered carriages for the use of the British Army.[110] After the end of the war, officers continued to apply for press warrants, including one that Murray approved for Captain Fraser in autumn 1765.[111] Following the Treaty of Paris, however, the use of press warrants, in general, declined and each order had to receive approval from Murray.[112]

Burton's press warrants, on the other hand, had not received Murray's endorsement and the governor took offence at the blatant disregard of his authority. The point of disagreement between Murray and Burton originated with the use of corvée to supply and defend the "Northern Department" and the "Upper Posts," a vast stretch of land that included the French forts of

Niagara and Detroit.[113] As a result, Murray embarked to limit the exploitation of habitants through impressment. Indeed, upon learning of the press warrants in early October 1765, he immediately ordered "injunctions to the Inhabitants of the Parishes the nearest to La Chine to furnish the men necessary for the sixteen battoes in question."[114] He condemned Burton and Christie, asserting that neither Parliament nor the provincial government of Quebec "ha[d] the legal power to impress men."[115] He added that British soldiers, "numerous as they [were] in this Colony," should have assisted in "transporting the King's Stores."[116] Furthermore, Murray consulted the attorney general of the province, who declared impressment illegal and "inconsistent with the Liberty of the Subjects in time of Peace and inexcusable at all times."[117]

To end the use of corvée on the supply routes, Murray ordered the termination of all press warrants. His reasoning echoed the 1708 seigneurial reforms of Jacques Raudot, which established the delicate balance of agricultural life in Canada. Murray argued that habitant impressment interfered "with the Seed time, the Harvest and tillage of the Ground."[118] He maintained that: "[the] subsistence of Canadians depends upon a punctual attention to and strenuous industry during these seasons, and that these Seasons are too short here to admit any interruption in the Business of agriculture."[119] Citing the fragile state of farming, Murray proclaimed: "to take a number of colonists from their domestik labours, is driving them into the Jaws of Famine."[120]

Despite all of the bluster and dramatic rhetoric, Murray added a caveat to his statement on the matter of press warrants. Indeed, while he ended the use of habitant labour during planting or harvest, he briefly mentioned that the transportation of goods could occur "in Summer when the people ha[d] leasure, and [would] voluntarily and cheerfully execute" orders of bateaux service.[121] As was done during the French Regime, Murray condemned the use of mandatory labour during the critical periods of planting and harvesting crops. He restricted the French policy of limiting corvée to the summer and late autumn to avoid overextending habitants. Later, during the American Revolution, the British Army would use the practices established by Murray's administration to mobilize Canadians on corvée. Indeed, habitants would work the same supply routes to the Upper Posts for which Murray had denounced Burton and Christie. In response, habitants collectively evaded corvée on these supply routes and petitioned the colonial government to relieve them from service.

THE GRAND VOYER OF THE DISTRICT OF QUEBEC AND CORVÉE, 1762–67

As peace negotiations with France began, the British started to experiment with corvée to repair the system of roads that knit the colony together. Indeed, work on roads, bridges, and ferries represented the form of corvée most consistently used by the British after the Conquest. The British retained most of the French customs related to corvée on public works. They preserved important components of the grand voyer but would ultimately, for the timebeing, split the responsibility between three chief surveyors in each district.[122] For habitants, the continuation of corvée on roads remained one of the few unchanged attributes of labour after the Conquest.[123]

While most likely not evident to habitants, the appropriation of the duties of the grand voyer represented a critical step for integrating their labour into a British imperial law code. Despite the routine of corvée remaining largely intact, Parliament established a familiar, but unequivocally British, set of laws to justify the maintenance of labour customs. As a post that did not exist elsewhere in the British Empire, the grand voyer and corvée inspired debate among colonial and metropolitan officials.[124] The integration of the office required an exhaustive inquiry into the everyday operations of habitant labour at the parish level.[125] In the end, the administration chose to maintain important pieces of the office and to incorporate the obligation of road construction into habitant concessions.[126] This bound habitants not only to the grand voyers in each district but also to a much larger colonial operation stemming from Parliament.

As early as 1762, the British demonstrated interest in maintaining the grand voyer. Indeed, while serving as military governor, James Murray submitted a description of the office to Parliament in his report entitled "The State of Canada under French Administration." In his entry on French Canadian offices, Murray described the grand voyer as the "inspector of the highroads." In a plea to Parliament, he stated that, "under proper regulations and restrictions," the grand voyer "seem[ed] to be highly necessary for the care and benefit of interior commerce."[127]

Road-building within the district of Quebec continued under the discretion of François-Joseph Cugnet during the British military occupation. Following the surrender of Quebec, Murray appointed Cugnet to the prestigious position of attorney general of the *Côte Nord* of the district of Quebec.[128] By

May 1762, Cugnet began serving as a temporary grand voyer in the district, repairing roads and bridges.[129] Despite not receiving full authority over the office until 1765, Cugnet laid the foundation of British corvée during his tenure as attorney general.[130]

Early uses of corvée under the military government required habitants in the district of Quebec to repair roads and bridges that had been destroyed by the war. As a result, orders of corvée centred on those communities most affected by the conflict. Most of Cugnet's directions focused on the immediate area surrounding the city, including Charlesbourg, the Bourg Royal, Cap-Rogue, and the Porte de Saint-Louis – a major entry point to Quebec.[131] In his first month of temporarily fulfilling the role of grand voyer, Cugnet issued twelve orders of corvée in his district, with an additional eleven following in June.[132]

While most of these orders focused on small-scale projects, several noteworthy orders exhibited Cugnet expanding the power of the military government over habitant labour. In particular, on 24 May 1762, Cugnet ordered the "militia of the government of Quebec" to repair "the roads and bridges immediately after the sowing."[133] This district-wide order mirrored orders from the grand voyer and intendant of New France. It maintained the hierarchy established and ironed out over the past six decades in New France, with the captains of the militia providing the intermediary role of executing colonial orders at the parish level. Cugnet also preserved the cycle of corvée, which would become a regular fixture under the British. Habitants would perform corvée on roads after the "sowing," something that dated back to Raudot's 1708 suggestions regarding seigneurial tenure.[134]

During August 1762, Cugnet continued to exercise his authority within his limited role in the military government. Following the repairs of pre-existing roads, he ordered corvée on several other infrastructure projects, such as building a road to the mill of Saint-Charles and communication routes in the second concessions of Saint-Joseph on the seigneurie of Deschambault.[135] The tasks he delegated also incorporated much of the auxiliary work that took place under the French Regime. For example, Cugnet ordered "six feet of fences" in the parish of Petite-Rivières. He reaffirmed British authority over corvée on these work projects and, in a September order, granted the militia captains "command of a corvées générale of all the habitants of their parishes after the harvest to open the necessary ditches on the roads."[136]

Following the Treaty of Paris and the installation of civil administration in Quebec, Murray officially appointed Cugnet to the position of grand voyer in the district of Quebec and entrusted him with expanding his operations.[137] Cugnet's appointment built upon his experience as attorney general. In particular, he retained most of the legal framework and labour routines associated with corvée on road construction.[138] Instead of reporting to the abolished Office of the Intendant as under the French, however, Cugnet followed the regulations of the newly formed Committees on Highways, Roads, and Bridges, which functioned as a semi-autonomous organization. These committees consisted of district surveyors, lawyers, and public officials.[139] Integrating the customs of corvée required careful bureaucratic organization that appropriated corvée while maintaining the recently established due process,principles, and precedent of English common law. For example, committees screened all corvée orders and petitions prior to laying them before justices of the peace.

One of Cugnet's first tasks involved generating a province-wide legal code for corvée on roads. Submitted to committee on 20 November 1765, his proposal provided a foundation for corvée in the province. First, he advocated that the role of grand voyer be split into three chief district surveyors. As was done under the French regime, he instituted a timetable for corvée that matched the agricultural seasons. He suggested the following order: "every inhabitant of the different Parishes of this Province may be held to furnish every year, between the time of their sowing their Grain" and the "time of cutting their Hay, the number of men and carts daily as shall be thought necessary for the reparation and keeping up the King's Highways." This order also included instructions for those habitants who lived in the "Towns" (or more urban areas) to also provide labour on the roads that passed through the community. Building on French corvée in the military, Cugnet fixed "the price of Men's day Labour and that of Carts," adding a wage of "two dollars per day" to compensate habitants for their time spent on construction. The "refusers" system also remained in place, with "a fine on those who refuse[d] to obey when ordered."[140]

In addition to roads, the British set out to expand riverine transportation across the St Lawrence. Cugnet's first major initiative included building ferries that would connect the north and south shores of the St Lawrence.[141] Corvée labour on ferries had already begun under the French Regime. During the construction of the Chemin du Roy, Lanoullier de Boisclerc ordered the construction of several ferries, most notably in a swampy section of the St Lawrence at the south end of Lake Saint Pierre that was prone to flooding. Moreover, ferries proved exceptionally useful in parishes that included tributaries of the St Lawrence that were too large for a single bridge.

Cugnet argued that a system of ferries was "of more importance than all the Extent of the South Shore, as there [was] no commodious passage on any of the rivers on which they may not erect bridges."[142] Furthermore, these tributaries also contained a "great floating of ice in the Spring," making traversing them by bateaux difficult and hazardous "for those that the breadth and current of the water [would] not permit." For these reasons, Cugnet reported that corvée on ferries was "absolutely necessary to settle the ferries of the rivers on which there [was] no possibility to erect bridges." The mobilization of labour fell to the entire community, and the militia captains would divide the work among all habitants. If they chose to "refuse to comply with this obligation" the parish risked losing "that right to the community of Inhabitants," or commune, a French system of land distribution that allocated land in the community for common use.[143]

The British expanded the pre-existing communication networks established by the French. This included a major initiative to expand highways into the interior of the colony branching from the Chemin du Roy. These roads, which the British called "out roads," routes, or communication roads, stretched into the rows of concessions allocated further from the river. In his report to Parliament, Cugnet asserted: "the inhabitants who live in the depths of the different seignories shall apply to the surveyor of their District [so that he] may mark out the roads of communication or out roads that will be necessary." For roads that led to the parish mill, seigneurs applied to the district surveyor. A general order issued by the grand voyer stated that mill roads would "be done at the expense of their tenants, who [were] obliged by their leases to bring Grain to be Ground."[144]

Cugnet maintained the importance of corvée with regard to building winter roads. Established by the Office of the Intendant in 1713, this custom required habitants to maintain their roads during the winter snowfall, primarily by placing poles on the edges of the road to outline the highway for travellers.[145] Indeed, Cugnet put local officers in charge of this obligation, stating: "[habitants] shall be required by the Bailiffs for keeping up the Winter Roads."[146] Habitants who ignored the winter work suffered the same fate as other refusers and incurred a fine for disobeying the order of corvée.[147]

To manage corvée on public works, Cugnet generated a bureaucratic hierarchy that integrated French custom with British common law. While the routines of corvée exhibited most of the identifiable characteristics of French custom, the orders now filtered through a British committee and habitant labour became subject to British courts. All major decisions required approval from the governor, but at the local level the district grand voyers retained discretion over the construction projects that took place within the province. These appointees travelled their district and reported to the committee on "works and reparations which shall be found necessary on the High Roads."[148] They convened at least once a year in Trois-Rivières to ensure that their observations matched a provincewide code "concerning the alteration of the King's High Ways."[149] District surveyors also collaborated with the justices of the peace and local bailiffs.[150] These men, appointed by the governor and lieutenant-governors, upheld colonial rule on the seigneuries. Furthermore, the three district surveyors were ordered to present a General State of the Highways in each District to the Justices at their Quarter Sessions.[151] Most petitions or habitant grievances that could not be rectified by the committee or local mediation would be directed through these courts.

The initial proposals for corvée under the civil administration shed light on how British officials integrated a foreign obligation of labour mobilization into their expanding imperial legal code. At the local level, British experiments with corvée laid the groundwork for larger structural changes to the colonial state. As Donald Fyson asserts, "many aspects of local criminal justice were determined by colonial legislation and policies, and the justices of the peace were appointed by central administration through a process that linked central and local interest."[152] Focusing on the "local" – the mundane routines of clerks, justices of the peace, and ordinary law – reveals the "preparatory developments such as the extensive social regulation, bureaucratization, and specialization" that historians often associate with the organs of state power.[153]

Corvée, in addition to other seigneurial dues and obligations that habitants owed to their superiors, remained intact during the transition from French to British rule. Despite significant changes to the administration of corvée, at the parish level work routines remained strikingly similar to what they had been in previous decades. British interest in preserving corvée, however, signalled an increasing centralization of the colonial government and its power over labour. Corvée, ironed out over decades of negotiations between habitants and officials of New France, functioned in the mid-1760s as a public tax. Fixed wages dictated the compensation of work performed on roads. British colonial judges, committees, and bailiffs decided the verdicts of habitant complaints and petitions. Corvée transitioned into a hybrid obligation of labour, in which common law courts ordained proper labour regulations in the parishes. Habitants' drudgery helped construct communication networks that connected Quebec to an enlarged, post–Seven Years' War British Empire.

THE COMMITTEES ON HIGHWAYS, ROADS, AND BRIDGES: COMMON LAW CORVÉE, 1765–67

Following the establishment of a corvée law code, the Committees on Highways, Roads, and Bridges set out to put habitants to work. While Parliament's legal representatives met to discuss further corvée reforms, committee member Adam Mabane ordered a survey of ferries that required repair. He asserted: "the ferrys over the different rivers in the province are in very bad repair & of the utmost consequence to the community."[154] The committee decided that seigneurs who owned land on which these ferries resided should privately arrange repair with their habitants. In particular, Mabane stated: "the Clerk of this Board should be ordered to write the different seigneurs to desire in the name of the council that they may repair & Furnish new [boats] where necessary."[155] Alternatively, seigneurs could surrender their rights to the ferry on their land and the Crown would seize all rights to the crossing. As noted above, habitants on corvée constructed a ferry that connected the north and south shore of the St Lawrence outside the city of Trois-Rivières. In addition to expanding the diversity of transportation in the region, ferries played an important role in transporting timber to the forges.[156]

On 2 December 1765, the committee, after "having read & confided the Acts of Parliament in England with relation to Highways," officially adopted corvée in the province of Quebec.[157] As per the suggestions presented to Parliament by Cugnet, the legal code not only appropriated corvée as a labour system but also integrated the pre-existing customs surrounding the organization and management of workers, albeit with several changes. Instead of the parish priest, the bailiff now posted the order of corvée on the parish church door after Sunday mass. Indeed, the committee ordered: "the Bailiff shall summon the parishioners at the Church Door eight days before the tome they intend working and that every Inhabitant shall be obliged to attend."[158] The meeting between the bailiff and habitants was laden with symbolism, physically embodying the transition of corvée labour from French civil custom to a British-appointed local representative of common law.

The newly ratified code standardized what had previously been customary working conditions for habitants. They worked eight hours a day on roads under the supervision of the captains of the militia. During this work period, habitants were responsible for bringing their own supplies and all "necessary utensils for mending the roads."[159] They also worked on auxiliary tasks associated with road construction, including taking "rubbish &c. out of any person's land, excepting houses and garden, for the reparation of roads."[160] To this end, habitants also constructed ditches "not to exceed ten yards" and fences that surrounded either side of the road.[161] Moreover, the community retained responsibility for maintaining and cleaning the roads, with parishioners in charge of "shrubbing" the highways or removing trees and underbrush that may interrupt travel.[162] Last, the committee preserved the *journées de harnois*, or days of the horse teams, and decreed: "whoever keeps a horse cart or other carriage shall be obliged to attend [the working party]."[163]

The British initially instituted a system of penalties that built upon the French custom of penalizing refusers. Under the French, the captains of the militia wrote the refuser's name in the parish rolls and presented this to the government court, or the Superior Council, during the *foy et homage*.[164] Similarly, bailiffs and constables levied fines against those habitants who evaded corvée. These fines were incurred based on the various different tasks that habitants ignored, such as road clearing or fence building, and could reach up to forty livres "per each neglect."[165] While the minutes of the committee do not indicate how quickly constables collected fines, the bailiff reported directly to the local justice of the peace and provided the names of offenders, implying that the punitive process of levying fines occurred within the eight-day time frame. Indeed, the collection of fines occurred during an "assessment" of the road that required habitants to pay fines for neglecting their work duty. The British also introduced a new position within the hierarchy of corvée, the "scavengers." Appointed by the justices of the peace, scavengers periodically surveyed the roads in cities and towns "to assess the people occupyers and owners of houses" and made sure that habitants cleaned and mended roads. In sum, the British generated standardized and streamlined penalties that dissuaded habitants from ignoring their corvée obligation.[166]

Seigneurs and militia captains resolved outstanding issues related to construction projects with the committee. This group of British legal authorities, surveyors, and the king's representatives in Quebec had considerable autonomy over dictating corvée labour policy. Habitants reconciled disputes over these community projects with the committee, and the Crown gave them full authority over setting legal precedent. Their recommendations formed a comprehensive British judicial system of corvée that generated a standardized procedure of petitioning grievances for retribution. They also established a clear chain of command with the deputy surveyors in each district fulfilling the committee's rulings.

Habitants took to these courts to dispute and contest construction projects. They submitted petitions, offering their collective grievances related to roads that the surveyors superficially imposed on their communities. They refused to work unless the roads benefitted them, and they evaded the obligation when they deemed the work too onerous. As they had done with the Office of the Intendant in the early eighteenth century, they could collectively petition to change the course of the roads or make the committee aware that a road would be better suited to a different location. For example, the habitants of the fifth concession of Saint Michel petitioned committee members for "a road sufficient for the Winter from the River Boyer to the Village Arlaka," which they completed "for the Benefit of the whole."[167]

Similarly, habitants also petitioned to maintain the upkeep of roads and to ensure that their neighbours kept their sections of the road clear of debris. Indeed, in November 1767, three habitants of the Lower Town in Quebec City travelled to a hearing of the committee, where they "represented that the Streets in the Lower Town [were] Extremely dirty and muddy," explaining that this "indanger[ed] the Healthy of His Majesty's Subjects and that an order to every inhabitant to remove the mud before his own house might be effectual to remedy that nuisance." Indeed, their neighbours had piled "Wood and Timber" on the path and consistently left "their carts and trucks standing in the streets to the danger and annoyance of his Majesty's subjects." This issue, the habitants reported, was complicated by "a number of Hoggs running loose about the Streets apt to destroy anything that may be left without guard." The committee ruled that that "all Inhabitants" should remove "their wood & timber piled in the Streets and … carry their trucks and carts out of the streets at night." The city police removed any "carts or trucks" and transport them to the king's wharf, where the offenders would pay a fine for "attending the removal" of their possessions.[168]

Most habitants petitioned the committee to convey collective grievances over road planning and to put forth alternatives for building orders. To achieve this, habitants could use their seigneur as an intermediary between the community and the colonial state. For example, on 19 December 1767,

Lotbinière submitted a petition on behalf of his habitants on the seigneurie of Vaudreuil. He asserted that the highway running through the seigneurie would best run "by a direct line, from the road of the first [rank] to that of the second [rank]," thus making travel more efficient for the community. He added that the habitants "of the two districts" agreed on this plan and that "next spring after the sowing" they would finish the project with a drainage ditch "of appropriate width and depth."[169]

Individual habitants could petition the committee on behalf of their community. On 19 December 1767 two habitants of Nouvelle Beauce, Charles Doyen and Joseph Praux, petitioned the deputy surveyors for "all the tenants and residents of the seigneurie" of Messieur Tachereaux. They asserted that "their means [could] not suffice to make such a considerable expense to be able to make this road perfect." The habitants emphasized that they believed the request was "unreasonable" and that the committee should have allocated more time for construction. The community had initiated work on a portion of the road, and the expenditures state that habitants served a corvée of four to seven days and that they received a cash payment for their labour. While the final outcome of this episode is unknown, petitioning the committee represented an outlet for habitant grievances related to corvée and allowed them to voice their discontent with projects they felt misused their labour. Indeed, the habitants stated in their petition that they "had to stop," and they made use of the opportunity to appeal to officials of the colonial state.[170]

On 28 December 1767, the Executive Council updated the legal code regarding corvée on roads, bridges, and ferries. Written by Cugnet, the order, entitled "Regulation for the Establishment, Maintenance, and Reparation of Roads in the Cities and Suburbs," laid out the fundamental principles that guided corvée under the British regime.[171] Building upon Boisclerc's tenure as grand voyer and Cugnet's previous "Observations," the new regulations incorporated French custom into the imperial legal code of Quebec. In particular, the document specified: "the habitants of the countryside will be required to maintain each of their frontage, both of highways and belts, to make and maintain bridges, [and additionally] work to repair and maintain by corvées [roads on land not yet conceded]."[172] Cugnet also specified several different tasks associated with corvée as involuntary service, including cutting down trees, removing rocks, filling in holes and crevasses, and opening drainage ditches.[173]

More important, Cugnet's "Regulation" reflected a shift in policy towards habitant labour mobilization. At the encouragement of Guy Carleton, the new governor of the province of Quebec, the local customs associated with corvée were also included in the legal code. This largely removed the justices of the peace's short two-year tenure of involvement in road construction, replacing their authority with the French strategy of having the surveyors, seigneurs, militia captains, and "ancien habitants" organize an "assembly of habitants" to decide on locations of construction projects. Initially started under Grand Voyer Bécancour, this procedure ensured that each individual parish or seigneurie decided the most functional locations for roads in its community. Indeed, Cugnet wrote that, "when habitants and censitaires concessionaires ask to change a road, royal or local," the grand voyer would "assemble the notables and ancien habitants of the parish in the seigneurie to communicate with them." The changes required "a plurality of votes," with the grand voyer providing the tiebreaker vote if the community was "divided between two sentiments."[174]

The reinstitution of these French customs further integrated corvée into an emerging imperial legal code in Quebec. Cugnet's "Regulations" were part of a broader scheme, on behalf of Carleton, to create a Canadian imperial constitution. From the beginning of his tenure as governor, he imagined a legal code that respected local French custom and seigneurial dues governed by an umbrella of English justice and common law.[175] In the following decades, corvée factored into that scheme and provided a powerful mechanism for the exercise of state authority over habitant life. While Carleton's reforms returned familiar intermediaries and community leaders as part of the decision-making process, the colonial state ultimately decided the mobilization of habitant labour. War, invasion, and the American Revolution tested the parameters of the newly instituted, experimental legal code and provided habitants with the opportunity to protest mandatory labour for the British colonial state.

CIVIL ADMINISTRATION IN QUEBEC

The chaotic post-Conquest legislation brought to light the challenges the British faced sculpting the corvée obligation to meet their own needs. Multiple forms of coercion overlapped with one another in the immediate aftermath of war, including pre-existing arrangements (such as corvée) to more British-inspired drudgery (like impressment). By 1767, Guy Carleton articulated a new direction for the province. He felt the profitability of Quebec hinged on maintaining the French custom that had predated the British arrival. This included corvée and, in the coming years, the British would rely heavily on that labour system for a myriad of tasks.

The provincial legal codes laid down by Cugnet provided a blueprint to legally justify the existence of corvée. It intertwined French custom with English common law practices generating a unique, hybrid labour code. In 1767, for habitants, the changes probably appeared miniscule. On the ground, little had changed – they still worked building roads and digging ditches for their militia captains. Elsewhere in the empire, however, a crisis slowly took form. Stamp Act protests and riots produced tension between the Anglo-American colonies and the metropole.[176] The habitants toiling on roads in 1767 could not have guessed that, in just ten years, the British would coerce them into a labouring force several thousand strong, pulling cannons and ferrying redcoats into a struggle that ultimately tested the very parameters of empire in North America.

CHAPTER 4

The Quebec Act and the Politics of Popular Protest, 1768–76

INTRODUCTION

From 1768 to 1774, Governor Guy Carleton led a parliamentary inquiry into the law codes of New France and the feasibility of reinstating seigneurial legal traditions in the province of Quebec. This culminated in the Quebec Act, which generated a direct linkage between the Crown, habitants, and corvée labour. Receiving royal assent on 22 June 1774, the Quebec Act reorganized the power structure of French Canadian landholders. In this manifestation of the seigneurial regime, the power to exercise "all Customs and usages" derived not from the decades of local social arrangements cultivated in New France but from the consent of the British Crown and Constitution.[1] Similar to legislation in the Anglo-American colonies, as Jack P. Green argues, the act demonstrated that the "King-in-Parliament was the supreme sovereign of the empire" and that all authority stemmed from ministers' "right to legislate in the colonies."[2] Based on their previous experience with British state-sanctioned corvée and the appropriation of their resources, habitants in Quebec recognized that increased colonial intervention threatened their livelihood. Indeed, they realized that Parliament placed imperial mercantile demands before the posterity of their families.

In May 1775, one month after the Quebec Act went into effect, the Continental Army launched a preemptive attack on Canada. The military campaign immediately tested the parameters of the recently reestablished seigneurial regime in the province. Throughout the six-month campaign, habitants defied state-sanctioned orders, attacked their seigneurs, and, in some cases, performed corvée for the Continental Army. While battle raged in the southern parishes of Quebec, another war, perhaps more important than the armed skirmishes, broke out between the British and Americans for the support of French Canadian habitants. Both armies publicly denounced their enemies' motivations and reached out to the habitants for support in the war. Regardless of their success or failure to garner the Canadians' allegiance, British and American High Commands centrally addressed corvée labour as a defining component of the campaign. The turmoil of war, in conjunction with the economic instability of both armies during the invasion, allowed habitants the opportunity to define their labour relationships and to negotiate their experience of corvée.

This chapter explores the ideological underpinnings of the British Empire in Quebec and the ways in which habitants responded to the political arguments taking place around them. Indeed, habitants were not separated from the tumult of the constitutional crisis taking place in the Anglo-American colonies. As American colonists protested imperial taxation in the streets of Boston, Philadelphia, and New York, French Canadians also began to question the legitimacy of British rule.[3]

The fallout of the Seven Years' War had serious political and economic consequences in all of North America, but especially in Quebec.[4] Enlarged by conquest, the British Empire had nearly bankrupted its treasury to defeat the French.[5] Transforming Quebec into a profitable venture became a priority for both Parliament and the king's officials in the province. Canadian political reform was thus refracted through an economic lens – any changes to seigneurial law codes would aim to harness habitant labour, extract Canadian raw materials, and drive down costs of production. Corvée played a prominent role in these discussions, and colonial officials continued to use the labour system to build public works. These revisions also echoed Parliament's efforts in the Anglo-American colonies as they attempted to draw British North America further under the direct control and supervision of the metropole.[6] The growing discontent of the thirteen Anglo-American colonies, however, ultimately allowed habitants a chance to respond to the labour initiatives of the British regime.

For these reasons, the Quebec Act belongs side by side with contemporary discourse on the Anglo-American taxation protests. Simply put, the Canadian legislation derived from the same chambers of Parliament that ratified the Stamp Act, the Townshend Act, the Tea Act, and the Coercive Acts. The same ministers debated the bills on the floor of Parliament and schemed to bring about legal justifications for their existence in the king's North American territories. Furthermore, colonists responded to these initiatives similarly. In the Anglo-American colonies, as Benjamin Carp argues, "Americans began to see the imperial government as an oppressor rather than a protector."[7] Politically mobilized colonists "coalesced into civic communities, defined the boundaries of the community, and contended with the challenges inherent in social and political change."[8] Like Parliament's centralized political reform in the thirteen mainland colonies, the Quebec Act pushed habitants into action and allowed them to articulate alternatives to British rule.

The American invasion of Quebec provided habitants the opportunity for a referendum on British colonial policies. Largely unprepared to defend the province, British officials in Quebec depended on Canadian habitants to provide corvée and militia service to thwart the American rebels. During the invasion, Governor Carleton issued a provincial decree that obligated all males to perform corvée in the defence of the colony.[9] Many seigneuries, however, used the invasion as a platform to publicly protest corvée in the military. They collectively petitioned, imprisoned their seigneurs, and aided the American rebels in their expedition north. Although the British defeated the Americans at Quebec City and repulsed the rebels during a lengthy counter-offensive, the invasion had long-standing consequences for labour mobilization. The British colonial administration had nearly lost the northern province and implemented new forms of coercion to ensure an obedient workforce. These labour policies not only shaped the lives of habitants during the American Revolution but also provided legitimacy for the obligation to perform corvée after the war ended.

ECONOMIC COLLAPSE AND POLITICAL REFORM, 1766–68

The challenges of integrating the newly created province of Quebec into the British Empire surpassed simply appropriating corvée and using habitant labour for the construction of public works. Indeed, corvée and the social arrangements that encompassed it depended upon the French seigneurial regime. To this end, British colonial officials disagreed on how much of French seigneurial law – if any – should remain in the provincial legal code.

Whitehall acknowledged that it had to maintain some elements of seigneurial law, such as rights to land, custom, and religion, which it had granted the French in the Capitulation of Montreal and the Treaty of Paris.[10] For an empire that prided itself on maintaining a composite monarchy that was free from arbitrary authority, this put ministers in an uncomfortable position.[11] As Denver Brunsman argues, "liberty was the protean ideological glue that helped hold together the British Atlantic."[12] Mainland and colonial Britons (with white skin) understood that, "at its most basic level, liberty meant freedom and arbitrary restraint from total subjection of another."[13] Corvée challenged this optimistic view of liberty and forced ministers to consider the consequences of integrating Canadian feudal practices into the empire.

Protected by an international treaty, however, Whitehall could not eradicate the vestiges of New France's feudal government and replace it with English common law. In particular, it feared that erasing New France's legal customs would provide a dangerous precedent that would give too much authority to one single branch of government, whether that be the colonial administration, the Parliament, or the king.[14] Eliminating a conquered territory's property and labour arrangements challenged the fundamental beliefs in the role of government and who should ultimately be responsible for organizing the legal codes of these colonies.[15]

Debates over the seigneurial regime also opened up complex issues pertaining to the Canadian economy. Prior to the Conquest, the French king owned all land in *demesne* and could seize unoccupied property deemed potentially profitable.[16] While the British Crown had similar precedent in its overseas territories, its acquisition of the French King's *demesne* meant appropriating the pre-existing seigneurial customs that governed this property.[17] Under the French, habitants were required to provide corvée on the king's *demesne* if called upon by the governor or intendant. Indeed, they harvested wood and surrendered raw materials deemed especially valuable to the Crown.[18] British merchants, equally interested in seizing these raw materials, debated which seigneurial customs and dues would need to be maintained and how the new colonial system would affect everyday lives of Canadian subjects.

The economic challenges of integrating Quebec's seigneurial regime into the British Empire were compounded by a postwar recession that left much of the population in poverty. Mandatory militia service and corvée during the Seven Years' War meant that many habitant families had fallen behind on their agricultural work.[19] In portions of the countryside, the British had burned habitant farms and, in the case of Quebec City, destroyed lines of communication and public infrastructure.[20] France's loss in the global conflict had deflated the value of the livre, especially in Canada, where British colonial officials remained undecided whether the currency would continue as the primary unit of exchange. Proposals, for example, suggested replacing livres with English pounds. As Parliament debated the measures, habitants and wage labourers were left with currency increasingly deemed obsolete and worthless in the face of replacement with British money.[21]

In addition to economic hardship in the countryside, Canadian merchants also suffered in the initial years following the Treaty of Paris. The war had upended over a hundred years of diplomacy with Indigenous communities that provided furs in the region's most profitable venture. In the postwar uncertainty, British merchants seized the opportunity to try to enter into the lucrative fur trade and replace French merchants who had long-standing ties to Native American tribes in Ontario and the Pays d'en Haut.[22]

In Quebec, disagreements between members of the new colonial administration and merchants over who would profit from the Conquest led to intense factionalism and internal unrest. Governor Murray defended maintaining French customs and found himself at odds with an ambitious group of British merchants that sought common law reform of Quebec's trade policies.[23] The dramatic in-fighting among Murray, other officials, and British merchants led to a series of hearings in London on the future of the province.

In 1766, Parliament ordered Murray and Burton to provide testimony in Parliament regarding the disagreements.[24] In the political vacuum left by factionalism, Murray's second-in-command, Guy Carleton, took over administrating day-to-day responsibilities pertaining to Quebec. Carleton decided to hold his own legal inquiry into French customs. With most political opposition replaced by newcomers, Carleton saw an opportunity to install several reforms that would streamline authority in Canada and give the British access to the resources they hoped to cultivate. His suggestions ultimately had long-standing consequences for habitant labour and the seigneurial regime in Quebec.

GOVERNOR GUY CARLETON AND LEGAL INQUIRIES, 1766–68

After taking his appointment as "Lieutenant-Governor and Administrator" in 1766, Guy Carleton set out to reform the political economy of Quebec. In his opinion, the economic inefficiencies plaguing the new province derived from a haphazardly composed post-Conquest government. Initial proposals after the Treaty of Paris had called for the replacement of *all* French customs with English common law. The change in regimes also meant that Parliament would eventually replace all French judges with appointed English justices of the peace. During Murray's "civil administration," for example, he dissolved the government courts of New France (Montreal, Trois-Rivières, and Quebec) and replaced them with two common law courts in Quebec and Montreal.[25] At the parish level, English bailiffs replaced French seigneurs as the primary state intermediary for mobilizing corvée. By the time Carleton took office the laws of the civil government remained undetermined and unclear, especially from the perspective of habitants who continued to perform corvée during these haphazard reforms.[26]

For Carleton, the easiest way to reestablish order lay in the seigneurial regime. As a result, a major part of his reforms stemmed from figuring out how to incorporate these customs into a Canadian constitution. Determined to integrate the province into the empire, Carleton and leading colonial lawyers deliberated the consequences of knitting feudal laws into that of their own "free" English procedures.

The British could not simply dismiss the seigneurial obligations protected by the Capitulation of Montreal, which had "preserved all properties and revenues of the seigniories and other estates."[27] Moreover, the terms of surrender had retained the "privileges, rights, honours, and exemptions" of the seigneurs, such as the cens, the grist mill banalité, and the custom of raising a corvée to work on the lord's demesne.[28] The Capitulation made provisions for all Canadians to retain their "entire peaceable property and possession of their goods, noble and ignoble, moveable and immoveable, merchandises, furs, and other effects, even their ships."[29]

Three years of using the Capitulation, as English lawyers saw it, had cemented the seigneurial regime in Quebec, and taking away property concessions would violate that Constitution.[30] As highlighted in chapter 3, the retention of certain characteristics of this regime led to a hybrid form of corvée, in which bailiffs, clerks, and judges administered work orders to the traditional feudal hierarchy of New France.[31] While officials carried on corvée for road building relatively smoothly, Carleton recognized that the provincial laws required clarification. For him, reinstating all French customs prior to the Conquest would not only satisfy war-weary habitants but also bolster the provincial economy and connect it to imperial markets.[32]

The first step towards drafting a provincial legal code required an exhaustive analysis of how the seigneurial and royal codes operated under the French regime. To achieve this, Carleton hired two Parisian lawyers, Elie de Beaumont and Jean-Baptiste Target, to analyze concessions granted to habitants under the Custom of Paris.[33] British administrators funded the inquiry to better understand the French laws concerning the king's right to timber, mining, and the obligations that habitants owed the Crown under the *ancien régime*.[34]

In particular, colonial officials hoped that habitants would harvest timber for the Royal Navy from the king's *demesne*. Indeed, the lawyers reported that the titles of concession under the French exhibited "a marked diversity in the right of His Majesty."[35] Each individual title contained different privileges regarding logging, with some "more onerous to the grantees, others less."[36] For example, many titles of concession granted the king full right to woods "near the sea and navigable rivers," stamped by the "navy hammer."[37] Other titles of concession allowed habitants to retain rights over portions of their lumber, in which case, the lawyers stated: "it is not possible to pretend the King can have a right to take all or any portion of such timber without indemnity."[38] In their verdict, the Parisian lawyers asserted that the British Crown retained "a right of preference and pre-emption over subjects, for the service of the navy, or his [the king's] royal houses, but a right which he exercised only on payment of the fair value." This obligation "of the King became that of the King of England when the sovereignty of Canada passed into his hands."[39]

The British Crown also profited from mines and minerals discovered on Canadian soil. Citing three royal codes, ratified by Charles VI in 1413, Charles X in 1563, and Henry IV in 1603, the lawyers reported that the Crown reserved a right to a "tenth part of all metals when purified and refined." Coal, iron, petroleum, slate, plaster, and chalk were exempted "from the duty of tenth," instead passing to private ownership. Companies or individuals seeking to start such ventures required permission, patents, or grants from the king that guaranteed access to minerals if needed for matters of state.[40]

Most important, Beaumont and Target articulated an imperial policy that Carleton could use for the foundation of a provincial constitution in Quebec. To achieve this, they cited a recent treatise written by Sir William Blackstone entitled *Commentaries on the Laws of England*. They specifically targeted Blackstone's fourth article, which focused on the relationship between English law and Britain's colonies. Blackstone subdivided these colonies into three categories of government: national, conquered, and ceded. National colonies, they argued "are those founded by Englishmen, established by means of improvement and prior occupation."[41] From their inception, these settlements abided by "the laws of England." Conquered and ceded colonies, on the other hand, "ha[d] already laws of their own" that allowed the king to "alter and change those laws." Until Parliament altered the foreign laws of the conquered or ceded territory, "the ancient laws of the country remain[ed], unless such [were] against the laws of God, as in the case of an infidel country." Quebec, these lawyers argued, fell under such jurisdiction, with all French customs remaining in effect until explicitly replaced by Parliament. Regardless of the pre-existing laws, all subjects and legal codes fell under the jurisdiction of Parliament, which had full control over the "distinct (though dependent) dominions."[42]

THE QUEBEC ACT DEBATES, 1768–74

After receiving the report from the Parisian lawyers, in 1768, Carleton reached out to William Petty, secretary of the Southern Department, to discuss creating a uniform Canadian constitution that reinstated most seigneurial customs. In a letter to Petty, he asserted that he had grown increasingly concerned about Canadian unrest, as the people were "not a migration of Britons, who brought with them the laws of England, but a populous and long-established colony."[43] They had, in Carleton's words, been "reduced by the King's arms to submit to his dominion on certain conditions."[44] Indeed, their "laws and customs were widely different from those of England," and they depended on these laws, especially with regard to their title deeds, which dictated property ownership. These same deeds also stipulated feudal obligations owed to landlords, such as corvée.[45] Any provincial constitution would need to incorporate these seigneurial customs.

Carleton also argued that the social relationships established under the French regime instilled order, obedience, and obligation in Canada. He stated: "this system of laws established subordination from the first to the lowest, which preserved the internal harmony they enjoyed until our arrival."[46] French custom "secured obedience to the supreme seat of government from a very distant province."[47] The British takeover of New France had "in one hour" overturned these customs, instead ratifying "laws ill adapted to the genius of Canadians, to the situation of the province, and to the interests of Great Britain."[48] In order to restore "life, limb, and property of the subject, within the limits of the power of His Majesty," Carleton believed that he should draft a new provincial code that restored full civil authority to seigneurs, with the British acting as the administrators and arbiters of justice.[49]

His plan called for the repeal of burdensome judicial institutions that had been put into place following the Treaty of Paris, such as the king's common law courts, instead suggesting it would be best to "leave the Canadian laws almost entire."[50] Carleton evoked England's history of past conquests in defence of such a strategy. For example, he cited "Edward the First after the Conquest of Wales" and articulated that the French civil law-based code would appease a conquered and subjugated people.[51] This also meant eliminating the "English justice and English offices," and having "gentlemen of the law, of integrity and abilities, with a knowledge of the French language" put into administrative offices.[52] Carleton framed the changes as not only political but also economic, stating that these reforms would streamline the collection of rents, taxes, and "arrangements essential to the King's service and the interests of Great Britain."[53]

The crux of any legal code in Quebec depended on maintaining seigneurial levies. As Carleton pointed out to Petty, the seigneurial regime dictated all economic and political hierarchies in the colony, and, because habitants and seigneurs had ironed out the boundaries of these relationships over the past 150 years, it made sense to integrate these into a provincial legal code instead of replacing them. The foundation of such reform rested upon the "title deeds" issued by the French. As discussed earlier, title deeds consisted of written agreements between seigneurs and habitants that set defined terms of rent, corvée, and *privileges extraordinaire*. In a draft of a provincial constitution, Carleton argued that these contracts defined all terms "concerning the rights, privileges, and pre-eminences" of tenure related to the state, seigneur, and habitant.[54] This included all "burthens, duties, and obligations to which [habitants] were subject."[55] The deeds also stipulated forfeiture of property and Crown-sanctioned annexation of land for the King's *demesne*.

Carleton proposed that "all grants made by the French King before the conquest of this country, and ... all land held under the immediate tenants of the Crown" have their title deeds honoured and fully reinstated.[56]

While Carleton undoubtedly sought to appease French Canadian seigneurs and habitants who believed that the British would replace integral parts of their law codes with those of the Isles, he also highlighted pragmatic imperial ambitions.[57] His ultimate goal was knitting Quebec into a larger British imperial economic network that extracted revenue, resources, and labour from its colonies.[58] He recognized that, for Quebec, French laws streamlined colonial state authority and reinstituted relationships that would ultimately ensure obedience from a conquered people. For example, Parliament could seize all "unused" land for logging and harness corvée labour for public works projects.[59] Moreover, by restoring the hierarchy associated with the seigneurial regime, intermediaries would bear the brunt of mobilizing labour and collecting taxes. Carleton imagined British officials grafted on top of a network of pre-existing relationships of obedience and obligation.[60]

His efforts persuaded the new secretary of the Southern Department, Charles Townshend, to initiate a formal parliamentary inquiry into reinstating all the seigneurial customs of New France. Ministers, however, grew concerned that if they restored all title deeds in full capacity then a stipulation allowing seigneurs to administer the *moyenne et basse justice* (a manorial court on their property that mediated community altercations, minor crimes, and the collection of taxes) would undermine British authority.[61] In response, Carleton led a subsequent inquiry into the authority of seigneurs and the feudal obligations that habitants owed them. Carleton admitted that "some of the privileges contained in [the] grants appear[ed] at first to convey dangerous powers into the hands of the seigneurs."[62] In truth, the French Crown had never fully allowed the *haute*, the privilege to organize such courts. Indeed, only a handful of mid-seventeenth-century Canadian nobles established these courts, instead deferring the time, money, and energy spent on cases to the "government" courts.[63]

The governor reassured Townshend that reinstituting full seigneurial authority over habitants would not undermine the Crown's authority over the collection of taxes and all other feudal obligations owed to the king. He cited the Custom of Paris (1664), which effectively eliminated these courts and stripped seigneurs of their privilege to choose judges. Noting this, Carleton assured Parliament that "even under the French government" these privileges "were so corrected as to prove of little signification to the proprietors."[64] Keeping courts also proved expensive and "too burthensome for the scanty incomes of the Canadian seigneurs."[65] He argued that the seigneurial customs would "secure a proper subordination from this province to Great Britain."[66]

Carleton's ongoing correspondence with Townshend forced sceptical members of Parliament to consider a new Canadian constitution. Indeed, ministers wanted to see Quebec transform into a functioning and profitable part of the empire. His economic arguments persuaded both government officials and wealthy merchants that the province required revised laws. Under Carleton's advisement, they permitted Francis Maseres, the attorney general of Quebec, to put together a list of suggestions on the current laws of Canada and those French customs that they should reinstate. In the meantime, Parliament sent instructions to Carleton to temporarily continue to make seigneurial grants and to honour French customs. Parliament's instructions stated that the governor should: "[grant all] lands which remain subject to our disposal, in fief and seigneurie, as hath been practiced heretofore, antecedent to the conquest."[67] They also re-established a version of the *foy et homage*, in which all seigneurial grants required "royal ratification" and registration "in like manner as was practiced in regard to grants held in fief and seigneurie under the French government."[68]

Alexander Wedderburn, the solicitor general for England and Wales, began collecting these various reports, concerns, and suggestions into a draft bill that would provide Quebec with a unified provincial legal code. Aided by Lord Dartmouth (secretary of state of the Southern Department), Carleton, and William Hey (chief justice of the province of Quebec), by June a draft of the bill made it to the House of Lords. Entitled "A Bill for Making More Effectual Provision for the Government of the Province of Quebec," later referred to as the Quebec Act, the legislation proposed reinstating seigneurial customs and privileges, establishing a legislative council at the discretion of the governor, and protecting the Roman Catholic faith in Canada.

On 26 May 1774, the House of Commons convened to discuss the bill. The debates surrounding the Quebec Act pivoted on three interrelated concerns associated with integrating the province into the British Empire. First, ministers grew wary of implementing seigneurial law in a North American province, especially one located so close to the thirteen Anglo-American colonies.[69] They feared that establishing seigneurial law would set a complicated precedent elsewhere in North America. For example, British migrants sent to any new colonies extending westward from Quebec (later named Upper

Canada) would have to reckon with French-derived seigneurial law.[70] While ministers understood the convenience of maintaining these laws in the area formerly known as New France, they balked at the idea that they would implement these customs in any new colonies. Additionally, the bill proposed subsuming Newfoundland and Nova Scotia under the same laws, angering British merchants in the fishing industry who believed that they would have to abide by French customs.

Second, debate also centred around the toleration of the Roman Catholic faith in Canada. As a province surrounded by Protestants, the opposition to the bill asserted that allowing Canadians the right to maintain their parishes could draw unwanted influence from the pope in Rome.[71] Indeed, as Phillip Lawson states, "religious toleration, the function of representative government, and the meanings of English law all come to the fore in the debate about Quebec."[72] Moreover, "at the root of British discomfort with the province in the immediate post-war period lay an inflexible political ideology, seemingly incompatible with the practical realities of governing seventy thousand or so French Canadians."[73]

Finally, most ministers agreed that Quebec would receive a criminal law code based on English traditions. They disagreed, however, on the extent to which jurors, justices of the peace, and bailiffs would take positions of leadership in French Canadian communities.[74] Debate also centred on the official language of the courtroom, especially in the Quarter Sessions, which had begun to operate "in a mixture of French and English."[75] Ministers questioned whether French Canadian habitants could understand, or agree with, the freedoms granted by a jury-based system of justice.

Debate over seigneurial obligations, such as corvée, factored heavily into the House of Commons discussion. Minister Thomas Townshend formed part of the opposition to the bill and raised scepticism over the implementation of French civil law in the British Empire. In particular, he saw the extension of seigneurial customs as problematic for areas that Parliament hoped to colonize with future British migrants. Townshend asserted that he was concerned over "carrying that system of law into a country where it was not extended at present."[76] He stated: "many gentlemen have bought large estates in Canada; even large seigneuries are now held by the British." These properties would need to convert to a foreign system of land tenure, taking "from the English subject his benefit of the laws of England."[77]

Empire, sovereignty, and subjecthood lay at the foundation of disagreements between the factions. These debates – whether on seigneurial customs, the Roman Catholic faith, or criminal law – revolved around competing visions of how each faction imagined Canadians in an enlarged British Empire. These discussions were undoubtedly amplified as a result of events in the decade after the Seven Years' War. The incorporation of Bengal, Spanish Florida, Canada, and Indigenous land into the Pays d'en Haut had shattered an emerging proto-nationalist identity of the empire as white, Protestant, and "free" under the English Constitution.[78] On one hand, as Hannah Weiss Muller has recently shown, staunch critics of the Quebec Act argued that "allowing French Catholics to continue living under French law and French tyranny would result in the failure to create British subjects";[79] on the other hand, supporters of a provincial code and imperial legal pluralism would, in theory, encourage obedience and connect Canada to the Crown's post-Conquest colonial landholdings.[80]

Carleton remained optimistic that Parliament could agree on a provincial code that fused French civil law and English criminal law. Indeed, he argued that Canadians, "by the introduction of the laws of the English government, and by the protection of the civil laws of their country[,] … were to become a happy people by change."[81] The "intelligent part of the Canadians think and hope," Carleton stated during his examination, that "their laws and customs may be continued."[82] Claiming to have spoken to habitants, he continued: "they had frequently expressed their desire and prayer to have their ancient usages restored to them; and stated that the form of government which came nearest their ancient usages would be most agreeable to them."[83]

During his examination, Francis Maseres, attorney general of Quebec, urged Parliament to preserve seigneurial laws of tenure. He defined these customs as "the laws relating to the mutual and reciprocal ties of landlord and tenant."[84] Additionally, he stated that the laws of tenure "oblige the tenants to pay their quit rents and corn rents and mutation fines, to their landlord, to grind their corn at his mill, and give him his meal-toll."[85] Any alteration of the tenure "would be taking away the seigneur's property, which cannot be done because it is granted by capitulation."[86] Parliament decided, however, that the Canadians' "laws, customs, and usages" derived from the king's "sole legislative authority," in conjunction with "the two Houses of Parliament."[87] To enforce the state's authority within the province, Parliament proposed a legislative council "to lay any taxes or duties within the said province" and dictate "making roads, erecting and repairing buildings, or for any other purpose respecting the local convenience and economy of [the parishes of Quebec]."[88]

Receiving royal assent in June 1774, the Quebec Act reorganized the power structure of French Canadian landholders. The act reinstated seigneurial property customs in full, but it also functionally eliminated the role of seigneurs as intermediaries between the colonial state and the parishes they represented. In New France, the absolutist regime had built in buffers against royal authority, most notably the seigneurs' power to redirect orders of corvée and the "assembly of habitants." Both functioned to report local needs and grievances to the king's officials. The Quebec Act, on the other hand, largely changed the influence wielded by these intermediary roles. Only by the "Advice and Consent" of Parliament did seigneurs receive the privilege of implementing customs at the local level. This direct link between the state and the community neglected what James Scott refers to as "the notion of a hierarchy of human needs, with the means of physical survival naturally taking priority over all other claims to village wealth."[89] Parliament's motivation was not lost on French Canadian habitants, who realized that the British sought to appropriate their labour to benefit an enlarged imperial economy.

THE AMERICAN INVASION OF QUEBEC, 1775

While Carleton drafted a provincial legal code and debated with ministers on the legitimacy of the seigneurial regime in Quebec, elsewhere in the empire a series of radical protests had ignited a rebellion against the Crown. Initially a referendum on Anglo-American taxation, the protests over the Stamp Act and subsequent bills had exploded into a dispute over the Constitution of Britain and the empire.[90] With a lack of representation in Parliament, the colonists declared that the taxes were a breach of their local assemblies' jurisdiction over internal affairs. Meanwhile, metropolitan officials argued that Parliament represented the empire in its entirety. Although Parliament reluctantly repealed the Stamp Act, the passing of the Townshend Acts in 1767 reinvigorated arguments over constitutional authority. As the debates progressed, the question of internal affairs evolved into a debate of sovereignty and empire. Parliament's ratification of the Tea Act, 1774, and subsequent Coercive Acts solidified Anglo-American unrest and resulted in colonists beginning to demand legal authority over internal and external affairs.

As early as 1774, American leaders made direct overtures to French Canadian habitants to join their rejection of an "omnipotent Parliament" and to reaffirm the sovereignty of local assemblies.[91] Indeed, these appeals to habitants were not peripheral – but central – to a burgeoning American leadership that located liberties, the ability to legislate, and taxation in the sovereignty of colonial assemblies. Meeting in Philadelphia, the delegates of the First Continental Congress (composed of twelve of the thirteen Anglo-American colonies) believed that they might find fertile ground for anti-British sentiment in the French Canadian habitant population. In their calls for Canadians to join their cause, the congressional delegates channelled a vision of widespread protest against "arbitrary government" and, to make their point, utilized corvée as an example of burdensome British policy.[92]

The Continental Congress published a series of letters in Quebec to provoke habitants to join their voices to dissent from imperial policies and to undermine British authority in the province. The first letter addressed to the habitants of Quebec dated 26 October 1774, attributed to John Dickinson, Pennsylvania delegate to the First Continental Congress, stated that the thirteen Anglo-American colonies had gathered in Philadelphia to "consult together on the best means of procuring deliverance from [their] overwhelming oppressions," and that the delegates had "judged it appropriate to address [Quebec] as one of its most interested parties."[93] In the letter, Dickinson condemned what Congress saw as the arbitrary authority exercised by Parliament over the king's North American colonies and the violation of local democratic customs. He asserted that British subjects have the "principal right" to share "in their government by their self-chosen representatives and are therefore governed by laws of their approval, and not by the edicts of those upon who he has no power."[94]

Dickinson explicitly highlighted corvée, and its connection with land tenure, as an oppressive burden thrust onto Canadians by the British colonial government. He pointed out that a right that all men should possess "consist[s] in the possession of land by virtue of slight annuities, and not by rigorous and oppressive corvées which often force the possessor to leave their family and occupations to do what in any well-regarded state should be the work of people hired expressly for this purpose."[95] Furthermore, he cast corvée as a representation of arbitrary authority, asking, "Who will defend your people from *lettres de cachet*, from prisons, dungeons, and tiring corvées, your freedom and life against arbitrary and insensitive leaders?" This call to action was not just rhetorical. Dickinson formalized Congress's plea to habitants to "enter into union with our colonies" against what the Anglo-American colonists interpreted as an increasingly despotic government.[96]

This anti-British sentiment certainly resonated with large groups of habitants. In the coming years, they would demonstrate their dissatisfaction with British policies in the public arena through protest, petitions, and mutiny. Canadian leadership, however, would not entertain Congress's appeal to join it in opposing Parliament's imperial jurisdiction. The Quebec Act, although recently ratified, had reaffirmed the positions of seigneurs as the landed elite with a full suite of services owed to them by their tenants. The act had satisfied other powerful Canadian social groups as well. The Roman Catholic clergy received protection of their faith, entitlements, lands, and tithes, and merchants counted on lucrative contracts with London for the sale of furs, timber, and iron.[97] At the upper echelon of the administration, the district officials remained loyal to Carleton, who had spent the past six years advocating for a provincewide legal code that reinstated French customs.

To the south, the British military occupation of Boston (1774) continued to escalate tensions across the thirteen mainland Anglo-American colonies. In response to the unrest, General Thomas Gage, acting military governor of Massachusetts, sought to seize ammunition depots of muskets and black powder located in New England villages. Troop movement in Boston provoked further agitation, with Massachusetts militiamen rallying to meet the British in the field.[98] This culminated in a series of skirmishes between New England colonists and professional British soldiers, first at Lexington and Concord, and later outside Boston at Bunker Hill. Following the king's dismissal of the colonies' offering of peace, delegates from each of the thirteen Anglo-American colonies formed the Second Continental Congress to discuss the crisis and a potential pathway towards reconciliation.[99]

Armed conflict in the imperial borderlands erupted in May 1775 after Benedict Arnold and Ethan Allen captured Fort Ticonderoga. In an attempt to protect the Anglo-American northern border from British retaliation, Arnold led a force composed of Continental regulars and militiamen on a raid of the fort at Saint Jean.[100] In response, Carleton immediately called upon the seigneurs' reestablished duty to raise the militia in their parishes. In the Richelieu, he proclaimed: "[the] noblesse of this neighbourhood were called upon to collect their inhabitants, in order to defend themselves."[101] For Carleton, the seigneurs demonstrated "great Fidelity and warmth for His Majesty's Service," but they lacked influence over their habitants.[102] Although the recently ratified Quebec Act legally required habitants to obey their respective seigneur, Carleton described the "minds of the People" as "tainted by the Cabals and Intrigues." As a result, he proposed conscripting Canadians into the militia and corvée to organize the defence of the province.[103]

For the British, the ability to raise corvée for the military stemmed from the sovereignty of the monarchy and Parliament. Utilizing his "virtue and ... the Powers and Authority given to [him] by His Majesty," Carleton issued a proclamation that declared martial law and ordered the captains in every parish to organize corvée.[104] On 19 October 1775, he posted an announcement in the *Quebec Gazette* that ordered all captains to enforce corvée in their respective parishes.[105] The governor ordered the corvée to "mow the hay, cut the oats or other grains" and "other plowing."[106] Additionally, he encouraged habitants to "repair and put in wintering state" the community infrastructure.[107] To achieve this, he appealed to their traditional arrangements of corvée duty, which consisted of labour on public works.

Carleton's order to the captains of the militia, however, also initiated a precedent of raising corvée labourers for the duties and objectives of the British military. As a proclamation ratified during a period of martial law, the labour that habitants performed reflected the necessities of providing food, supplies, and infrastructure for the defence of the province. Indeed, as the Canadian militia prepared for the siege of Quebec City, Carleton expected habitants who remained in the parishes to perform labour to sustain the local economy.[108] Additionally, all habitants ordered to perform corvée worked under the auspices of a British-appointed district commander. Organized, efficient, and bureaucratic, High Command incorporated corvée into the rigid hierarchy of the military.

In an attempt to undermine British authority, American soldiers delivered pamphlets to the parishes in Quebec.[109] Published by John Hancock, president of the Second Continental Congress, the pamphlets denounced the Crown and encouraged an alliance between the Canadians and the Continental Army. To persuade the habitants, he utilized the politicized language of the rebellion. Indeed, Hancock believed that the legislative encroachment of the Crown created "a feeling of common danger" between the rebelling colonies and Quebec, in which both were "equally doomed to ruin by a common despotic administration."[110] Moreover, the conflict bound "the fate of the Protestant & Catholic Colonies" together in a common cause to overturn the perceived British tyranny.[111]

The attacks occurred eleven months after royal assent of the Quebec Act and just one month after the law code's formal implementation in the province. Ultimately, the larger conflict, referred to as the American invasion of Quebec, generated a series of Canadian protests against corvée labour and seigneurial obligations that the British believed they could exploit to curtail American aggression. During the invasion, outright rejection of feudal obligations, such as corvée, illustrates what Sergio Serunlikov describes as the "politics of insurrection."[112] In these protests, habitants "began to articulate contractual notions of legitimacy that challenged" the local landed elite.[113] Colonial hegemony "rested not on the dominance of alien institutions but on the power of defining the social meaning of such institutions."[114] Armed responses against their seigneurs symbolically articulated the peasants' dismissal of the local agent of state authority, followed by a communal decision to undermine the legitimacy of British law by aligning with American political objectives.

Three forms of protest defined the actions of French Canadian habitants. First, insurgent habitants subverted colonial political institutions through demonstrations of symbolic authority. Public demonstrations and communal oath-taking degraded British officials and stripped corvée "of its function as a ritual of state authority."[115] For example, the habitants of Berthier convened a secret meeting at which they promised to collectively destroy the property of those who aligned with British interests.[116] In the Quebec parish of Cap Santé, a farmer named Frans Germain also organized a series of secret meetings in his parish. At these gatherings, the captain of the militia, Joseph Louis Pagé, organized the men in his parish to perform corvée to support the Americans. When three men – Joseph Mate, Louis Nicolas Mate, and Pagé du Bois – refused to work for the rebels, the militia captain fined them and confiscated their country carts for the transportation of supplies.[117] Public acts of defiance demonstrated the application of peasant concepts of communal justice and political legitimacy.

During this period of instability, habitants also subverted the political order utilizing familiar symbols and settings in their parish traditionally used for collective gatherings. The parish door (the location of parish announcements and work orders since the early eighteenth century) transformed into an arena of public protest. Several habitants across the côtes of Quebec used this space to publicly denounce the British and, in some cases, declare their intentions to serve the rebels. These calls to action could, more significantly, come from important voices in the community. For example, in Saint-Féréol, a "highly respected" parishioner named Chrétien Giguere "repeatedly boasted, at the church doors, of the rebels' strength and power in order to persuade [the people] that the town was very much threatened."[118] Furthermore, these statements seemed to have a real impact on the decisions of the community. In Saint-Laurent-Ilse D'Orléans, the captain of the militia, Marc Dufrene, "shouted at the church doors that those who do obey Congress' orders would be looted." Several of his milice helped the American army, with François Baby commenting that men in the parish "played a significant role in last fall's rebellion."[119]

Second, ritual acts of insurrection condoned public performances of violence against seigneurs to invert the social hierarchy. Habitants imprisoned, held hostage, or attacked militia captains as well as mid-level British military officials. Indeed, the imprisonment of seigneurs suggests a symbolic reassertion of moral accountability in which habitants played an active role in deciding the distribution of their labour. On one hand, these actions most likely functioned to articulate habitant grievances that their seigneurs failed to address; on the other hand, the targets of these attacks suggest a much larger disdain for all intermediaries of the British colonial regime. For example, in the parish of St Charles, the community arrested its loyal militia captain and "held him captive from morning to night" in a local house until "he quickly changed his conduct" and demonstrated sympathy to the rebellion.[120] The habitant population of the province harnessed sovereignty to legitimize their actions, while simultaneously subordinating British colonial influence.

A dramatic example of habitant violence directed towards their seigneurs occurred in the aforementioned seigneurie of Berthier-en-Haut.[121] At the end of July, James Cuthbert, the seigneur of Berthier-en-Haut, dispensed a message to his peasants notifying them of their mandatory service in the militia.[122] The habitants collectively responded that, "if he had anything to communicate, he might come to them." Sometime later, Cuthbert and his tenants met at a central point on the seigneurie, and he "made a preemptory demand of their services on the French system, being their seignior." After publicly refusing to take up arms against the Americans, they took an oath that, "if one of them offered to join the [British] government, they would directly burn his house and his barn and destroy his cattle." They continued: "if General Carleton should attempt to compel them into service, they would repel him by force." Several months later, at the end of September, Joseph-Marie Godefroy de Tonnancour, lieutenant of the Trois-Rivières militia, arrived in Berthier, notifying the habitants that he would "return in a few days" to conscript them into service. When a company arrived in Berthier several days later, the Canadians surrounded Tonnancour and seventeen others and took them hostage. After debating whether to send them "to the provincial camp near St. John's," they decided to let the nobles go in exchange for a pardon.[123]

In some parishes, gender and familial relationships played a critical role in deciding the political alignment of the community. Canadian women, for example, publicly denounced the Crown and convinced their neighbours to side with the rebel invaders.[124] In Pointe-aux-Trembles, two wives of local militiamen "went door to door to defame those who, last fall, [had] talked the young men into marching [with the Royal Emigrants]."[125] The women told the men that they "would be slaughtered" if they continued to follow the British and that "they would not have to obey such orders" from the militia captain. These public defamations seem to have occurred somewhat regularly in the parishes. Indeed, Augustin Chabot's wife, in the parish of St Pierre-Ile-d'Orléans, also went "door to door" to convince the community to side with the Continental Army.[126] According to the habitants, she "made a strong impression on them with her subversive spirit."[127] Women also organized meetings in their private residences to persuade men to support the rebels. During the invasion, a widow of a militia soldier "often held and presided over gatherings in her house" in an attempt to "bolster the people's spirit against the government, and urged them to side with the rebels."[128] These meetings apparently consisted of discussion over siding with the Americans and "strong drink."[129]

Wives of men eligible for corvée utilized both the public and private spheres of the community to weaken the British war effort. In Berthier-en-Haut, following the capture of Tonnancour, several women in the community demonstrated solidarity with their rebellious husbands, shouting praise as the habitants paraded the mortified militia captain through the parish. They eventually imprisoned the captive officers in the house of Jean-Baptiste Buron. A soldier who accompanied them recalled that: "after they were made prisoner, all the women they passed on the road mockingly called out to their husbands: 'You certainty had a good hunt today.'"[130] Publicly shaming British officers allowed Canadian women the opportunity to voice dissatisfaction with the colonial regime and invert the gendered social hierarchy.

Third, political acts of resistance also functioned to undermine the foundations of the colonial regime and thereby to strengthen the military prowess of the invaders. For parishes that openly sided with the American war effort, only by eliminating any sign of British colonial dominance could habitants claim sovereignty over their individual community. In the Richelieu, the invasion prompted several Canadian parishes to join the rebellion against the Crown. Indeed, following Carleton's orders to provide militia and corvée in defence of the province, the "Chamblies parishes" rose in revolt, siding with "the Bostonians."[131] These parishes actively supported the Continental military effort, sowing "the idea in all other parishes to not take up arms against the 'Bostonians.'"[132] According to a militia captain present during the insurrection, the Chambly habitants argued that the Anglo-American colonists "had come to draw us out of oppression" and tyranny of the British Crown.[133] They proved convincing, and most seigneuries in the region failed to provide militia and corvée.

The insurgency in the Richelieu frightened British officers who depended on Canadian labour for the defence of the colony. The Chambly syndicate played a critical role aiding the American invaders, first blockading Fort Saint-Jean and then seizing "several carts filled with provisions, herds of animals, and munitions."[134] The Chambly habitants accompanied the "Bostonians" in a failed assault on Longue Point, helped attack Montreal with Major John Brown, and convinced parishes on the island to support the Continental Army. During the raids, the British captured twenty-five of the insurgent Canadians, shackling them "hand and foot" in Montreal.[135] To dissuade the remaining disaffected habitants, Carleton "sent an English officer" to relieve all seigneurial obligations of the Richelieu parishes and pardon those who had risen with the Americans.[136] He ordered the habitants to "retire each to his home," an order that they "immediately complied with."[137]

Areas of militant habitant resistance correlated with seigneuries that had borne the brunt of corvée labour in Britain's imperial schemes. For example, in Trois-Rivières, the parishes that experienced the most economic disruption from the St Maurice corvée protested service in the military. Instead, habitants provided assistance to the invading American army in the form of labour, food, and sentry duties. Gentilly and Bécancour, two parishes that supplied wood for the iron mines from 1760 until 1764, both openly aided in the rebel invasion and the movement of supplies.[138] Elsewhere, the habitants of Pointe Lévy assembled an abundant number of fascines, in one case reaching up to two thousand bundles, for American fortifications.[139] In St Henry, habitants built two hundred ladders and moved wooden beams taken from the grist mill to the construction site of a redoubt.[140] Additionally, habitants transported wheat, flour, and various other provisions to American camps.[141] In five parishes, habitants on corvée built, operated, and guarded signal fires that stretched through five parishes and alerted incoming ships of their position.[142] This process of negotiation crystallized communal labour relationships and accentuated the ability of habitants to demonstrate their dissatisfaction with the British state.

During the occupation many parishes, however, did defy the American invaders and remained loyal to the Crown. Loyal habitants refused to allocate their energy to the American war effort. Some members of the community deserted their parish in an effort to discontinue their labour for the American army. Ultimately, the failure of both the British and the Americans to fully utilize seigneurial obligations demonstrates the limitations of extracting labour from a conquered population. Moreover, the ability, and relative ease, of the people who performed corvée to decide who reaped the benefits of their production suggests that the individual habitant consecrated his loyalty within an acute, perceptive awareness of the boundaries of mandatory labour in the military.

On 31 December 1775, in the midst of a blizzard, the Continental Army launched a final, desperate attempt to capture the city of Quebec. Carleton's combined forces of British professional soldiers and Canadian militiamen repulsed the Continental regiments and forced the remainder of the invaders to retreat. Following his victory over the Continental Army, Carleton appointed three commissaries to travel to each parish in the three districts and to assess the loyalty of the militia in the community. From 22 May to 18 July, François Baby, an owner of several seigneuries in Montreal; Gabriel-Elzéar Taschereau, the seigneur of Nouvelle Beauce; and Jenkin Williams, a British lawyer, travelled through fifty-six parishes in the districts of Quebec and Trois-Rivières.[143] Carleton assigned them to review the size of each parish militia, punish any subjects who performed corvée or armed service for the Americans, and order each parish to aid the British military in any way they deemed appropriate. Each parish would receive a full, detailed report of the names of individuals eligible for militia or corvée duty.

The entrance of the envoys into the community reflected the restoration of the social order envisioned in the Quebec Act. Prior to their visits, Baby, Taschereau, and Jenkins gathered evidence and allegations of militia duty or corvée performed for the Americans. Typically, they arrived at a new parish promptly by 9:00 a.m.[144] The commissaries then assembled the militia and physically inspected each individual habitant. After the inspection, they read charges of disloyalty to the Crown and dismissed, punished, or publicly humiliated the militia captains who had supported the Americans. This ceremony included verbal confirmation that the captain had accepted a commission from the rebels, followed by a ritual burning of the documents associated with the Continental Army.[145] For record-keeping purposes, the envoys wrote the names of habitants who had demonstrated "great Zeal" for the Americans.[146] Once it did not "seem that the spirit of rebellion reign[ed]" in the community, Carleton's advisors ordered the new militia captains to enforce corvée.[147] No matter which parish they attended, the envoys always obliged the parish to cheer "Long live the King" before exiting the community.[148] The inspection, the public humiliation, the cleansing of the community, and the order of corvée demonstrated "elaborate rites of carefully calculated performances of state power.[149]

The Quebec Act had deteriorated the local customs of habitant communities and replaced these arrangements with new exploitive relationships in the name of the fiscal-military state. Through imperial law, Parliament generated a direct linkage between the state and peasant, increasingly marginalizing the position of seigneurs as intermediaries. Following the mobilization of the British Army in Quebec, habitants contested, and would continue to contest, this exploitive manipulation of their labour customs. While the presence of full-time professionally outfitted regiments limited what habitants could do to protest, during the remainder of the Revolution they put forth their own definitions of proper labour mobilization and stifled Britain's ability to wage war from Quebec.

PART 3

Workers of the Revolution, 1776–83

A still greater call upon the Canadians will be for the transport of all Provisions, Artillery, Stores, & Baggage from the Repositories to the Water and afterwards to the carrying Places. This service may at the opening of the Campaign require two thousand men, besides a very large proportion of Carts and Horses & will happen at the time of sowing the corn.

– Lieutenant General John Burgoyne, Memorandum and Observations Relative to the Service of Canada, submitted to Lord George Germain, Colonial Office Records, series Q, vol. 13, p. 16, LAC.

Figure 5.1
Thomas Davies, *View of the Lines at Lake George* (1759).

During the American Revolution, the British positioned corvée labourers at a critical supply depot on the northern end of Lake George. In 1777, the American rebels raided the portage, and most of the corvée workers fled the area, while some were taken prisoner. This painting depicts a British encampment on the southern end of the lake with the Adirondacks rising high above the water on either side.

CHAPTER 5

The Northern Campaign and the Battle of Saratoga, 1776–77

INTRODUCTION

On 22 June 1777, Lieutenant General John Burgoyne wrote a letter to Lord George Germain, secretary of the Southern Department, detailing the state of his campaign. Just two months into his expedition to Albany, Burgoyne experienced serious issues with his communication lines. The supply train running from Fort Saint-Jean in Quebec was moving too slowly for the general's liking. Burgoyne identified corvée labourers, or the lack thereof, as the primary cause of his army's glacial pace. Most of the one thousand labourers he expected to bring with him had not shown up at the militia muster.[1] He wrote to Germain, "it is with mortification I must add to these circumstances others of considerable disappointment. The assistance of Canadians beyond the limits of the Province … will be little or nothing."[2] Burgoyne, the highest-ranking military officer north of New York City, failed to compel French Canadian habitants to march beyond the jurisdictional boundary of Quebec. Indeed, he lamented: "the Country yet has not afforded a single working party further than those upon the road & upon the transport directly within the boundaries."[3] Standing in front of Parliament in 1778 to defend his failures on the campaign, Burgoyne cited the Canadian corvée as one of the primary reasons he had advanced slowly towards the rebels in Albany. In front of the House of Commons, he stated: "the corvées, which are detachments of provincials without arms, to repair roads, convey provisions, or any other temporarily employments for the King's service, could not be obtained in sufficient number, nor kept to their employments."[4]

Despite Burgoyne's claim that "the corvées" had not "kept their employments," hundreds of French Canadian corvée labourers *did* participate in the British Army during the 1777 Northern Campaign.[5] Wage lists indicate that habitants worked in the province repairing roads, transporting supplies by bateaux, and driving carts. The campaign was won and lost as much on the supply routes as it was in Saratoga. Burgoyne needed French Canadians to provide their labour for the expedition against the Anglo-American rebels. Conscripted into drafts, Canadians performing corvée did everything they could to assert their autonomy within the rigid discipline of the military. Collectively, they refused to work for the British Army when High Command violated their recently reinstated seigneurial customs. They deserted work camps, fled on horseback, stole bateaux, and, when the situation suited them, argued that the British had violated the very customs the Quebec Act had sought to restore.

Following the expulsion of the American rebels from the province in 1776, Carleton ratified legislation that forced habitants to perform corvée for the British military. In what was referred to as the Acts of Militia, Carleton inaugurated a transformed "King's corvée" and, more important, a new relationship between habitants, the state, and the military. Indeed, corvée during the 1777 campaign functioned more as a form of mandatory wage labour than as a civil obligation to the province. Burgoyne's massive expedition required an equally large number of labourers, and military officials targeted the contractual relationship between seigneur and habitant to fulfill those needs. During the four-month expedition, the British Army's surging demand for workers in Quebec caused widespread protests. Desertion and evasion forced the governor to ratify a new provincial code regulating the use of corvée.

The American Revolution presents a unique opportunity to study the consequences of war, law, and labour in colonial North America. During the course of the conflict, Governors Carleton and Haldimand attached corvée labourers directly to military regiments, from which they served under the chain of command of the British military. Instead of local militia captains, Carleton created a branch of the army to oversee the mobilization and execution of corvée. It was called the Commissaries for Transport by Corvées, and the governor appointed three military officers (one from each district) to ensure that parishes met their quotas and that work continued as scheduled. These commissaries allocated fixed wages to compensate habitants for their participation on the supply routes.

The successes and failures of British High Command's attempts to mobilize corvée for the army during the American Revolution adds considerably to our understanding of the colonial fiscal-military state. Indeed, Brewer asserts that "the highly centralized character of the English state, the proficiency of bureaucracy and the legitimacy accorded to parliamentary statute meant that it was extremely difficult in England to offer overt resistance to taxes," while in the Americas "metropolitan power was far removed."[6] He argues that, as a result, "state power declined in the periphery." In contrast to the Anglo-American colonies, the habitants witnessed the full deployment of the British fiscal-military state during the Revolutionary War. The dual pillars of the British state – war and taxation – became inextricably linked to corvée labour. On one hand, Burgoyne required an incessant number of Canadian labourers to transport his supply train; on the other hand, the very customs that he intended to use allowed habitants to protest and evade service in the military despite the overwhelming presence of professional soldiers in the province.

THE BRITISH COUNTER-OFFENSIVE, 1776

After thwarting the American rebels' attack on 31 December 1775, Carleton sheltered the remnants of the joint British and Canadian soldiers within the city's fortifications, where they awaited reinforcements scheduled to arrive in the spring. While the rebel commander's leader, Colonel Benedict Arnold, attempted to organize a siege, the remaining Americans suffered losses from winter weather, illness, and fatigue. Reinforcements arrived with Lieutenant General John Burgoyne in June 1776, and the British took to the offensive to expel the invaders.

A counter-offensive launched from Quebec City required workers to transport supplies, ammunition, provisions, and men to pursue the enemy. With several thousand professional soldiers under British High Command, Carleton harnessed corvée to facilitate the movement of the army. To accomplish this, he authorized two forms of corvée labour for the campaign. The first form of labour primarily involved repairing roads and operated under the traditional relationship between the habitants and their seigneur. Indeed, Carleton targeted the seigneurs' reinstated privileges to meet the demands of the British Army. Within the districts of Quebec, Montreal, and Trois-Rivières he appointed new, loyal militia captains to organize labour. In the immediate aftermath of the invasion, corvée primarily sustained the maintenance of roads within their parishes. Using the hierarchy of the communities and the customs of New France, Carleton appropriated the cultural form of labour to ensure the security of the province.

The governor also inaugurated an experimental iteration of *corvée militaire*, in which habitants served under the command of individual regiments in the British Army.[7] Under the French, habitants had served corvée during wartime on public works, fortifications, and auxiliary tasks for the military, such as building signal fires during the War of Austrian Succession. The captains of the militia oversaw the mobilization of this labour and managed the distribution of corvée among the community. In the latter years of the Seven Years' War, squads of corvée had also aided the *troupes de la marine* in their counterattack on Quebec City.

Harnessing these pre-existing relationships, Carleton raised corvée as a body of workers attached to regiments of the British Army. Habitants serving corvée took direct orders from British senior officers and operated strictly in a labouring capacity. Indeed, these groups of habitants became known as "the Corvée," a collection of workers drafted by the recently reinstated feudal obligation to the Crown whose only purpose was to act as a labour force for their attached regiment.[8] These detachments were composed of habitants from multiple parishes and under the command of the army. Rather than overseeing the deployment of corvée, the governor required captains of the militia to round up habitants to work for senior officers of the British Army.

In the spring of 1776, Parliament commissioned Lieutenant General John Burgoyne, Brigadier General Simon Fraser, and Major General William Phillips to command the British Army in the northern colonies. These three officers raised, organized, and managed corvée for the needs of their commands. In the district of Montreal, the corvée worked on infrastructure, provided supplies to the army, and helped transport soldiers. Additionally, road repair took place on the destroyed main highway connecting the St Lawrence at La Prairie to Fort St Johns.[9] Indeed, Phillips ordered the "assembling of the country people with their tools" to repair roads and to assist "in the present circumstances of the artillery."[10] In the Montreal seigneurie of Varennes, the corvée transported soldiers over the St Lawrence to avoid "over fatiguing the Troops."[11] During July, habitants worked to reconstruct "the King's works" and fortifications destroyed by the rebels.[12]

While their responsibility managing corvée diminished, the captains of the militia in each parish played an important role for the British Army's corvée detachments. In addition to drafting male habitants from their community, Carleton also appointed the captains of the militia as disciplinary intermediaries of the state. Indeed, in July 1776, a contingent of "the Corvée" attached to the "King's Works" in Quebec City deserted its duties and "returned home."[13] The governor required "the Officers of Militia of the parishes to which the Deserters belong[ed]" to appoint a "careful Canadian" to collect them and return them to the site "against the execution of which no excuse whatsoever [was] to be admitted."[14] The militia officers would then "send them to the Army under an escort taken from the Troops."[15]

The transportation demands of fully outfitted British regiments in Quebec also required captains of the militia to enforce *corvée de harnois*, or the requisition of carts for the army. During July 1776, this work primarily took the form of supplying bateaux for the king's troops who were pursuing the American rebels who had retreated to Crown Point in northern New York.[16] Carleton pushed military officials, such as Major Hector Cramahé, and parish militia captains to requisition bateaux from "volunteers," "workmen," and "the parishioners" of the communities surrounding Montreal.[17] In conjunction with the riverine vessels, on 25 September 1776, the governor required all habitants in the "Montreal suburbs and the Isle d'Perot" to send equipment to Saint Jean, and he ordered the captain of the militia in La Prairie to "furnish the carts necessary for the equipment."[18]

Carleton efficiently deployed corvée detachments with British regiments during the 1776 counter-offensive. Squadrons of habitants mended roads destroyed by the Americans, transported troops, and provided the carts necessary for the movement of supplies. With the American Army routed in the Champlain Valley, Carleton, British High Command, and Parliament planned their next move. Working with his subordinates, Burgoyne planned a northern campaign directed towards Albany to leave Quebec the following year. Witnessing the effectiveness of corvée labour attached to the military, he intended to draft at least one thousand habitants to follow his army during the offensive.[19]

The Quebec counter-offensive formed the first campaign of a series of attacks whose purpose was to knock out rebel activity in the northern colonies. While French Canadian habitants ferried supplies and provided *corvée de harnois* for the British in Quebec, simultaneously a second far larger army under the command of General William Howe attacked Long Island and nearby Brooklyn Heights. After a quick route, the rebel commander-in-chief of the Continental Army, George Washington, led a hasty retreat from Long

Island and, eventually, the New York seaport fleeing the British. By the end of 1776, the British had both expelled the Americans from the province of Quebec and secured the city of New York, Westchester, and northern New Jersey from patriot interference.[20] Corvée for the military had proved fundamental to British success in Canada, and, in the following year, Burgoyne would seek to harness habitant labour to capitalize on these opening successes.

PREPARATION FOR THE NORTHERN CAMPAIGN, 1777

In the winter of 1777, Parliament appointed Burgoyne as the senior officer for a military expedition to Albany. The campaign, Parliament hoped, would finally put an end to the rebellious activity of the Anglo-American colonies. As he began making preparation for the expedition, Burgoyne demonstrated interest in utilizing a corvée to build fortifications, repair infrastructure, and transport supplies. Indeed, in a letter written in March to Germain, he stated: "[a] great Call upon the Canadians will be for Workmen at the Fortifications of Sorell, St. John's, Chamblee, and the Isle aux Noix."[21] He continued: "[a] still greater call upon the Canadians will be for the transport of all the provisions, Artillery Stores & Baggage from the Repositories to the Water and afterwards the carrying Places."[22] Utilizing the recently ratified Quebec Act and seigneurial customs, Burgoyne targeted corvée as a resource that the British Army could exploit during the campaign.

The demands for labour in the army put pressure on Carleton to construct the legal mechanisms necessary to draft Canadians into service. In his briefing, Burgoyne estimated that the upcoming campaign would "require 2,000 men, besides a very large proportion of carts and horses."[23] To provide the troops required by the British Army, Carleton proposed a conscription of mandatory militia service for all males between the ages of sixteen and sixty.[24] On 27 March 1777, Carleton prepared a military ordinance that set the terms of service for Canadians in the British Army. Each parish militia captain would draft the necessary number of men into a company that served under the district commander.

Habitants not conscripted into the armed militia would fulfill their service through corvée. The governor wrote: "the remainder of the inhabitants may be employed on corvée and the service of transport."[25] Describing this labour as "second class," Carleton stated: "every owner of land en roture [*sic*] will be liable to corvée or to furnish wagons or boats on account of the tenure of his land."[26] He continued that raising the corvée must "require much care to obviate complaints and discontent and avoid taking the inhabitants from the necessary cultivation of the soil."[27] The governor specified that seigneurs and parish priests had exemptions and could not "be commanded upon any corvée."[28] Additionally, these workers were "to be paid the wages for each man for each journey," with British officers ensuring that they fairly compensated habitants.[29]

The social arrangements prepared in the March ordinance were put into effect the following month. Entitled the Acts of Militia, Carleton's legislation solidified the relationship between corvée and the British military. Written by the governor, article 11 exempted from military service: "the seigniors stiled here seigneurs primitifs the noblesse, so acknowledged under the ancient government of the country PROVIDED ALWAYS that nothing in this ordinance contained, be construed to exempt the seigniors, or noblesse, from rendering such personal services agreeable to the antient usage, and which they are bound by the tenure of their lands, whenever the governor, or in his absence the lieutenant governor, or commander in chief for the time being, shall judge to call upon them the same."[30] Carleton ordered the landholders to exercise their duties in accordance with the military activity of the province. The Acts of Militia produced a new form of corvée, one in which the duty of habitants now provided service directly to the fiscal-military state.

However, in May, as Burgoyne addressed his army, only several hundred Canadians had obeyed the order. The lieutenant general expressed his displeasure at the low turnout of the Canadian militia stating: "when the plan of my expedition was framed, the ideas of Government respecting armed Canadians went to six times the number of those Companies were they compleat and permanent." In particular, the Canadian militia experienced a high level of desertion. Burgoyne wrote Carleton exclaiming that "McKay's Company of Canadians lost twenty men by desertion, & Monin's ten the same night."[31] Furthermore, he disapproved of the penal system established by the Militia Acts, which sanctioned fines and confiscation of property as punishment for desertion. Burgoyne reiterated the failure of these reprimands, declaring: "the men being bachelors & without property in their parishes the penalties of furnishing doubly the King's Convoys does not affect them, nor in general are they capable of paying the fines."[32] The lack of enthusiasm towards militia duty most likely also stemmed from the intersection of the campaigning season and "the time of sowing corn."[33] Living in a primarily

Figure 5.2
Friedrich Von Germann, *Ein Canadischer Bauer* (1778).

Arriving in Canada with German soldiers hired by King George III to fight in the American Revolution, Friedrich Von Germann painted thirteen watercolours of soldiers and civilians who participated in the conflict. Here, Germann portrayed a French Canadian habitant dressed in traditional clothing of the region, a capot or blanket coat tied with blue ribbons and a sash to close the garment. The habitant is also wearing First Nations–style leggings with ties around the knee.

agricultural economy, most men within the parishes ordered to furnish the militia would have had limited time to farm between the thaw in April and the onset of winter in late October.

To compensate for the lack of militiamen present for service, Burgoyne suggested that a one-thousand-man corvée accompany his army.[34] Indeed, he stated: "to remedy in some measure this deficiency I have to propose to your Excellency a Corvée of a thousand men to attend the expedition for a limited time for the purpose of labour and transport."[35] The corvée, he believed, would save the soldiers: "from the harassing duties which at the outset of a Campaign your Excellency well knows are productive of disease and the ranks will be properly full for their service in arms."[36] Burgoyne exhibited "confidence that the Corvée of working men" would be "palatable to the Country if [Carlton] thought [it] proper to issue a proclamation limiting the time of their service."[37]

Carleton complied with Burgoyne's orders to raise the labourers but also admitted the limitations of forcing habitants to continue with the army to Albany. While Burgoyne urged Carleton to utilize seigneurial privileges as a mechanism to raise the workforce, the governor understood that corvée existed primarily as an agreement between the seigneur and tenant (*corvée seigneuriale*) or the Crown and the province in which the habitant lived (*corvée générale*). In a response to Burgoyne's orders, Carleton agreed to "order the Horses and Corvées [Burgoyne] require[d] if upon mature consideration [he thought] it [was] advisable," but he stipulated that Burgoyne "[could not] depend upon them eithre, and [was] Apprehensive it would rather tend to provoke the People still more."[38] Not only had Parliament only recently reestablished seigneurial custom, but, even under the French, the jurisdiction of the king's corvée only extended to labour within the province. Carleton admitted that he did not "know by what Law they [could] be compelled to go beyond the Limits of the Province, or we [could] punish their Disobedience."[39] Burgoyne's orders to raise a corvée, and Carleton's compliance in fulfilling the quotas, articulated the fundamentally new relationship between the fiscal-military state and French Canadian parishes. The Crown required seigneurs to exercise their right to raise a corvée strictly for military purposes.

As a formal apparatus of the armed forces, the British Army issued "the corvée" orders through a chain of command.[40] Rather than serve directly with the Canadian militiamen, Burgoyne attached the corvée to the supply train.[41] Carleton issued orders to Major General William Phillips, who then dispensed orders to the three district commissaries of transport by corvée. Each regional commissary also replenished the corvée when workers deserted and reinforced mandatory labour in communities along the route to Lake Champlain.[42] Carleton chose the commissaries based on their previous experience harnessing corvée on public works. For Montreal, the governor appointed Saint-George Dupré, a French Canadian major in the district militia who had experience with transportation during the American invasion. Similarly, in Trois-Rivières, Tonnancour took on the responsibility of mobilizing corvée as he had during the rebel invasion. Finally, Carleton made François Baby commissary in the district of Quebec. One of the wealthiest seigneurs, Baby and his family operated several large seigneuries in the province, all of which used corvée labour for public works and agricultural purposes. Baby had also led the investigation into habitant participation with American rebels and had personally overseen the reinforcement of seigneurial law.

The commissaries of transport by corvée shared several characteristics that made them ideal intermediaries for mobilizing labour in the parishes. Perhaps most important, each of the commissaries had French ancestry and aided the British during the tumultuous Murray administration.[43] Each of the commissaries derived from families with long-standing roots in the economically profitable fur trade and were well known for their collaboration with British merchants, politicians, and officials. Baby, for example, represented the interests of Canadian merchants and seigneurs during the Quebec Act debates and had advocated for the institution of French customs. Despite their wealth and social status, each of the men had also remained loyal to the British during the American invasion of Quebec and had distinguished himself as a French-descended royalist in that conflict. In Carleton's military schema, they played the important role of connecting the British military hierarchy with the habitant population.

Moreover, Carleton established a duration of service for the corvée. As in the Canadian militia, the labourers served a six-month tenure with the army until "the first of November[,] being the time they expected the Winter to set in."[44] All labourers consented to corvée duty "upon the faith of being dismiss'd." Additionally, the army provided them with the option to remain with it "of their own free will and Inclination."[45] The governor notified Burgoyne that the army should dismiss all "married men sent on Corvée" so that they could "return home for their harvest."[46] He hoped that "those sorts of services might be made as little burdensome to the people, as the exigencies of the King's business could allow," and he recognized that continued corvée depended on habitants maintaining their farms.[47]

As an incentive to perform corvée for the military, on 12 July, Carleton established a uniform system of "allowances to the inhabitants for transporting provisions, Artillery, and other stores for the use of His Majesty's forces." A labourer's compensation directly stemmed from the branch of the military to which the supplies belonged. As a result, the commissary general and his deputies paid the corvée "for the Transportation of provisions," while the "Commissaries and Conductors of Artillery" paid them for moving artillery and ammunition. The actual amount of specie an individual received depended on the supply route. Shorter distances paid "half a dollar a day and one Ration of Provision," while longer routes generously allotted between three and five shillings per day with "no provision." As an allowance, Carleton's orders provided direct monetary compensation for the labourer's raw output of energy and correlated with the expected distance of travel.[48]

Corvée labourers also received provisions as a reward for transporting supplies. Indeed, Carleton ordered Dupré to make sure the "Different Corvée [were] supplied" throughout the transportation of baggage.[49] Workmen who transported supplies from Chambly to the portage, or Chambly to Sainte-Thérèse, received "one Ration of Provisions" consisting of beef, pork, flour, bread, peas, and oatmeal.[50] Rum rations undoubtedly passed down to the corvée labourers along with Madeira wine, if they could afford it, as well as tobacco rations. Workers fulfilling their six-month contracts received blankets and shoes for their participation in the supply train.[51] Material goods issued to Canadians continued to solidify the contract between labourer and state. Just as the Board of Trade and Commissary of Provisions compensated professional soldiers for their service, so the value of corvée translated into a physical reward for their progress – food and materials to sustain the potential and kinetic output of an individual human's exertion.

The 1777 corvée that accompanied Burgoyne's army derived from each of the three districts of the province. Unlike the French, who mobilized "the environs" or côtes near where they needed the labour, Burgoyne's army required a steady and long-term body of workers to follow his route towards Albany.[52] To this end, Carleton attempted to use the Acts of Militia to draft one thousand corvée men to attach themselves to the military for a six-month period.[53] High levels of desertion, especially in the opening months of the campaign, make reconstructing the demographic of the labour force difficult.

All three districts certainly remained active during the expedition. Initial returns of corvée suggest that the captains of the militia drafted five hundred from the district of Quebec, three hundred from Montreal, and three hundred from Trois-Rivières.[54]

Despite the enticements and allowances, the commissaries struggled to meet their quotas. In addition to a reluctance to join the British Army, desertion plagued the supply lines as Burgoyne moved south.[55] Indeed, Hector Cramahé commented: "there is so little dependence to be placed upon these Corvées after they are raised."[56] During June and July, many habitants worked the portage at Fort Saint-Jean, the depot that supplied Burgoyne's army on the Richelieu. According to official statements made by the commanding officers, habitants reported to fulfill their obligation and then fled to their parishes. The governor ordered High Command to take "every step to apprehend the deserters."[57] Although the Militia Acts stipulated a five-pound penalty for desertion, Carleton was reluctant to impose fines on the habitants.[58] Instead, he decided to use the commissaries, militia captains, and seigneurs to catch the fleeing habitants or replace the deserters with other men from the corresponding parish.

CORVÉE LABOUR DURING THE NORTHERN CAMPAIGN, 1777

After raising the corvée in June, Carleton ordered the labourers to advance from Quebec with the British Army towards Chambly and Saint-Jean. Before departing, Burgoyne prepared an expansive, mobile depot of goods, including approximately one thousand horses and cattle appropriated from the habitants of the province.[59] The corvée travelled in the rear of the army with the supplies, provisions, and ammunitions, navigating carts and baggage down the central road from Montreal to Saint-Jean.[60]

Carleton standardized the corvée system of transportation by cart based on the expected route the habitant would travel. Five separate routes existed and correlated to specific sites of high-volume supply movement: Chambly to the little carrying place, Chambly to Sainte-Thérèse, Longueuil to Chambly, La Prairie to Saint-Jean, and Lachine to Montreal.[61] On these journeys, the corvée acted as drivers of supply carts. Carleton outfitted each cart, carrying "5 Barrels of Flour or 4 Barrels of Beef and Pork" with two horses.[62] Although carts varied in size, a general order issued by Burgoyne later in the campaign forbade placing more than ninety pounds of supplies onto a cart. The duration of travel depended on the specific route taken, with the longer journeys making "Two Trips a day" and the shorter distances "three trips a day."[63] Work transporting supplies, constructing roads, and repairing bridges not only took place during the day but also "continued all Night."[64] Despite not having "any covering Party" to directly oversee the labour, soldiers received orders that "the most vigorous exertion [was] to be used" to keep the corvée on duty.[65]

In an effort to acquire as many horse teams as possible, British High Command called upon habitants to fulfill their obligation to provide carriages and horse teams for supply movement.[66] As an expedition, the enormous amount of supplies, ammunition, and people needed to transport goods required an equally onerous number of horse teams. As early as June, Burgoyne and his quartermasters experienced a shortage of horses while still in the province of Quebec. They requested that Carleton reinforce the Acts of Militia to send "a number of Horses" for the "body of Canadians ordered for Corvée to attend upon the army."[67]

To achieve the acquisition of horse teams, the British fiscal-military state appropriated habitant resources and labour. Jacob Jordan, seigneur of Terrebonne and paymaster general, utilized the Acts of Militia to gather the *corvée de harnois* (horse teams) necessary for supply movement. Facing a shortage of carts, Jordan ordered "from the Country as many [carts and horses] as [would] make up for [Burgoyne's] deficiency."[68] These habitants, drafted from each of the three districts, worked the supply routes along the Richelieu. Pulled away from their families and farms during the critical period in the agricultural cycle, habitants received wages for working the supply routes. The demand for horses increased as the campaign continued, and Brigadier General Francis Maclean authorized an "increase to the allowances made to those people for the purposes of feeding themselves and Horses."[69] By October, disgruntled habitants began to petition the administration, citing the use of their carts and horse teams as a primary grievance of corvée duty. Indeed, they petitioned the administration, citing the army's "perpetual want of drivers owing to their being ordered for Corvées" as a major grievance against wartime service.[70]

On the way to Chambly, the army encountered difficulty moving the supply carts. Indeed, Captain James Murray Hadden of the Royal Artillery noted: "being incumbered with many carts &c. destined for our expedition our march was much retarded by the badness of the roads."[71] According to

Burgoyne, the commanding officers raised the corvée in part "to repair roads."[72] Prior to the expedition, Carleton implemented a centralized system of transportation that divided the roads of Quebec into two categories: high-roads and bye-roads. The king's high roads extended "thirty feet wide, with a ditch of three feet on each side [to] prevent the snow from being collected in heaps on the road."[73] Bye-roads existed "on the line of division between two concessions, of twenty feet wide on each side."[74] In wartime Quebec, Parliament appointed the seigneurs to be in charge of construction, upkeep, and repair of the roads. Seigneurs raised corvée "according to their ancient duty and custom" to build and repair the section of road that passed through their property.[75] Indeed, the maintenance of roads fell to "the joint labour of the people of the parish in which … such lands lie."[76] An appointed surveyor, a province-wide grand voyer, oversaw the completion of the project, while captains in the local militia served as *sous voyers* and dictated construction within the community.[77] If road construction was "too burthensome for the people of one parish" militia captains conscripted the joint labour "of two or more parishes."[78] The corvée also "kept in constant good repair" the fences that lined both styles of road.[79] Under royal order they erected "well-guarded" fences on "strong well fixed rails, of four feet high."[80] In the initial phases of the campaign, the corvée worked to efficiently supply the army and to repair roads.

Upon reaching Chambly and Saint-Jean, the corvée worked on the "Transport of provisions and stores."[81] As a result of the size of the supply train, in a letter to Major General Riedesel, Burgoyne ordered: "as there are not a sufficient number of vessels for all the regiments, the baggage must be transported by water." Burgoyne's army primarily used bateaux to transport supplies and soldiers over waterways and, in some cases, rapids.[82] Issued in 1776, an official document from the Admiralty Office listed the dimensions of a bateaux as thirty feet (nine metres) in length, six feet six inches (two metres fifteen centimetres) in width, with a depth of two feet and one and one-half inches (sixty-five centimetres). References to bateaux in other documents, however, suggest that the vessels varied in size and proportion, with the larger bateaux reaching forty-five feet (13.5 metres) in length. Prior to the expedition, the commissary of transport hired a private contractor in Quebec to construct the vessels for Burgoyne's army. Each bateaux fit twenty-five to thirty soldiers, or five barrels, within the vessel and transported a variety of supplies, ranging from barrels of provisions, ammunition crates, to light artillery.[83]

The rapids near Chambly stretch several kilometres and required manual labour to safely guide the bateaux to landing points. In the places with an especially "strong current," soldiers and corvée men hauled the bateaux onto shore using cords attached to the vessel.[84] To guarantee the portage of the vessel, teams of labourers or soldiers tied the cord through a hole in the front of the stern and pulled the bateaux to shore. Once on land, the corvée loaded the supplies onto carts and pulled them over the portage. A separate group drove the bateaux across the portage on carts pulled by six horses. The corvée portaging the vessels made four trips to the "carrying place" in a single day. To maximize the goods that could be transported over the portage, the army waited for "moderate" weather. After Burgoyne proceeded down Lake Champlain, nearly the entire corvée remained at Saint-Jean to unload baggage across the portage and to continue shipment to the primary army.[85]

In late June, Burgoyne's army surrounded Fort Ticonderoga and prepared for a siege. After brief skirmishing, the American forces abandoned the fort and retreated south down the Champlain corridor. On 6 July 1777, Burgoyne garrisoned a contingent of soldiers, consisting of the 62nd Regiment of Foot, the Brunswick Regiment Prinz Friderich, and commissioned officers of the provincial Royal Highland Emigrants. As Burgoyne pursued the American forces towards Albany, the garrison emerged as a critical supply depot and served as a hospital for wounded soldiers. Burgoyne appointed Louis Rousseau and Jonathon Clarke, assistant commissaries general, in charge of distributing provisions and resupplying the army.

On 10 July, Carleton secured approximately five hundred corvée labourers from "this district" of Quebec "to follow" Burgoyne's army "out of the Province."[86] By 24 July, four hundred corvée garrisoned Ticonderoga and Mount Independence with British and German regiments.[87] Carleton placed the corvée under the command of the commissioned officers of the Emigrants. First, Lieutenant David Price took "charge of all the Canadien Corvées" until early August, when "by the orders of his Excellence Sir Guy Carleton," Price transferred command of the corvée to Lieutenant Francis Dambourgess, also of the Royal Highland Emigrants.[88] Thomas Hatfield, one of the captains of bateaux, also utilized a portion of the corvée to aid in managing supply vessels.

At Fort Ticonderoga, the corvée primarily acted as stevedores "transporting commodities" by bateaux to the Lake George Landing and unloading excess baggage sent back to Ticonderoga for storage. Indeed, following a skirmish near Fort Anne, Burgoyne "strongly recommended" soldiers "to take as little baggage as possible" in the advance. The rest of the material, "heavy baggage &c. was mostly sent to stores appointed at Ticonderoga." The corvée also unloaded fresh provisions arriving from Saint-Jean. The general officers supplied Rousseau with accounts "of the number of rations they [chose] to be daily supplied with." Bateaux carrying fresh provisions generally fit four to five men along with the barrels of supplies and ammunition. In an effort to protect the supplies, soldiers used "oil clothes &c." in "covering the provisions ashore and afloat." To ship supplies over land from Ticonderoga to the army, the commissaries of transport employed around 180 carts pulled by "between 20 and 30" oxen.[89]

RESISTANCE TO CORVÉE LABOUR DURING THE NORTHERN CAMPAIGN, 1777–78

Many of the corvée workers who transported supplies, constructed roads, and drove horse teams within the province of Quebec and with Burgoyne in New York exhibited agency in alleviating the hard labour they owed to the military. They disobeyed work orders, refused to leave the province, deserted the army, and petitioned the legislature for losses collected during the campaign. Most habitant responses to corvée took on the characteristics of what James C. Scott refers to as "everyday forms of peasant resistance," or the "prosaic, but constant struggle between the peasantry and those who seek to extract labour, food, taxes, and interest from them."[90] In revolutionary-era Quebec, resistance to corvée took on both pragmatic and symbolic meanings. Habitants certainty deserted their obligations for practical reasons, such as needing to return to their dwellings for the harvest. Their evasion of corvée, however, also represented a statement to their colonial overlords. As Scott states, no matter how "partial or imperfect their understanding of the situation," peasant societies are "gifted with intentions and values and purposefulness that condition their acts."[91] Habitants resisted corvée by putting forth their own definitions of proper labour arrangements, which contradicted the objectives of the fiscal-military state.

For example, Burgoyne struggled to entice the corvée to travel any further than the jurisdictional boundaries of the province. The habitants understood their obligation to the seigneur and state as a contractual agreement, and they refused to travel further when they felt the military had violated that contract. In a letter to Germain he labelled them a "considerable disappointment" in that they refused to go "beyond the limits of the Province."[92] Indeed, as the army progressed, the habitants offered not "a single working party further than those upon the road & upon the transport directly within the boundaries."[93] Moreover, they ignored "pressing encouragements, injunctions, & orders."[94]

The corvée workmen also deserted the supply train to evade distressing labour. Major General Phillips wrote to Carleton on 17 June 1777 to pass on "reports from the Quarter Master General's Assistants that the Corvées necessary for the Transport of the Army from Chambly to the Portage and from the Portage [had mostly] run away in such a manner that the Transport of Provisions [was] near stopt."[95] To remedy the desertion of labourers, on 26 June 1777 a group of corvée consisting of 248 "men from the district of Quebec" embarked for Saint-Jean.[96] Around 247 followed the next day, accompanied by forty-four whom Carleton explained had "been sent to replace deserters."[97] As further incentive to work, Carleton also offered payment to "one part" of the corvée.[98]

The British Army, with Burgoyne in New York, experienced a high level of corvée desertion. Moreover, corvée desertion correlated with periods of high distress and combat. On 18 September, Colonel John Brown and his American detachment of five hundred soldiers raided the landing place at Lake George. Along with successfully appropriating supply depots by the lake and repatriating their own prisoners, Brown also imprisoned a handful of the Canadians acting as stevedores. With no one left in charge of them, on that same day "a great many of them deserted" Fort Ticonderoga and Mount Independence "a dozen at a time."[99] Indeed, several labourers mounted horses "found in the woods" or "found Battauex" between Ticonderoga and Crown Point to make their escape.[100] At Saratoga, Burgoyne also experienced high levels of corvée desertion.[101] Following the Second Battle on 7 October, Burgoyne initiated a large-scale retreat to Schuylerville. On the evening of 12 October 1777, all the "Canadian drivers of wagons, carts, and other services found means to escape [the army]."[102] During periods of martial engagement, the corvée deserted their posts to avoid being captured and having to perform labour for the army.

Mistreatment and overuse of corvée prompted habitants to desert the army. By the end of the campaign, disgruntled habitants began to petition and protest the use of corvée in the British Army. As early as September, the seigneur of Longueuil wrote to the governor that he had "just been informed of the extreme abuse of corvée."[103] The grievances trickling back to High

Command included the conscription of people whom the army promised would "not be ordered on corvée" and the lack of compensation paid to those "Corvée ordered for the service of the King."[104] Elsewhere in the district of Montreal, in Saint Ours, the militia captain took "double [the workers] and more from the other company," which led to vexation among the countrypeople.[105]

Corvée labourers in New York fared little better. The demand for workers on the supply routes around Lake Champlain and Lake George led to exploitation at the hands of overdriven army officers. Reports of corvée abuse from those habitants who "had crossed the Lake had disgusted them so much" that High Command feared retaliation if the squads of workers did not return home by the end of their contracts.[106] In an attempt to reconcile the discontent, Cramahé ordered that the habitants in New York be exempted "entirely from Corvées" and that payment for those workers on the lakes be increased upon "their arrival at Quebec."[107]

In addition to discontent on the supply routes, habitants exposed to front-line fighting rightfully feared that the American rebels would punish them for their service in the British Army. Following Brown's raid on Ticonderoga, Americans took at least two Acadian "drivers of carts" and fourteen Canadians prisoner following Burgoyne's surrender.[108] Under the terms of Burgoyne's surrender, the Americans sent all corvée labourers in New York back to their province on the condition that they would not pick up arms against their cause. Strangely, however, the Americans transported the two Acadians to a Rhode Island prisoner of war camp, where they served as translators for the Continental Army.[109] These two men eventually escaped the prison and fled back to Fort Saint-Jean, where they received compensation for their hardships.

On 16 October 1777, Burgoyne surrendered his regiments and signed the Articles of Convention at Saratoga. Article 9 of the convention released "All Canadians and persons belonging to the Canadian establishment," including the "sailors, batteaumen, artificers, drivers, independent companies, and followers of the army," from imprisonment and permitted them to return to Canada.[110] In early November, the British retreated from Fort Ticonderoga to the province of Quebec.[111] As winter set in, all corvée retreated from New York with the army.

The experience of harnessing the corvée for the Northern Campaign fundamentally altered the relationships between habitants and the fiscal-military state. Burgoyne's overuse of corvée amplified Canadians' mistrust of colonial policies. To protest their grievances, they failed to arrive on work detail, refused to travel outside the jurisdictional boundary of the province, and deserted the army. The resilience of the habitants ultimately shaped Britain's imperial experiments in Quebec and demonstrated the autonomy of the Crown's subjects when it came to articulating their own definitions of proper labour arrangements.

Corvée during the Northern Campaign illuminates the fraught social arrangements put into place by the British fiscal-military state in post-Conquest Quebec. British High Command, including Burgoyne and Carleton, had harnessed every possible mechanism of state authority to coerce habitants into the labour force. Building on the seigneurial customs restored by the Quebec Act, Carleton mobilized French Canadians for drafts of labourers. Increasingly, corvée became tied to service in the military and financial compensation through predetermined wages. Habitants protested nearly every step of this process, evading corvée conscription or deserting the army in an attempt to discontinue their labour. In the coming years, court cases over corvée desertion, and the British Army's failure to enforce military corvée, ultimately resulted in a postwar return to civilian obligations that had existed under the French regime.

CHAPTER 6

The Upper Country and Mounting Challenges to Corvée, 1778–83

INTRODUCTION

On 17 September 1778, two Acadians and six Canadian militiamen arrived at Fort Saint-Jean, all of them claiming that the Americans had taken them prisoner during Burgoyne's Northern Campaign.[1] While the rebels had captured the militiamen during a skirmish at Bennington, the two Acadians – David Belliveau and Basil Leblanc – had worked as "bateaux men" and performed corvée at the Lake George landing place.[2] In September 1777, Colonel John Brown had orchestrated a surprise attack on the British at the lightly garrisoned Fort Ticonderoga and, in the process, had seized the squads of corvée men at the critical portage between Lake Champlain and Lake George.[3]

The story of the Acadians' escape illustrates the extraordinary, inter-imperial struggles in which corvée labourers found themselves embroiled. While the ancestry of Basile Leblanc is unknown, it is likely that he immigrated to Quebec in 1755 along with David Belliveau as part of the Acadian Expulsion, which witnessed tens of thousands of French-speaking Acadian Roman Catholics exiled from Nova Scotia during the Seven Years' War.[4] Many sought refuge in New Orleans, the Caribbean, and South Carolina, in addition to a sizeable number of exiles integrating themselves into the fabric of the ruins of Canada. These two men settled in the seigneurie of Bécancour, most likely purchasing a title deed and assimilating themselves into the newly created province of Quebec.[5]

Although evidence does not specify when they joined the British Army as bateaux men, Carleton most likely conscripted them as part of a June 1777 order that gathered corvée "men from the district of Quebec" to "replace deserters."[6] From Fort Saint-Jean, they then travelled south with the five hundred corvée labourers sent to Fort Ticonderoga during Burgoyne's Northern Campaign and ended up in the squads working the supply routes at the carrying place.[7] After Colonel John Brown raided Fort Ticonderoga and consequently captured the men working the portage, the rebels took them prisoner and "they were sent to Portsmouth, Boston, Albany, and Hartford."[8] They recalled later that "they were employed by the Rebels, at all the above places, as Interpreters."[9] At some point, according to their own account, Belliveau and Leblanc also started to act as informal spies, collecting information on the rebel army and any news related to troop movement should they find a way to return to Quebec.

On route to Rutland, the two imprisoned Acadians made their escape. Stealing a canoe that they found on Otter Creek in Vermont, they fled to Crown Point "and went into a House where there were two men belonging to the Flag of Truce, who said … they had no orders to take them prisoners" and advised them "to depart instantly lest a Scout should arrive."[10] From Crown Point, they travelled north into the Richelieu and ended their year-long journey at Saint-Jean. They supplied the British garrison with all of the intelligence they had collected on the Continental Army and provided invaluable information on troop movement in New England.

From the Acadian Expulsion to Burgoyne's Northern Campaign, to espionage, Belliveau and Leblanc found themselves navigating an increasingly complex network of trans-imperial borderlands formed during the eighteenth century. They were not alone – thousands of corvée workers under both the French and British regimes participated in colonial wars and supplied the resources upon which these empires depended. Corvée workers were, in short, instrumental to the construction of empire during the eighteenth century. In peacetime, both regimes depended on Canadian corvée to collect resources for their empires and to transform the northern colony into a profitable venture. These resources connected corvée to a sprawling, entangled network of labour in the early modern Atlantic World. During war, corvée workers constructed the symbols of empire. They raised forts, redoubts, picket lines, and served as stevedores at major portage points as far south as Lake George and as far west Lake Ontario. In conjunction with other forms of coerced labour, they supplied the French and British Empires with the workers needed to make colonies function on a daily basis.

A particularly illustrative example of how the British used corvée to achieve imperial aims involved fortifying the Pays d'en Haut after Burgoyne's defeat at Saratoga. With the military effort shifting south towards the Carolinas, the new governor, Frederick Haldimand, sought to shore up defences in the garrisoned province of Quebec. This included a new series of defensive works within the St Lawrence Valley as well as a gaze westward towards the Great Lakes. Corvée, the administration reasoned, could provide the labour for the first leg of this journey. It established a far-flung network of water transport and swept up French Canadian habitants in that effort.

Indeed, the end of the Northern Campaign did not signal the end of military corvée in Canada. To the contrary, the sheer number of habitants mobilized during the expedition made corvée more visible to colonial officials, ministers in Parliament, and British High Command. Haldimand stepped into a position of leadership amidst unrest in the countryside over the abuses of corvée. Petitions concerning the "perpetual want of drivers" had gained support not only from habitants but also from prominent seigneurs in the district of Montreal.[11] Mass desertions and corvée evasion displayed habitants' discontent with the labour system.

Rebel movement in the Great Lakes, however, threatened the posterity of British supremacy in the region. As a result, Haldimand's policies towards corvée continued to match the demands of the fiscal-military state in Quebec. The presence of two full regiments garrisoning the province meant that the mandates for corvée persisted until the end of the war. As filtered down the chain of command from Germain, Haldimand's new objectives included fortifying the St Lawrence Valley and, more important, ferrying supplies to the western posts on Lake Ontario and Lake Erie.[12] In an effort to make mandatory working drafts for the military more appealing, he ensured that habitants would not have to serve on rotations outside of the province.[13] Like Carleton, however, the new governor expected habitants to leave their homes, report for work duty, and fulfill their obligations to the state.

THE UPPER POSTS AND THE REVOLUTION IN THE BORDERLANDS

To mitigate the military's "extreme abuse of corvée," which had plagued the rural parishes during Burgoyne's campaign, Haldimand initially only authorized work orders that had habitants labouring in their district.[14] His strategy quickly pivoted, however, towards the protection of Quebec's borders.

In corresponding with Haldimand, Germain reinforced the importance of shoring up resistance to rebel activity in the borderlands, stating: "the security and Defence of the province must, however, be the primary object."[15] Securing the western edges of empire in North America directly affected this initiative. The secretary of the Southern Department added that Haldimand "should be particularly attentive to what passe[d] in the Rebellious Provinces on [his] Frontier" and that he should "discover any designs that may be entertained of making an attack upon Canada."[16] As a result, Haldimand planned on mobilizing Canadian habitants to ferry supplies to the professional soldiers garrisoning the region's defensive works.

In the same letter to the governor, Germain proposed utilizing corvée labour for these purposes. Reassuring Haldimand that the five thousand British soldiers in Canada would "be full sufficient to defend the province in its present state against any attack from the Rebellious Provinces," Germain called for "a Corps of Canadians, not exceeding 1,000 men" to operate supply lines for the military. He provided Haldimand with a clear directive to mobilize habitants, stating that "the private men of such Corps [should] be taken by Draughts from the Militia, or by way of Corvée, to serve a limited time." These rotations would "be relieved by Draughts in succession" during the campaigning season.[17]

In order to facilitate the defence of the province, Haldimand compiled an extensive survey of rebel activities in the borderlands. The "Upper Posts" consisted not only of several critical fortifications on Lake Ontario, such as Fort Oswego and Fort Niagara, but also of the western most outposts of Detroit. These fortifications, seized by the British during the Seven Years' War, figured into a larger imperial scheme that solidified the Crown's influence in the western borderlands of eighteenth-century North America. In an effort to control trade in the Great Lakes, the British sought Indigenous alliances, especially with the Odawa Nation.[18] In the absence of highways and bridges in this region, the British – as the French before them – utilized the waterways, carrying places, and portages on the Upper St Lawrence. A British military presence in the Great Lakes reaffirmed long-standing alliances with Indigenous communities that were essential to the maintenance of the fur trade in the interior of North America.[19] These waterways also provided passage to the Ohio and Mississippi River valleys and offered the British an opportunity to reinforce their presence in the interior of North America.[20]

Forts, such as Niagara and Detroit, also defended future British imperial interests – the prospective surveyors' maps of an expanded Canada. Alan Taylor argues that Parliament and the Crown saw this territory as a potential "settler society" that "wove a web of property lines to demarcate thousands of farms privately owned."[21] Most important, this westward territory would generate "revenue and power by surveying those lines and selling sovereign title to the enclosed parcels."[22] To this end, the British military effort in the Upper Country contended not only with the active American rebellion but also with the imperial geopolitics of the waterways of the Great Lakes.

As the main body of the British professional army swung into the southern colonies, the governor grew increasingly concerned about rebel raids on these lightly defended borderland posts. In his report on the defences of the province, he wrote: "the upper posts may be easily cut off by [the] Oswego River."[23] He continued: "roads have already been marked by the Rebels to the inhabited parts of the Province [and they] have explored every part of the Country, and know it well."[24] The military situation of the rebellion was compounded by economic fears that raiding parties could seize outposts of the fur trade and that, should this happen, "America most probably [would] be lost to Great Britain for ever."[25]

Haldimand's priority to fortify Britain's imperial borders came at a point in the war at which the morale of French Canadians appeared – at least by the accounts of the governor – to be wavering. Coming out of the 1777 campaign, he wrote: "by all accounts, we still have amongst us many favorers of Rebellion, who are indefatigable in their endeavour to poison the Minds of the Canadians, and to swerve them from their duty and allegiance." He continued: "the Seeds of Jealousy and Dissension between the Colonies have long been sown, they are ripe for breaking out."[26]

In an attempt to compel Canadian loyalty and to dissuade revolt, Haldimand advocated that Parliament reiterate the "levying and drafting out of the Militia of the Province." This not only rendered "them useful to the Interests of Great Britain" but also reinforced the "Laws and Customs of Canada" laid forth in the Quebec Act. In particular, he cited the act's property rights clause that reestablished "the Noblesse of the Province to the Influence they once possessed over." Strengthening seigneurial hierarchies, he reasoned, would "restore obedience and subordination [among the] People, and the Savages."[27]

Initial plans from Britain sought to harness corvée under the same legal pretexts of the previous year. As early as March, William Knox, under-secretary of state, wrote to Haldimand that Quebec required new fortifications to defend against an American invasion. Knox proposed a citadel in Quebec City to protect the bluffs on the St Lawrence. He asserted that any fortifications in cities, however, would require "a considerable expense." Knox further suggested that Haldimand make use of corvée in that district for: "the People, holding their lands upon the Tenure of services to the Crown, are subject to be called upon for [procuring and transporting materials] as well as other purposes of Government." Indeed, a corvée for the Citadel would have had "great diminution of the publick expense."[28]

For British High Command, the appropriation of habitant labour through the obligation of corvée remained a priority not only for the defence of the province but also for the larger imperial schemes of the Crown. Colonial administrators and military officers continued conscripting the agrarian labour force to construct the symbols of empire in Quebec – roads, trade routes, and fortifications. As these efforts dragged on, however, they started to create real strains on Canadian communities, and habitants evaded corvée whenever possible. The burdens of this work sparked widespread discontent, especially in the districts of Montreal and Trois-Rivières. Pulled from their plough for the war effort, habitants began to articulate a formalized resistance to corvée mobilization.

MOUNTING CHALLENGES AND DISCONTENT WITH LABOUR

From 1778 to 1780, squads of habitants reluctantly provided corvée in each of the three districts of the province. The organization and management of corvée remained the same as in the previous campaign. Haldimand renewed the commissions of the Commissaries of Transport by Corvée for each district and put them in charge of ensuring that the parishes met labour quotas.[29] François Baby resumed command of corvée in the district of Quebec.[30] St George Dupré continued his control of Montreal habitants and Tonnancour returned to oversee work in the district of Trois-Rivières.[31] The three district commissaries received orders from the governor and British High Command to mobilize agrarian labour. After that, orders continued to filter through the parish captains of the militia who drew up rotations for work duty.[32] Unlike the haphazard system of compensation on the Northern Campaign, all habitants providing corvée for the military received wages in return for their work.[33] Indeed, during the remainder of the Revolution, corvée ceased to function as a "custom" and acted more as a mandatory form of wage labour. The military drafted habitants into squads, deployed them where they deemed fit, and paid them a fixed wage for their labour.[34]

Military personnel typically replaced traditional intermediaries of corvée mobilization. The Commissaries of Transport in each district served as the point of contact for all corvée-related inquiries. On the ground, habitants received orders from a range of senior or high-ranking officers in the professional army. Captains Edward Foy and Robert Matthews served as the governor's military secretaries and corresponded with officers overseeing the building projects in Sorel and Montreal.[35] Lieutenant Colonel Thomas Carleton, younger brother of the former governor, managed the implementation of corvée on the Upper Posts from the Lachine supply depot.[36]

Perhaps most important, military personnel also assumed duties once carried out by parish community members. For the most part, the British Royal Engineers, helmed by William Twiss, largely replaced the Office of the Grand Voyer for building infrastructure in the seigneuries occupied by the army.[37] Haldimand also continued the Carleton-era policy of elevating influential or politically connected seigneurs to "district" militia captains. These three captains managed militia conscription and corvée mobilization in Montreal, Trois-Rivières, and Quebec. At the parish and seigneurial levels, militia captains witnessed their influence diminish, as the district commanders assumed the duties of raising corvée. Little to no mention of parish assemblies suggests that Haldimand replaced their role in mitigating corvée exploitation by a rigid chain of command flowing from senior officers.

The expressions of power and authority wielded by these individuals also continued to deviate from any sense of traditional corvée custom. Orders for labourers often reflected arbitrary objectives that failed to benefit the communities from which the workers derived. Officers wrote to Haldimand justifying corvée mobilization for local tasks almost exclusively in terms of the strategic plans of the military. Construction on fortifications served to quarter the British and German regiments garrisoning Sorel, not the defensive requirements of the community.[38] Habitants ferrying supplies to the Upper Posts provided soldiers in distant Michilimackinac or Oswegatchie with provisions, while Canadians received small allowances.[39] Carriages and horse teams requisitioned for *corvée de harnois* transported raw materials to Chambly when soldiers required it.[40] In sum, corvée in the latter years of the

American Revolution continued to devolve from a practice rooted in French custom based upon obligation to one's land tenure and now owed to a formal detachment of the British military compensated in wages.

The arbitrary authority the British wielded over corvée was not just put into practice but also articulated in writing by the highest-ranking men in the empire. Germain, for example, suggested that Haldimand simply conscript "a Corps of Canadians … to be taken by Draughts from militia, or by way of Corvée to serve a limited time." He expanded on this, asserting that, by way of militia or corvée, the men would "serve a limited time" and eventually "be relieved by other Draughts in Succession." In this iteration, militia service or corvée would suffice to defend either the "Frontier" or "the Coast of the Atlantick." He believed that either mechanism resided well within the purview of the fiscal-military state, regardless of recently reinstated seigneurial customs.[41]

Corvée primarily took place on two interconnected supply routes that ran through the province of Quebec and that mirrored the activity of the army. The first supply route centred around the confluence of the Richelieu and St Lawrence Rivers at the seigneurie of Sorel. As a large village at this critical junction, Sorel had been occupied by the British immediately after the 1775 American invasion. During earlier campaigns of the Revolution, habitants from the seigneurie primarily provided carts and bateaux for the movement of supplies and troops.[42] By 1778, as Haldimand reinforced both the Richelieu and the district of Montreal, the village transformed into a garrison for parts of the British 34th Regiment of Foot and a loyalist regiment called the Royal Yorkers.[43] To house the soldiers, Haldimand authorized a corvée in the surrounding côtes to aid in the gathering of wood and the construction of lodgings.[44]

The preliminary plan required habitants from nearby communities "to build hangars and other buildings for the use of the King's Service at Sorrel."[45] Edward Foy commanded the local captains of the militia to draft ten men from their parishes and transport them to Sorel to aid in the construction. Nine of the parishes complied, including Point du Lac, Yamachiche, Rivière du Loup, Maskinogé, Berthier, Lanoraie, Lavaltrie, La Baie-du-Febvre, and Saint-François. In total, Foy calculated ninety men on corvée for the collection of timber at Sorel.[46] An additional contingent of habitants would provide "a certain number of carriages to pull a quantity of pieces of timber intended to build hangars and other buildings for the use of the Troops."[47]

A general order to neighbouring parishes stipulated that habitants provide "two horses" at a "reasonable price for their work."[48]

Construction on the Sorel buildings began in September 1778. By the end of the month, the army had broken ground on barracks, lodgings, and storehouses, with habitants primarily collecting wood for the buildings.[49] The officers at the sight reported to Haldimand that "forty Horses, twenty carriages [were] employed for [the] Service of Timber," with the "different branches of Service" working together on "Saw Pitts and Store Houses."[50] From their account, the habitants had complied with their obligations and requested that Haldimand "regularly" continue "the number of Canadians" reporting for corvée at Sorel.[51]

The scope of the Sorel projects increased significantly during October and November. British High Command designated Sorel as a critical site for the defence of the province and thus enlarged the initial plans for construction. By the end of November, the reporting officers relayed to the governor that two soldiers' barracks neared completion, along with two officers' barracks, kitchens, storehouses, a market house, and "a log house to lodge the Canadians on Corvées."[52] Additionally, High Command ordered the construction of redoubts "close to the gorges" and a series of pickets to bolster the earthworks.[53] The commanding officers proposed a completion date of New Year's Day, which meant that the Canadians serving their obligation would need to stay at least partially through the winter months.[54] Despite the unusual circumstances of lodging the corvée during the winter months, habitants participated in the construction projects until completion, with Lieutenant Ensign William Twiss commenting that he was "apprehensive that many of the Canadians would have deserted, from the severity of the Weather."[55]

Throughout the remainder of the war, Canadians on corvée continued to operate out of Sorel. From 1779 through 1781, the newly constructed military posts acted as British operations in the Lower Richelieu. Haldimand instituted a standardized system of corvée conscription in the district to ensure that the parishes surrounding Sorel continued to supply a steady rotation of men for the transportation of bateaux. He specifically directed: "the government of Three Rivers will furnish what men may be necessary for the Corvées on the Sorel."[56] Work orders for these projects derived from Commissary of Transport Tonnancour and then passed down to "the captains and other officers of the militia for Corvée."[57] In busy periods of supply movement the surging demand for labour led to disarray during the mobilization process. Habitants voiced "great inconveniencies" signing up for work duty under their local militia officers and ignored the commissaries charged with conscription.[58] As a result, Haldimand ordered: "it is expedient for the service that such orders [of corvée] be sent in the name of the Quarter Master," who would keep track of habitants reporting for duty.[59]

Utilizing this streamlined system, the British Army enforced corvée with the commissary of transport drafting habitants to aid in the transportation of bateaux to and from Montreal and Quebec City. Reportedly, many of the "Corvée men" drawn from nearby parishes begrudgingly participated, with one officer commenting: "[they] come in slower than they ought to."[60] To ensure that habitants willingly obeyed, the commissaries of transport stopped corvée during the winter when Lake Saint Pierre froze and paid close attention to an "equitable distribution [of labour]" that ultimately "could be made consistently with the good of the King's service."[61]

British officers elsewhere in the province often complained that habitants disobeyed work orders and demonstrated a general disinterest in performing their obligations. In October 1778, while mobilizing corvée for the supply routes on the Upper Posts, Colonel Thomas Carleton reported that habitants in the environs of Montreal "are very refractory, and pay no regard to the Captains of the Militia." He encouraged using the Brunswick troops to enforce labour orders at those parishes as "the most effectual means of bringing them to reason."[62] He echoed this sentiment in a letter to the governor sent later in the month, stating that the army was short bateaux "to be sent to the Lakes, owing to disobedience and desertion of the inhabitants." He continued: "the Canadians pay little regard to orders that are not enforced."[63] The challenges of both mobilizing and enforcing corvée on the Upper Post supply routes would continue through the remainder of the war.[64]

Corvée at Sorel and on the supply routes of the Upper Posts was compounded by seigneurial obligations and day-to-day maintenance required of habitants. During the latter years of the American Revolution, these work orders often overlapped with the British military effort in Quebec. The custom of *corvée de harnois* (requisitioning horse teams and carriages) continued in the parishes and directly supported local tasks needed by the army. For example, in 1778 William Twiss requested that his officers be: "furnished with an order, from the Col. of Militia, to all Captains of the Militia, and Inhabitants, that they shall when the Service requires it, furnish … their horses and Slays to draw out the Timber." Like Burgoyne's supply lines in the Richelieu, these rotations of horse teams compensated habitants for their participation. Men providing *corvée de harnois* received "four livres per day for one man, and one horse." The army would also supply them with "provisions, but no rum, to feed his horse, or horses."[65] Near the end of the war, in 1782, militia captains distributed a requisition for carts and carriages in the environs of Chambly to aid in the transportation of provisions.[66]

While the general upkeep of infrastructure most likely declined due to the volume of corvée required on the Upper Posts, the maintenance of parish roads and bridges still fell on habitants.[67] During the Northern Campaign, Carleton and his council had adopted a comprehensive ordinance on road building that reinforced the corvée customs that had existed since the Conquest.[68] Road repair in the previous years had primarily revolved around facilitating the transport of Burgoyne's army, and post–Northern Campaign road building returned to mundane drudgery. In1778, for example, Jean Baptiste Magnan, the grand voyer, ordered habitants of Saint Etienne to build a highway between two ditches on the southwest side of the seigneurie.[69] He authorized similar work orders in the following years, including road repair in Lauzon and the construction of a thirty-foot (nine-metre) highway – with two ditches – in the environs of Quebec City.[70]

CORVÉE ON THE UPPER POSTS AND LIFE AS A WORKER, 1778–80

Notwithstanding the growing complaints from military personnel, dozens of habitants did show up for corvée, albeit in smaller numbers than High Command had expected. The largest amount of corvée labour allocated to the military post–Northern Campaign supplemented the transportation of supplies to the Upper Posts.[71] Following Burgoyne's defeat, British High Command fortified the western region of the province for defensive purposes to buffer against a potential invasion from American rebels. Meanwhile, the bulk of the British Army in North America invaded the colonial South, and military policy in the north pivoted towards protecting assets in the Great Lakes. For the British, this included a number of key fortifications that rested on "carrying places" or trade routes on the Lakes.[72] Haldimand collectively referred to these forts, such as Detroit, Michilimackinac, and Niagara, as the Upper Posts, and he garrisoned soldiers there to maintain diplomatic Indigenous relationships related to the fur trade.

The fiscal-military state's demands for labour reflected this shift westward. Colonial officials planned to use corvée to ferry bateaux to the Upper Posts.

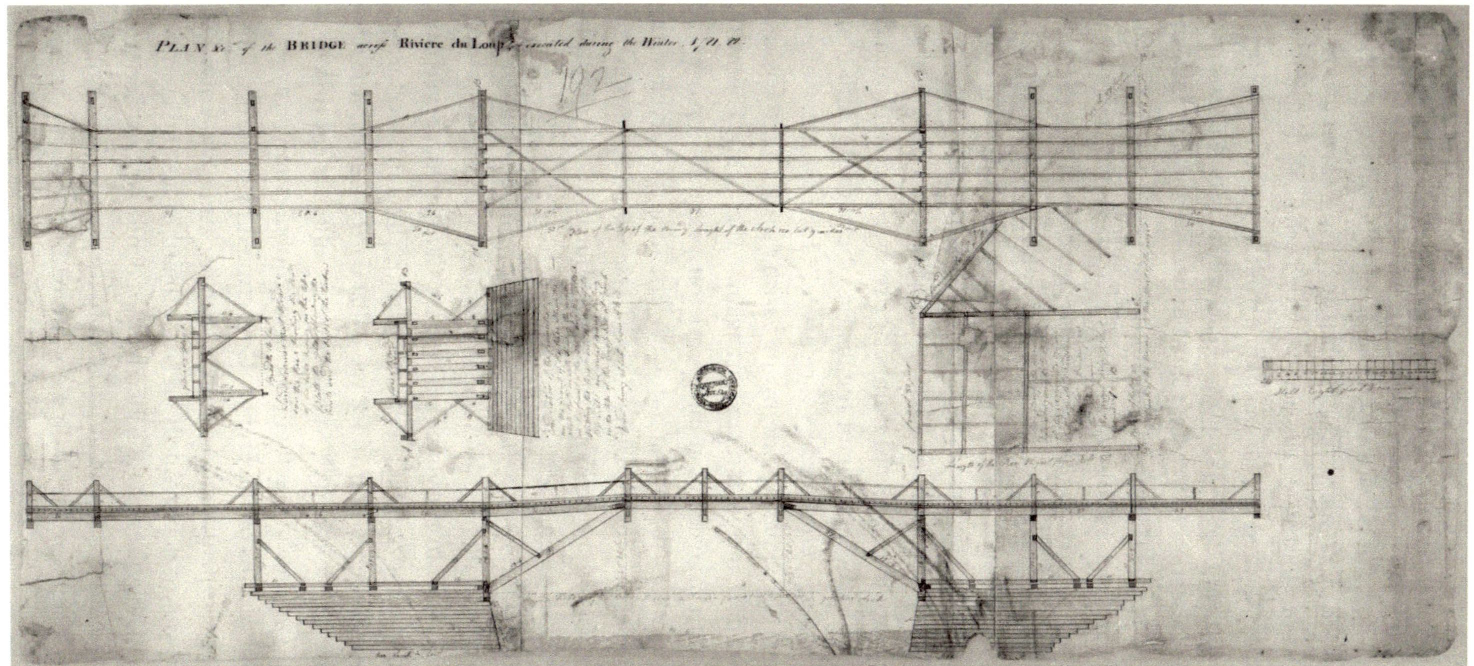

Figure 6.1

Plan &c of the bridge across the Rivière du Loup, executed during the winter of 1781,82 (1781–82).

Despite the overwhelming demand for workers on the Upper Country supply routes, the maintenance of roads and bridges still fell on habitants. Pictured here is a blueprint for a bridge in Rivière-du-Loup, a small seigneurie northeast of Quebec.

As was done with the corvée squads working at Sorel, Haldimand enforced a strict hierarchy to conscript Canadians into service.[73] The governor's orders for work were executed by St George Dupré, the commissary of transport by corvée in the district of Montreal.[74] He then delivered orders to the parishes, where militia captains drafted quotas of eligible militiamen to serve corvée at two locations supplying the Upper Posts – Lachine and the Cedars.

The evasion and desertion of French Canadian workers in summer and autumn 1778 met with a swift repression from colonial authorities. Colonel Thomas Carleton informed Haldimand: "[the] difficulties we have met in our transport to the Upper Posts have arose from the disobedience of some of these Parishes," and he suggested using British soldiers to coerce the reluctant communities into submission.[75] Haldimand agreed and ordered soldiers to garrison the "refractory parishes" and supervise the mobilization of corvée for the trade routes.[76] St George distinguished between the "good and bad subjects" to ensure that a record number of refusers received punishment.[77] Despite military occupation of the district, the parish of Vaudreuil continued to collectively refuse orders for corvée.[78] In response, Colonel Carleton ordered the Grenadiers to occupy the parish throughout the winter to organize the transport and get it set to start again in the spring. Following the thaw in early 1779, the governor granted Carleton a commission over the transportation of supplies, providing him with "the means of accelerating the Transport of Provisions for the Upper Posts."[79] He would attempt to ensure that habitants obeyed the demands of their authorities and provide labour for the movement of supplies.

Despite the difficulties related to habitant desertion and disobedience, in 1779 the British Army did manage to establish successful corvée rotations to the Upper Posts. As it did in Burgoyne's Northern Campaign, corvée continued to function as a form of coerced wage labour. Habitants performed a set number of tasks for a predetermined wage that correlated with the duration and difficulty of the labour.[80] While military officials continued to frame corvée as a "custom," the actual routine of mobilization strayed far from the feudal obligations of the French. Conscripted by the army, habitants had little choice, other than desertion, in participating. Moreover, the army once again began to deploy them far from their homes and communities. Continuing the hierarchy established by Burgoyne and Guy Carleton, officers marched habitants out of their parishes to the supply depots on the St Lawrence, where they worked loading and unloading bateaux destined for Lake Ontario.

Returns of wage and cargo lists allow a partial reconstruction of life on these supply routes to the Upper Posts. Corvée began, as aforementioned, with orders from the commissary of transport instructing specific parishes to report to one of the supply depots on the St Lawrence River. The captain of the militia continued to hold responsibility for ensuring that the parish met the army's quotas for workers.[81] The habitants then travelled to one of two different depots that supplied the Upper Posts. The first, Lachine, was located just south of Montreal and acted as a launch point for the route.[82] Additionally, the Lachine Rapids on the St Lawrence hindered the transportation of bateaux and required careful supervision to ensure safe passage. This first contingent of habitants, working with professional soldiers, ferried the bateaux to a second supply depot at "the Cedars."[83] From there a contingent of corvée temporarily halted the bateaux until specially designated habitants piloted them to Carleton Island at the mouth of Lake Ontario.[84] After safely arriving at the island, the pilots unloaded the supplies destined for Fort Niagara and returned to the Cedars.[85]

Most habitants worked loading and unloading bateaux at the two depots. Alongside soldiers, they filled bateaux of various sizes with barrels of provisions, supplies, and ammunition. These items ranged from military equipment to the more mundane utilitarian goods for everyday use. For example, in 1779, five bateaux leaving from Sorel included two medium barrels of brass ordnance for the artillery, fourteen horse harnesses, two drag chain pairs, four powder horns, for steel spikes for nailing guns, and an assortment of twenty different entrenching tools, such as pickaxes, spades, felling axes, and hatchets.[86] Alongside the military equipment, habitants loaded raw materials, including sheep skin, leather buckets, tanned hides, wool, and flannel.[87] Finally, they packed utilitarian items that soldiers needed during their garrison. Candles, tin tubes, grease, ladles, ropes, and sponges rounded out the cargo destined for Niagara.[88]

Squads of habitants on corvée also piloted the bateaux and personally oversaw the movement of supplies. These men joined the supply route at Lachine in the spring and remained with the bateaux train until they completed the journey in July. From June to July 1779, fifty habitants served corvée as bateaux pilots in between Lachine and Carleton Island. These men left in individual expeditions that ranged in size from one single vessel to eight bateaux and canoes. For example, six habitants worked "transporting Artillery Stores from Lachine to Carleton Island for "8 Dollars," accompanied by "three men for [the same trip] at 6 dollars." Although the wage lists do not specify why certain habitants earned more money for the expedition than others, the nine men collectively worked together to safely transport three bateaux. The largest expedition of eight bateaux left Lachine on 8 July and included thirty-three men piloting them. Subdivided into two sixteen-person squads, they "transported three bateaux loads of Artillery Stores from the landing to the embarking place." One man hired "as conductor" must have overseen the management of the larger supply train leaving on the St Lawrence.[89]

Financial accounts from these supply routes indicate that habitants made these journeys over a five-month period from March to July.[90] Supporting documentation also suggests that men serving on corvée should unload provisions and head back as soon as possible, presumably for the upkeep of an efficient supply line. Indeed, in July 1779, Haldimand wrote to Captain Daniel Robinson at Fort Oswegatchie that he should "not upon any account whatever, the approach of an Enemy excepted, delay the Return of Men sent to [his] Post upon Corvée." He added that their return "may be very prejudicial to the Service in the Transport of Provisions etc. to the Upper Posts."[91]

Following Burgoyne's campaign, corvée remained a critical piece of British military efforts in the north. While habitants played an important role in the construction of fortifications on the St Lawrence, their duty to perform corvée in the Upper Posts and Great Lakes represented a departure from previous policy. The military paid the wages of men who came from various parishes of Montreal and huddled together on bateaux to ferry ammunition to the forts in the borderlands of the province. Even over the course of the American Revolution, the customs had changed considerably as the British attempted to harness the potential of the working population. The burdens of corvée, especially on the Upper Posts supply lines, would prompt a series of petitions and court cases to challenge the fiscal-military state's use of habitant labour.

PROTEST AND COURT CASES ON THE UPPER POST CORVÉE, 1778–80

Despite the colonial administration's attempts to standardize corvée, habitants consistently protested mandatory labour in the military. The Lachine-Carleton Island supply route proved onerous to the parishes of the district of Montreal, especially because, under the captains of the militia, civilian corvée continued with the building of roads and bridges.[92] Overextended following the previous campaign, several parishes directly challenged the use of corvée. They collectively protested the British fiscal-military state and provoked colonial officials to punish them for their perceived disobedience. While officers fumed over habitants' evasion of conscription, the colonial courts demonstrated reluctance to legally punish deserters. In 1780, a large-scale, coordinated desertion of habitants on the Lachine-Carleton supply routes prompted a legal battle over punishment for evasion. The outcome would eventually set the stage for the corvée regime after the American Revolution, with habitants returning to civilian duties that primarily benefitted their communities.

The Haldimand administration's official policy towards corvée desertion combined financial punishments and public demonstrations of state authority. Based on Carleton's Militia Acts, 1777, all habitants who deserted their obligations received a five-pound fine for their disobedience.[93] Fines, however, proved difficult to collect. British officers insisted on utilizing corvée outside of habitants' home communities and thus encountered challenges finding deserters who had escaped from the military and could not be located. If a disobedient habitant could not be found and fined, the punishment fell to the parish from which the habitant derived.[94] In theory, this meant that the parish captain of the militia would need to replace the deserter with another community member.[95] By 1778, the British state offered financial compensation to the replacements filling in for the escapees.[96]

During Burgoyne's campaign, the presence of several military regiments and the mechanisms of colonial state authority had – at least partially – mobilized replacements for deserters.[97] Although desertion remained endemic throughout the campaign, the gravity of the expedition and its importance for the war effort prompted high-level British officers to pressure militia captains to round up replacement corvée labourers on the supply routes. By 1778, the immediacy of corvée conscription had significantly decreased as the war effort moved outside the province. To be sure, British officers continued to come up with schemes for the potential uses of corvée, but the militia captains grew increasingly reluctant to provide a never-ending stream of workers for the fiscal-military state.[98]

The turning point for corvée policy occurred on the Lachine-Carleton Island supply route. As mentioned above, many habitants did willingly participate in these services and piloted bateaux to Lake Ontario for the Upper Posts.[99] Within months, however, habitants began deserting that route in what was reported as a conscious choice to discontinue their labour for the military. Thomas Carleton commented in November 1778: "bad weather has occasion'd the desertion of almost all the Canadians intended for the last brigade of provision boats."[100] Initially, Carleton's solution for desertion included garrisoning British regiments in disobedient parishes to oversee the mobilization of labour.[101]

While this strategy worked in the short term, military conscription for corvée further agitated parishes that bore the brunt of work on the supply route. Indeed, by 1779, the British fiscal-military state's policies towards corvée began to deteriorate. First, habitant families started to apply to the courts for exemptions from mandatory labour. Appeals for exemptions put increased pressure on both colonial officials and habitant communities. On one hand, British High Command needed to maintain workers on the supply routes. Indeed, in a letter to Brigadier General McLean, Major Robert Matthews asserted: "[the] exigencies of the King's Service, in the present situation of affairs, require the aid and assistance of every good subject."[102] People "requesting an exemption from Corvées" detracted from the pool of eligible labourers, and those seeking exemption should "give every assistance" to encourage them to serve their obligation.[103] On the other hand, French Canadian parishes grew increasingly dissatisfied with corvée and protested the annual conscriptions through desertion.

Significantly, the Upper Post supply lines put real strain on the workers in Canadian parishes. These riverine and lake-based routes, stretching from Detroit to Lachine, affected more than just the immediate environs of Montreal. The resources destined for the west derived from a complex system of ferries and carrying points along the St Lawrence. These nodes proved critical to the British's military priority to preserve its imperial objectives in the Pays d'en Haut. As a result, the burdens of corvée on the Upper Posts played out along a chain of parishes that encompassed a large portion of the province.[104]

The strain put on communities outside the immediate environs of Montreal to assist in this operation prompted formal complaints from community leaders. In January 1779, the militia captains of the parishes around Sorel approached St George, appealing to the "very great burden, that this part of the country [was] liable to on account of Corvées."[105] Indeed, as a primary hub of corvée activity for fortifications, habitants in Sorel bore the brunt of both construction and ferrying supplies further south on the St Lawrence.[106] Senior officers in the British Army carefully considered these grievances. At the beginning of the campaigning season, Haldimand agreed that "it [was] necessary to reserve the Corvée in the District of Montreal, as much as possible[,] for the Transport of the Upper Posts" and that the construction at Sorel "should be taken from the District of Three Rivers."[107] This subdivision of labour alleviated those workers in and around Sorel, but the pool of habitants from around Montreal continued to find mandatory corvée on the western routes disagreeable. The flood of requests for exemptions increased the pressure on the administration to respond to calls for the reform of corvée.[108]

The disputes over exemptions, desertions, and conscription reached a breaking point in 1780, when an unknown but significant, number of "Corvée men" deserted their posts at Lachine, and the "Commissioners of the Peace" failed to "summon those deserters of [the previous] fall" to public hearings. The "difficulties which occurred [in autumn 1780] in that Branch of the Service" prompted a military investigation into the punishment of deserters and the application of conscription on the supply routes.[109] According to the reports submitted to Haldimand, the mass "desertion of the Corvée Men [the previous] fall" led to a "very great expense and the stores and Provisions were much damaged."[110]

Several high-ranking British officials put forth proposals to increase state authority over corvée mobilization and punishment. The enforcement of criminal charges for corvée evasion represented a significant change in legal policy or. as Donald Fyson asserts, "it is hard to argue that enforcement of the corvée service reflected anything but the desires of the central administration to control of the rural inhabitants."[111] Indeed, he continues that corvée evasion was "prosecuted under official regulations … and largely by official prosecutors."[112]

Proposals for disciplinary action reflected a real urgency to maintain supply routes to the western borderlands of empire in North America. Haldimand himself lamented that sustaining these forts with materials depended on habitants providing corvée. As early as 1778, he wrote: "the Transport of provisions to the Upper Posts is much retarded by the people in the district of Montreal, being occasionally employed on Corvées in other parts."[113] Moreover, he highlighted the "great inconvenicencies and delays" over the mobilization of the "Corvée men."[114] St Leger also commented on the slow process of harnessing the labouring potential of habitants, stating that the "Corvée men" arrived for duty "slower than they ought to [have done] in such pressing times as these."[115] Importantly, the urgency behind this correspondence stemmed from a need for the British military to maintain the physical presence of the empire in the woodlands of North America. Corvée played a critical role in this concept of imperial warfare – providing the raw output of labour necessary to ferry ammunition, provisions, and weapons to the borderlands.

In general, these British officers encouraged Haldimand to prosecute deserters in public trials that would reinforce state authority while simultaneously dissuading other habitants from deserting. Colonel Carleton appointed a captain in the British Army to work with St George "to prosecute to legal conviction such of the militia as might disobey the orders for Corvées."[116] He was charged "with the Prosecution of the Disobedient or deserted Corvée men."[117] Despite the disciplinary rhetoric, justices of the peace remained reluctant to convict habitants for desertion. Carleton reported to the governor: "amidst the number of commissioners of the Peace for Montreal, there may be several who from lukewarmness to their service, or a mistaken tenderness for the people, have acquitted some of the disobedient Corvée men improperly."[118]

Other high-ranking officers encouraged further action to discipline habitants who deserted corvée on the supply lines. In particular, the process of paying money to workers on the Lachine supply route only to have them desert forced military personnel to constantly recruit more habitants from parishes in the region. To remedy this Captain James Maurer in Montreal, for example, suggested that John Burke, the clerk of the peace in Montreal, should be able "to prosecute the Canadians for not appearing or Deserting when ordered for Corvée." He continued that, in an attempt to discourage further evasion of duty, men deserting corvée should be "immediately prosecuted."[119]

Robert Matthews approved the measure in 1782, with the "Clerk of the Peace" designated with the "full power to prosecute all such offenders" and "Canadians as failing in their duties when ordered for Corvée."[120] He tasked John Burke with prosecuting corvée evasion and desertion and ordered him to "punctually exercise" this authority.[121]

As Fyson's study on the post-Conquest criminal justice system shows, desertion cases were brought before two justices of the peace. Plaintiffs could speak to their innocence or attempt to justify their actions in breaking the colonial ordinances, but, as Fyson highlights, a majority of desertion cases ended with convictions. Indeed, following the enforcement of criminal statutes, corvée desertion cases in Montreal had a conviction rate of "between sixty and seventy percent," and most instances "were often brief affairs."[122] Habitants convicted of being guilty of "refusing to provide corvée labour for the king" were then prompted to pay the fine laid out in the militia ordinances.[123] Although the Sessions did have an appeal process for those convicted individuals with a fine of more than £10, most, if not all, habitants "avoided appeal and clemency."[124] He highlights that "an appeal from a summary conviction was a lengthy and costly process, almost inevitably involving lawyers, and the punishments imposed by the justices in cases that could be appealed, generally moderate fines, were not worth the effort."[125] In short, the hearings were a financial and symbolic demonstration of the British justice system and enforced the colonial state's claim on habitant labour.

By the time that Matthews tasked the clerk of the peace empowered with prosecuting disobedient habitants, the American Revolution was effectively over.[126] Cornwallis's surrender to Washington in 1781 ended major offensive activity in the Anglo-American colonies. Skirmishes, hostilities, and evacuations punctuated the closing years of the American Revolution before the official treaty signing in 1783. During the final year, corvée labour on the supply routes dwindled, and habitants returned to their communities after five years of conscription. The battle between British High Command and habitants over corvée ended in a stalemate, with no evidence that the courts had punished the deserters.

Epilogue

In the wake of the politically turbulent court cases over corvée desertion on the Upper Country supply routes, the labour system entered a new phase. The ordinance that empowered the clerk of the peace to prosecute deserters made corvée a difficult and potentially finically crippling obligation to evade. While many local militia captains tried to ignore enforcing the summons for criminal prosecution, overwhelmingly the colonial state relied on the justices and British-appointed subdelegates to enforce these labour policies.

Hundreds of habitants faced criminal prosecution for their evasion, or desertion, of corvée during the closing years of the American Revolution. As Donald Fyson asserts, "we can see a more general rise in recourse to public prosecution in the enforcement of the justices' police regulations," especially regarding corvée infractions.[1] Evasion during the War of 1812 also caused a flurry of such prosecutions, with Fyson stating: "[the] king's counsel were ordered to prosecute corvée infractions, with the result that 'many person in different parts of [Montreal] district were prosecuted, which had the desired effect of making the inhabitants more obedient to the corvée law.'"[2] Clearly, the criminal prosecutions of corvée fundamentally changed the ways in which habitants interacted with the colonial state.

Despite a return to peace for most of the province, corvée continued on the Upper Country supply routes. Indeed, seigneurial records from the Baby family demonstrate that Montreal and its neighboring environs of Longue Pointe and Pointe aux Trembles provided corvée at Lachine as late as 1785, two years after the Revolution had officially ended.[3] As occurred in the wartime years, men labouring at the transport site were compensated with wages for their work.[4] Obviously, the British colonial state still sought the use of habitant labour to meet the demands of supply transportation in the North American borderlands.

The Upper Posts remained a considerable operation for the British Empire. Men conscripted from the environs of Montreal to perform corvée transported wood, ammunition, and "baggage of the Troops" to the outposts on the Great Lakes.[5] The British supplemented short-term rotations of corvée with artificers, shipbuilders, sailors, and day labourers. Following the discontent of the American Revolution, and presumably the obligation to work for the military via corvée, many Canadian habitants continued work on the supply routes for wages and navigated the western waterways of the Great Lakes.[6] In sum, corvée continued to remain a critical component of military transportation in post-revolutionary Quebec.

The end of the war also meant that life in rural seigneuries returned to agricultural routines, with corvée primarily transitioning back to work on local roads. For most habitants, this meant a return to the drudgery of repairing roads, which the conflict had largely prevented. In late 1782, Governor Haldimand appointed Jean Renaud as grand voyer, who set about mobilizing corvée for road repair.[7] His overhaul of the Canadian road system continued through 1793, with habitants working to repair pre-existing roads and to build new highways that facilitated travel.[8]

Much of the work that took place during the immediate postwar period centred on repairing public works that had fallen into disorder during the war. A major part of this initiative included mobilizing habitants to collect timber for the reconstruction of bridges. Most orders that Renaud issued between December 1782 and February 1783 dealt with repairing bridges. For example, on 11 January 1783, Renaud ordered the habitants of Saint-Laurent to "transport the pieces of wood necessary for the reparation of the bridge of the parish."[9] Given the season, the grand voyer also ordered habitants to fix winter roads that ran through their communities, such as "the winter route" he ordered in Saint-Joseph.[10] The hierarchy of corvée remained the same. Orders filtered down from the grand voyer to the militia captains, who organized corvée in their individual parishes to complete the work.

Renaud embarked on his own ambitious project to construct a post-road to Fort Howe on Lake Témiscouata in 1783, an endeavour that included several portage-points to facilitate the delivery of the Royal Mail.[11] Records attest to Renaud enlisting around 185 Canadian militiamen to perform corvée on the post-road, which stretched "twelve leagues and sixteen *arpents*."[12] The militiamen came from several parishes, including "twenty militiamen from [Kamouraska]" and "fifty men to work the road [from Rivière-Oulle]."[13] The work included all of the auxiliary tasks associated with road construction, including building ditches and portage points in the marshy region east of the St Lawrence River. The "good men" performing corvée received wages and rations for their labour on the highway.[14]

As early as 1781, the Committees on Highways, Roads, and Bridges also reformed and started to hear habitant petitions and grievances regarding road construction.[15] During the war, the committees seem to have disbanded, with road construction channelled through the grand voyer for all civil matters, and the Royal Engineers taking over maintenance highways for supply routes.[16] In 1781, the committee regrouped and renewed the hearing of petitions. At least two petitions came through the committee during those years, including one concerning a new pathway passing through Henry Caldwell's farm on the Rivière Saint-Charles.

A former soldier and member of the Legislative Council during the American Revolution, Caldwell had purchased the land on the Saint-Charles in 1778.[17] He cultivated "a farm at the little river," where, in 1783, Renaud authorized a corvée for a new pathway "which would shorten the distance of the King's Highway." This proposal also included a new bridge over the river. After discussing the matter with Caldwell, the grand voyer offered "to get the habitants of the neighbouring parishes that benefitted from said road to make it." The habitants of the nearby parishes seemed to have disagreed because Renaud returned to Caldwell and relayed that he had no "legal authority to oblige them to." In order to fence in his section of the unfinished road, and complete the bridge, Caldwell appealed to the committee. His desired outcome, he stated, was that the committee should ratify the initial proposal "by which the Grand Voyer may be legally authorized to oblige the parishes that benefit from said road to compleat it."[18]

While the outcome of this petition is unknown, Caldwell's retelling of the incident reflects three important dynamics of corvée in post-revolutionary Quebec. First, Caldwell's description of events demonstrates that litigating civil issues of road maintenance and construction had returned to the province following the turmoil of the previous years. Indeed, Caldwell first approached the grand voyer, then the committee, to have this matter resolved. Second, Caldwell's account is illustrative of the typical local squabbles that had been taking place since the early eighteenth century. Similar disagreements over road, bridge, and fence construction appear in the records of the intendant in New France. Finally, the reformation of the committee highlights that litigating corvée had returned to civil authorities. During the war, the Royal Engineers often took over organizing corvée. The petitions submitted to the committee in 1783 reflect a sense that, in Quebec, corvée on roads had reverted to some sense of normalcy.

*

On 3 September 1783, the American delegates John Adams, Benjamin Franklin, and John Jay met with the Crown's representative David Hartly at the Hôtel d'York in Paris. Together, they signed the Treaty of Paris, ending the American War for Independence and formally recognizing the United States of America. The same day, two lesser-known agreements referred to as the Treaties of Versailles, 1783, ceded Florida back to the Spanish Empire in exchange for islands in the Bahamas. This series of treaties transformed North America on the same scale as had the 1763 iteration of negotiations following the Seven Years' War. Quebec, Nova Scotia, Hudson Bay, and the Pays d'en Haut were the only British colonial landholdings remaining on mainland North America, a drastic reduction for an empire that had for twenty years stretched from the Arctic to the Caribbean.

The loss of the thirteen Anglo-American colonies and Florida affected Britain's larger imperial labour strategy. In the wake of revolution, British officials in Canada turned to increasing anglophone settlement, composed of former American loyalists and a wave of Irish migration, particularly to the "Eastern Townships."[19] In the meantime, French Canadians hung in the balance, with their seigneurial customs having been reinstated by the Quebec Act but, with the advent of war in the province, never fully used. Allan Greer's scholarship on the Lower Richelieu attests that "the feudal burden" of the seigneurial regime persisted for Quebecois into the late eighteenth and early nineteenth centuries. After the war, habitants went back to cultivating small farms and offering feudal dues such as lods et ventes, the goods and services owed to a seigneur under French civil law.[20]

Overall, British administrators shifted their focus away from the Atlantic World towards their burgeoning empire in the Indian Ocean. As H.V. Bowen states, "[British] imperial interests began the long-term process of shifting away from the Western Hemisphere to the East." The imperial backbone of this empire also began to change, creating a polity that "was multi-national and multi-faith in character and contained a bewildering array of institutional and organizational forms." Canada, and corvée labour, remained important but had started to fit a larger imperial strategy that encompassed Britain's expanded empire.

In 1791, British officials incorporated corvée into the law code of the newly created province of "Lower Canada." The influx of British American loyalists (also known as United Empire Loyalists) to the Great Lakes region following the American Revolution necessitated a legal reform in the province of Quebec, still governed by reinstated French civil law. Parliament's solution split the former province into two separate entities. Upper Canada occupied the Great Lakes region and received a law code based on British common law. For this reason, anglophone migrants did not perform corvée, and their landholdings were held under British property regulations.

Lower Canada, centred around the St Lawrence Valley, retained many of the measures reestablished by the Quebec Act. The newly created territory maintained the familiar customs of tenure that had existed since New France, including the cens, lods et ventes, and banalité.[21] Habitants also continued to pay a tithe to the local parish church. French Canadian corvée remained active through the early nineteenth century, and military records attest to the British harnessing corvée for public works during the War of 1812.[22]

As occurred with the outbursts of protest during the American invasion of Quebec, nineteenth-century French Canadians contested seigneurial dues, especially if they found the rents, customs, or labour particularly onerous. In the lead up to the Lower Canada Rebellion, for example, Allan Greer points out that "petitions from rural seigneuries complained of a variety of different 'abuses,' though the most common grievances concerned rents, refusal of free grants, and mill monopoly."[23] In these moments of heightened tension, habitants harnessed accepted British traditions of protest, such as petitioning, to address long-standing dissatisfaction with the local landholding elite. Patriot leaders co-opted the language of these complaints and channelled them to fuel an uprising centred on reforming land tenure in the region.[24] The labour customs, and seigneurial tenure, endured until the Seigneurial Act, 1854, which abolished all feudal obligations enshrined in French civil law or custom.

*

This book shows the complex, and often important, situations in which corvée labourers found themselves entangled during the eighteenth century. To be sure, the first generation of migrants from France in the seventeenth century experienced a vastly different version of these customs than did wage labourers conscripted to perform corvée during the American Revolution. Even more specifically, father and son could have experienced different laws governing corvée, different projects and work routines, and perhaps even different officials who spoke a different language overseeing the labour. For example, while the earliest migrants practised an agricultural corvée on the seigneur's estate, by the beginning of the eighteenth century increased royal intervention in colonial warfare demanded a more grueling, state-sanctioned variation of mandatory labour that prioritized work on fortifications and roads. Each generation of habitants faced unique challenges in its struggle for autonomy within this compulsory, and often bothersome, system of labour.

The story of two brothers from Boucherville, Jean Baptiste and Adrien Lamoureux, help illustrate the evolution of corvée over just one generation. Born in 1669 in Longueil, Jean Baptiste Lamoureux eventually settled in the seigneurie of Boucherville, where he would marry Marie Gareau and raise a family.[25] Jean was born shortly after the Custom of Paris revised corvée policies and came of age during the initial conscriptions of labourers and militiamen for the Nine Years' War.

His brother Adrien turned sixteen at the start of the conflict and was thus also eligible for service in the militia.[26] During the early eighteenth century, the brothers also likely participated in the reconstruction of a parish church.[27] By that time, both Jean and Adrien had witnessed one major change in corvée policy, with Jacques Raudot's 1707 clarifications in the wake of the Nine Years' War.

The two brothers worked on the stone enclosure surrounding Montreal. As discussed in chapter 1, Bégon ordered the environs of Montreal "to provide corvée on the openings of the compound." Squads of habitants contributed *journées d'hommes* and were "employed to draw stone from the quarries and amass it on the fields." The habitants on *journées de harnois* also worked "with the pack animals to load the lime necessary" and transport the materials to the worksite outside Montreal.[28]

The two brothers obeyed the intendant's orders. Jean, now forty-six years old, provided four days of work with horse teams carting materials to the worksite.[29] His brother joined him, offering two days of *journées de harnois*.[30]

While the tax lists do not indicate their enthusiasm for corvée, they certainly worked together when called upon "to furnish the necessary Courvées for the wall of the city," and their captain of the militia, Louis Menard, signified as much in the seigneurial rolls.[31]

Jean aged out of the corvée requirement in 1729 when he turned sixty, and Adrien joined him shortly afterwards in 1731. The Lamoureux family undoubtedly would have heard of the confrontation between their neighbours in Longueuil and the governor as well as the regional, widespread discontent over corvée obligations on the Montreal enclosure.[32] Their children and relatives likely participated in other major initiatives of the French colonial state. For example, Boisclerc called upon Boucherville habitants to provide corvée during the construction of the King's Highway. Habitants built a series of auxiliary roads in the seigneurie, including a twenty-four-foot (seven-metre) highway accessible to "habitants of the second, third, fourth, and fifth ranks of Boucherville."[33]

There can be no doubt that Jean and Adrien Lamoureux's work facilitated local needs. They built roads that enabled travel through their seigneurie, dredged ditches, and hauled materials with carts for the enclosure around Montreal. On a larger scale, the two brothers were entangled in a much greater process taking place on both side of the Atlantic. Their labour connected to a sprawling network of roads and bridges that lay at the heart of France's economic ambitions in the New World. Their hands helped erect the Montreal fortifications and the veritable symbols of empire in North America.

Many other French Canadian habitants experienced a similar transformation of their labour customs. Highlighting the compensation of corvée underscores just how much customs had changed since the early eighteenth century. Under the French, the initial mass corvée on the Quebec fortifications was carried out under custom, obligation, and obedience to the monarch. Workers received rations for their tenure at the city, working on ten- to fifteen-day rotations.[34] Despite the ambition of the fortifications, however, a majority of corvée under the French primarily remained a local affair, with neighbouring environs providing support for public works. By the end of the American Revolution, corvée resembled a system of coerced wage labour, with standardized, fixed wages paid to workers from many parishes gathered by the British military to work far-flung supply routes into the Great Lakes.[35] This wage labour system persisted until Britain's abolition of corvée in the mid-nineteenth century.[36]

In sum, corvée workers did more than simply fulfill their royal obligations to build roads, bridges, fences, and fortifications: they often found themselves thrust into the middle of seismic transformations taking place in contested arenas of the Atlantic World. They participated in a number of the most dramatic martial engagements of the eighteenth century, including the siege at Carillon (1758), the counterattack at Saint-Foy (1760), and the Battle of Saratoga (1777). These imperial conflicts often extended into the borderlands of North America, where corvée carried the symbols of the empire aboard bateaux to western outposts. As previously discussed, Britain's tenuous hold over the Great Lakes resulted in the establishment of military garrisons to protect their claim to this land during the American Revolution. The fiscal-military state of the empire in their western outposts required a consistent supply of weapons, ammunition, and raw materials. The trade route that developed from Montreal to Lake Ontario became a lifeline for supplies during the latter years of the conflict, and it largely depended on habitants ferrying these supplies.[37] Both French and British officials expected obedience and obligation in times of war and in times of peace, and corvée labourers transformed into critical lynchpins of construction and supply transportation.

Habitants also constructed the arteries of empire in Canada – highways, bridges, and ferries – that connected French and British merchants to the interior of North America. At the start of the eighteenth century, Canada contained clusters of local footpaths and roads centred around the commercial activities of Quebec and Montreal. By the end of the American Revolution, twenty-four-foot (seven-metre) highways crisscrossed both shores of the St Lawrence. These highways facilitated profitable enterprises, such as the fur trade with the Indigenous communities of the Pays d'en Haut. They also allowed the transportation of goods, ideas, and people to the settlements dotting the region.

From the Nine Years' War to the American Revolution, habitant communities witnessed the transformation of corvée labour in North America. Over nine decades, under two imperial regimes, the labour system had irrevocably changed. What initially started as a conscription of habitants to build fortifications around New France's two main cities had, by the close of the eighteenth century, become a critical source of labour for the British fiscal-military state. The colonial officials who administered corvée in Canada had also changed. Generations of habitants in the parishes of the St Lawrence watched as French, then British, administrators wrestled with the labour system. From the mutiny at Longueuil (1717) to the desertions on the Upper Posts (1783),

French Canadians often defied corvée orders when they felt that officials had overstepped the boundaries of labour customs in the northern colony. Corvée highlights the entangled relationships between law and empire in the eighteenth century and the communities of habitants that protested unremunerated labour in the North American borderlands.

Notes

INTRODUCTION

1 Trudel, *Les débuts du régime seigneurial au Canada*, 197. See also Frégault, *La civilization de la Nouvelle-France*; and Desloges, "La corvée militaire à Québec au XVIIIe siècle," 333–56.

2 Trudel, *Les débuts du régime seigneurial au Canada*, 165.

3 Greer, *Peasant, Lord, and Merchant*, 123.

4 Ibid., 140.

5 Historians also refer to this form of labour as "the King's corvées" because these orders disseminated from the superior council or intendant, the representatives of the King in New France. The phrase "King's corvée" derives from Guy Frégault, *La civilization de la Nouvelle-France*. Louise Dechêne uses the term "corvées général" to describe the same type of labour.

6 McDonough, "Building the Roads," 98.

7 Gowas, *Church Architecture in New France*, 69.

8 Intendants also played a role in organizing corvée in France, but the distribution of those orders stemmed from the provincial authorities and the king's councils in those provinces. See McDonough, "Building the Roads," 112.

9 McDonough, "Building the Roads," 104.

10 Desloges, "La corvée militaire à Québec au XVIIIe siècle," 336.

11 On the original seigneuries subdivided by the Company of One Hundred, see Grenier, *Brève histoire du régime seigneurial*, 56–60. For a breakdown of rural seigneuries in New France, see Grenier, "Gentilshommes Campagnards de la Nouvelle France," 21–43.

12 Moogk, *La Nouvelle France*, 181–5.

13 Choquette, *De Français à paysans*, 121–8.

14 Grenier, *Brève histoire du régime seigneurial*, 120–1.

15 The grand voyer became the point-person for all corvée orders on highway construction and road building. See Dider, "Subdélégués et subdélégations dans l'espace atlantique français," 248.

16 Wilson, "Rethinking the Colonial State," 1295; and Scott, *Domination and the Arts of Resistance*, 45.

17 On the French seigneurial customs, see Grinberg, *Écrire les coutumes*; Mauclair, *La justice au village*; and Thompson, "Custom Law and Common Right."

18 Daniels and Kennedy, *Negotiated Empires*; Wilson, "Rethinking the Colonial State," 1294–322.

19 Brewer, *Sinews of Power*; Stone, *Imperial State at War*.

20 Armitage, *Ideological Origins of the British Empire*. See also Pagden, *Lords of All the World*.

21 Scott, *Seeing Like a State*, 24.

22 Blais, "La representation en Nouvelle France," 51–75.

23 Levasseur to the Minister, 12 November 1707, Québec, AC, C11A, vol. 27, pp. 25–9, LAC; and Vaudreuil to the Minister, 18 May 1725, AC, C11A, vol. 47, pp. 149–54, LAC.

24 Monsieur Longueuil to Carleton, 26 September, 1777, reel 15, Haldimand Papers, LAC (hereafter HP).

25 Dechambault, Memorie sur les Milices en Québec, series B, vol. 17, pp. 114–27, HP.

26 The concept of the "fiscal-military state" derives from Brewer, *Sinews of Power*; and Stone, *Imperial State at War*.

27 Greer, *Property and Dispossession*, 77. For a ground-breaking recent monograph on the early settlement of Canada and the impact of colonization on First Nation communities, see Lozier, *Flesh Reborn: The Saint Lawrence Valley Mission Settlements through the Seventeenth Century*.

28 "Carte du Lac Champlain depuis le Fort de Chambly Jusques au desus du Fort St. Frederic, dans la Nouvelle France," (1739) PH901, box 2001422127, no. 4147269, LAC.

29 Hocquart to the Minister, 28 September 1740, AC, C11A, vol. 73, pp. 105–9, LAC; and Vallette de Chévigny to the Minister, 12 September 1738, AC, C11A, vol. 72, pp. 248–9v, LAC.

30 Murray, The State of the Government of Quebec, 1762, reel 4, mss. 21667, pp. 1–31, HP; Gage, The State of the Government of Montreal, 1762, reel 4, mss. 21667, pp. 43–50, HP; Haldimand, The Present State of the Government of Three Rivers in Canada, reel 10, mss. 21681, pp. 4–15, HP.

31 Grenier, *Brève histoire du régime seigneurial*, 56–60.

32 Grinberg, *Écrire les coutumes*, 71. Sylvie Perrier also addresses the creation of "peasant legal cultures" through French civil law. See Perrier, *Des enfances protégées*.

33 Grinberg, *Écrire les coutumes*, 72.

34 Ibid.

35 Mauclair, *La justice au village*, 138.

36 Thompson, "Custom Law and Common Right,"100.
37 Greer, *Property and Dispossession*, 154.
38 Ibid., 156.
39 Ibid., 159.
40 Trudel, *Les débuts du régime seigneurial au Canada*, 175.
41 Greer, *Peasant, Lord, and Merchant*, 122–3.
42 Ibid., 125,
43 Greer, *Property and Dispossession*, 189.
44 "Titre II, Droits Extraordinaire," in *An Abstract of Those Parts of the Custom of the Viscounty and Provostship of Paris, which were received and practiced in the Province of Quebec, in the Time of the French Government*, 30. The section focusing on the cens appears in "Titre III, Des Censives es Droite Seigneur-uaux," 34.
45 Greer, *Property and Dispossession*, 171.
46 Trudel, *Les débuts du régime seigneurial au Canada*, 197.
47 Numerous titles of concession from the late seventeenth and early eighteenth centuries are held at Library and Archives Canada and the Bibliothéque et Archives Nationales du Quebec. In Ontario and Quebec archives, these documents are archived in "seigneurial collections." The primary collection that I consulted is Fonds de la Familie Ramezay, Seigneurie Sorel, Titles of Concession, MG18-H54, LAC.
48 The seasonal characteristics of corvée referenced in this paragraph derive from an evaluation of 116 separate orders. These represent every order of corvée issued by the Intendant's Office from 1708 to1729.
49 Dechêne, *Habitants et Marchands de Montreal au XVIIe siècle*, 153–5.
50 Bégon, Ordonnance entre M Laliberté et autres habitants des Isles Bouchard et le Seigneur Desjordy, 3 June 1714, C-13588, Fonds Intendants, pp. 324–8, LAC.
51 Ibid.
52 Liste d'habitants qui ont fait du sucre et qui on bûché du bois, Seigneurie de Sorel, Fonds de la Familie de Ramezay, pp. 1381–2, LAC.
53 Dechêne, *Habitants et Marchands*, 144.
54 Gowas, *Church Architecture in New France*, 69.
55 Dechêne, *Habitants et Marchands*, 144.
56 Ibid., 201.
57 Banks, *Chasing Empire across the Sea*, 22.
58 Ibid., 23.
59 Ibid., 25.
60 Ibid., 25–7.
61 Greer, *Peasant, Lord, and Merchant*, 123.
62 Podruchny, *Making the Voyageur World*, 29.
63 Gould, "Entangled Histories, Entangled Worlds," 767–8.

64 Dubois, "The French Atlantic," 147.

65 Benton, *Law and Colonial Cultures*, 255.

66 On African slavery in Canada, see Trudel, *Canada's Forgotten Slaves.*

67 On Indigenous slavery, see Jetten, *Enclaves amérindienne*; and Rushforth, *Bonds of Alliance*. Recently, new scholarship has shed light on the attempts of the broader European empires to enslave Indigenous people. See Negrin, "Native Women Work the Ground," 90–110; and Kruer, *Times of Anarchy*.

68 Gigi, "Building an Empire."

69 Gigi, "Materiality of Empire."

70 Hardesty, *Unfreedom*; Linebaugh and Rediker, *Many-Headed Hydra*; Rockman, *Scraping By.*

71 Carleton to William Petty, "Despatch of Governor Carleton to the Earl of Shelburne regarding the Administration of English Laws in Canada," 24 December 1767, in Munro, *Documents Relating to the Seigniorial Tenure in Canada, 1598–1854* (hereafter DST), 227.

72 Armitage, *Ideological Origins of the British Empire*. See also Pagden, *Lords of All the World.*

73 Wilson, "Introduction," 12.

74 The Anglo-American colonists' protests against "arbitrary authority" derives from: Green, *Constitutional Origins of the American Revolution*; Gould, *Persistence of Empire*; and Pagden, *Lords of All the World.*

75 Scott, *Domination and the Arts of Resistance*, 2.

76 Ibid., 4.

77 Ibid., 4–5.

78 Ibid., 95.

79 Roseberry, "Hegemony and the Language of Contention," 350.

80 Rama, *Lettered City*, 7.

CHAPTER ONE

An earlier version of this chapter appeared in Tomczak, "Corvée Labour and the Habitant 'Spirit of Mutiny,'" 19–47.

1 Michel Bégon, Ordonnance pour les courvées des fortifications de Montreal, 6 November 1714, Fond Intendant, C-13588, pp, 438–40, LAC. A comprehensive definition of the term "habitant" can be found in Greer, *Property and Dispossession*, 172.

2 Vaudreuil to the Council of the Marine, 17 October 1717, Quebec, Archives des Colonies, C11A, vol. 38, pp. 121–4v, LAC.

3 Ibid.

4 For a recent analysis of corvée in eighteenth-century France, see Conchon, *La corvée des grands Chemins au XVIIIe siècle*. For the translation of metropolitan policies of corvée in New France, see Desloges, "La corvée militaire à Québec au XVIIIe siècle," 333–56; Banks, *Chasing Empire across the Sea*; and Dechêne, *Le Peuple.*

5 Hardesty, *Unfreedom*; Linebaugh and Rediker, *Many-Headed Hydra*.

6 Rushforth, "Origins of Indian Slavery in New France," 778–808; Little, *Many Captives of Esther Wheelwright*.

7 Rushforth, *Bonds of Alliance*, 20–1.

8 On "negotiated empires," see Daniels and Kennedy, *Negotiated Empires*; Wilson, "Rethinking the Colonial State," 1294–322. See also Roseberry, "Hegemony and the Language of Contention," 355–66.

9 Choquette, "Center and Periphery in French North America," 200–1.

10 See the construction of Fort Saint-Jean, see Boisclerc to the Minister, 5 November 1748, AC, C11A, vol. 89, pp. 220–1v, LAC.

11 Many bridges were constructed to facilitate the transportation of supplies in the colony and were an integral part of the Chemin du Roi. See Beauharnois and Hocquart to the Minister, 14 October 1733, AC, C11A, vol. 60, pp. 80–4, LAC. For ferries, see Beauharnois and Hocquart to the Minister, 14 October 1733, AC, C11A, vol. 60, pp. 80–4, LAC.

12 Hamilton, *Fort Ticonderoga*, 40–1.

13 On Lake Champlain, see Varin to the Minister, 2 November 1748, AC, C11A, vol. 92, pp. 295–6v, LAC. On the colonial cities, see Levasseur to the Minister, 10 October 1701, AC, C11A, vol. 19, pp. 254–5, LAC.

14 Stanwood, *Empire Reformed*.

15 Charbonneau, Desloges, Lafrance, Quebec, *Fortified City*, 32.

16 Levasseur to the Minister, 10 October 1701, AC, C11A, vol. 19, pp. 254–5, LAC.

17 Louvigny to the Minister, 21 October 1706, Quebec, AC, C11A, vol. 25, pp. 25–46, LAC.

18 Levasseur to the Minister, 10 October 1701, AC, C11A, vol. 19, pp. 254–5, LAC.

19 Levasseur to the Minister, 1 October 1705, Quebec, AC, C11A (transcript), vol. 22, pp. 325–61, LAC.

20 Conchon, *La corvée des grands Chemins au XVIIIe siècle*, 41.

21 Levasseur to the Minister, 15 October, 1705, Quebec, AC, C11A, vol. 22, LAC.

22 Louvigny to the Minister, 21 October, 1706, Quebec, AC, C11A, vol. 25, pp. 25–46, LAC.

23 Ibid.

24 Ibid.

25 Ibid.

26 Louvigny to the Minister, 6 November 1707, Quebec, AC, C11A, vol. 27, pp. 25–9, LAC (transcript).

27 Louvigny to the Minister, 21 October 1706, Quebec, AC, C11A, vol. 25, pp. 25–46, LAC.

28 On the carting of materials and construction of palisades, see Louvigny to the Minister, 21 October 1706, Quebec, C11A, vol. 25, pp. 25–46, LAC. On digging trenches, see Louvigny to the Minister, 6 November 1707, Quebec, C11A, vol. 27, pp. 25–9, LAC (transcript).

29 Ramezay and Bégon to the Minister, Montreal, 7 November 1715, AC, C11A, vol. 35, pp. 25–9, LAC.

30 Ibid.

31 Louvigny to the Minister, 21 October 1706, Quebec, AC, C11A, vol. 25, pp. 25–46, LAC.

32 Ibid.

33 The number of habitants that participated in corvée is based on a compilation of tax lists that list the days worked by each individual habitant for the Montreal fortification project. The Quebec City corvée was larger than that of Montreal and we can assume would have required a similar number of workers. See Fonds de la Familie de Ramezay, Rolles de l'Îsle de Montreal, vol. 35, C11A, LAC; Rolles de Varennes, Saint-Michel et Saint Theresa, vol. 35, pp. 343–5; Rolles de Rivières-des-Prairies, vol. 35; Rolles de Lachine, vol. 35; Rolles de Boucherville, vol. 35, pp. 340–2; Rolles de Vercheres et Isle d'Bouchard, vol. 35; Rolles de Isle d'Jesus, vol. 35; and Rolles de Lachenaie, 1715, vol. 35, C11A, LAC.

34 Louvigny to the Minister, 21 October 1706, Quebec, C11A, vol. 25, pp. 25–45, LAC. On digging trenches, see Louvigny to the Minister, 7 November 1707, Quebec, C11A, vol. 27, pp. 25–9, LAC.

35 Clearing underbrush was a common task of corvée labour for road construction. See Bégon, Ordonnance des principaux habitants du la paroisse de l'Ancienne Lorette concernant les chemins, 24 June 1713, Fonds Intendant, C-13588, pp. 207–9, LAC.

36 Louvigny to the Minister, 21 October 1706, Quebec, C11A, vol. 25, pp. 25–46, LAC. On digging trenches, see Louvigny to the Minister, 6 November 1707, Quebec, C11A, vol. 27, pp. 25–9, LAC.

37 Louvigny to the Minister, 21 October 1706, Quebec, C11A, vol. 25, pp. 25–46, LAC. Corvée woodcutting derives from Bégon, 25 November 1721, Fonds Intendant, C-13588, vol. 5, pp. 445–6, LAC.

38 Information on the noise created by oxen derives from British sources observing corvée. See Captain Money, "Captain Money called in and examined by General Burgoyne," in Burgoyne, *State of the Expedition*, 56.

39 Louvigny to the Minister, 21 October 1706, Quebec, AC, C11A, vol. 25, pp. 25–46, LAC.

40 On the location of the bateaux, see Louvigny to the Minister, 6 November 1707, Quebec, AC, C11A, vol. 27, pp. 25–9, LAC. See also "Dimensions of Bateaux," Naval Documents of the American Revolution, vol. 6, ed. William Bell Clark. On the number of men within a bateau, see General Orders, *Journal of Captain James Murray Hadden*. On the supplies Burgoyne ordered to be stored in the bateaux, see Orderly Book of the 47th Regiment, Grenadier Company Major Acland's Battalion, "Sunday, River Sable Lake Champlain,

Brigade Orders," "Tuesday, Camp at River Sable, 10 June 1777, Brigade Orders and After Brigade Orders," and "Tuesday, Camp at River Bouquet, 17 June 1777, Brigade Orders."

41 Hadden, *Journal of Captain James Murray Hadden*.

42 Levasseur to the Minister, 12 November 1707, Quebec, AC, C11A (transcript), vol. 27, pp. 31–45, LAC.

43 Louvigny to the Minister, 21 October 1706, Quebec, AC, C11A, vol. 25, pp. 25–46, LAC. Levasseur to the Minister, 12 November 1707, Quebec, AC, C11A (transcript), vol. 27, pp. 31–45, LAC.

44 Louvigny to the Minister, 21 October 1706, Quebec, AC, C11A (transcript), vol. 25, pp. 25–6, LAC.

45 Ibid.

46 Ibid.

47 Ramezay and Bégon to the Minister, Montreal, 7 November 1715, AC, C11A, vol. 35, pp. 25–6, LAC.

48 Louvigny to the Minister, 21 October 1706, Quebec, AC, C11A (transcript), vol. 25, pp. 25–6, LAC.

49 Ibid.

50 Levasseur to the Minister, 12 November 1707, Quebec, AC, C11A (transcript), vol. 27, pp. 31–45, LAC.

51 Louvigny to the Minister, 21 October 1706, Quebec, AC, C11A (transcript), vol. 25, pp. 25–6, LAC.

52 Ibid.

53 Time restrictions on corvée were eventually implemented in 1708 following an investigation into the use of corvée in New France. See Jacques Raudot, Mémorie de Raudot, 1708, Archives des Colonies, séries C11G, Correspondance général, F-421, pp. 66–9v, LAC.

54 Louvigny to the Minister, 21 October 1706, Quebec, AC, C11A (transcript), vol. 25, pp. 25–6, LAC.

55 Levasseur to the Minister, 12 November 1707, Quebec, AC, C11A (transcript), vol. 27, pp. 31–45, LAC.

56 Ibid.

57 Habitants "whispered of mutiny" several times in the first three decades of the eighteenth century. It appears once in documents related to the Quebec City corvée and twice in documents discussing the Montreal fortifications. On Quebec City, see Levasseur to the Minister, 12 November 1707, Quebec, AC, C11A, vol. 27, pp. 31–45, LAC. On Montreal and mutiny, see Vaudreuil and Bégon, Projet du memoire de Roi, 23 May 1719, AC, C11A, vol. 40, pp. 301–5, LAC; and Vaudreuil to the Minister, 18 May 1725, AC, C11A, vol. 47, pp. 149–54, LAC.

58 Raudot investigated a number of corruption charges, with the seigneurial regime and corvée just being one part of a larger investigation.

59 Jacques Raudot, Mémorie de Raudot, 1708, Archives des Colonies, séries C11G, Correspondence général, F-421, pp. 66–9v, LAC.
60 Raudot, Ordonnance qui oblige les habitants du gouvernement de Montreal pour la bâtisse en pierre du fort de Chambly, 16 November 1709, Fonds Intendant, C-13587, vol. 3, pp. 196–8, LAC.
61 Minister to Beaucourt, 7 July 1711, AC, série B, vol. 216, p. 164, LAC; and Vaudreuil to Raudot, 7 November 1711, AC, C11A, vol. 32, pp. 195–204, LAC.
62 Ramezay to the Minister, 17 September 1714, AC, C11A, vol. 34, pp. 354–61, LAC.
63 Ibid.
64 Ibid.
65 Vaudreuil and Bégon, 20 September 1714, AC, C11A, vol. 34, pp. 228–61v, LAC.
66 Bégon, "Ordonnance pour faire les ouvrages de enceinte de la ville de Montreal par corvées," AC, C11A, vol. 34, pp. 328-9v, LAC.
67 Gideon, Sub-Engineer, to the Minister, 19 November 1713, AC, C11A, vol. 34, pp. 114–6v, LAC; and Vaudreuil to the Minister, 16 October 1716, AC, C11A, vol. 36, pp. 81–2v, LAC.
68 Rolles de l'Île de Montreal, 25 March 1715, AC, C11A, vol. 34, pp. 351–2, LAC.
69 All records derive from AC, C11A, vol. 34, LAC. For l'Isle d'Jesus, Charles Dazée [Dazé] et François Renaud, 17 March 1715, 348; Lachenaie, Charles Dazée, 15 March 1715, 348; Rivière-de-Prairies, 17 March 1715, 346; Varennes, Saint-Michel, et Saint-Theresa, Jean Lemire, 25 January 1715, 343–4; and Vercheres et Isle d'Bouchard, Daniel Tetro [Tetreau], 25 January 1715, 342.
70 Vaudreuil to the Council of the Marine, 17 October 1717, Quebec, AC, C11A, vol. 38, pp. 121–4v, LAC.
71 l'Isle d'Jesus, Charles Dazée [Dazé] et François Renaud, 17 March 1715, AC, C11A, vol. 34, p. 348, LAC.
72 Lachenaie, Charles Dazée, 15 March 1715, AC, C11A, vol. 34, p. 348, LAC.
73 l'Isle d'Jesus, Charles Dazée [Dazé] et François Renaud, 17 March 1715, AC, C11A, vol. 34, p. 348, LAC.
74 Ramezay and Bégon to the Minister, 7 November 1715, AC, C11A, vol. 35, pp. 15–52v, LAC.
75 Ibid.
76 Vaudreuil and Bégon, Projet du memoire de Roi, 23 May 1719, AC, C11A, vol. 40, pp. 301–5, LAC.
77 Ibid.
78 Ibid.
79 Ibid.
80 Chaussegros de Léry to the Minister, 20 October 1732, AC, C11A, vol. 58, pp. 203–7, LAC.
81 Bécancour issued six orders for roads in the seventeenth century. Several of these focused on Notre-Dame-des-Agnes, with the first order on 20 February

1683. See Cahier 1, Fonds Grand Voyer, p. 59, Bibliothéque et Archives Nationales du Quebec (hereafter BANQ).

82 Jean Talon, "Pour la construction d'un pont sur la rivière Saint-Pierre," Inventaire des ordonnances des Intendants de la Nouvelle France, vol. 3, p. 259, BANQ; and da la Barre, Notre-Dame-des-Agnes, 22 February 1683, Fonds Grand Voyer, p. 59, BANQ.

83 Jean Talon, "Pour la construction d'un pont sur la rivière Saint-Pierre," Inventaire des ordonnances des Intendants de la Nouvelle France, vol. 3, p. 259, BANQ.

84 McDonough, "Building the Roads," 17.

85 Ibid.

86 Robichaud, "Relier Québec et Montréal par le Chemin du Roy," 4.

87 McDonough, "Building the Roads," 15.

88 Rushforth, "Origins of Indian Slavery in New France," 801.

89 Ratified in 1709, Jacques Raudot's "Ordinance on the Subject of Slavery in Canada" codified slavery in New France and defined the legal characteristics of an individual's enslavement. In particular, enslaved Indigenous nations and Africans were purchased as "full property," barring them from purchasing their own title deeds for land. See Raudot, "Ordinance by Intendant Raudot on the Subject of Slavery in Canada," 13 April 1709, Centre de Quebec, Ordonnance des Intendants, E1, S1, P509, Archives nationales du Quebec.

90 Greer, *People of New France*, 55–6.

91 The largest corvée tax list is from the 1715 Montreal corvée for construction of the outer wall. The list contains names of each habitant and the days that they were required to serve but makes no mention of their status in the community. That list can be found in Ramezay, Rolles de l'Îsle de Montreal.

92 Becancourt, Pour le grand chemin de la côte et seigneurie de Saint-Anne, 18 May 1710, Fonds Grand Voyer, Cahier 1, p. 10, BANQ.

93 Bégon, Ordonnance concernent les Chemins du petit village on la seigneurie de Notre Dame, 10 June 1719, Fonds Intendant, C-13588, pp. 361–3, LAC; Bégon, 28 June 1720, Fonds Intendant, pp. 465–6 , LAC; and Bégon, 18 June 1723, Fonds Intendant, vol. 6, pp. 433–5, LAC.

94 Bégon, 13 April 1718, Ordonnance au sujet des chemins, clôtures et fossés de côtes de la Bouterillere et de la Grande-Anse, Fonds Intendant, C-13588, vol. 5, pp. 291–3, LAC.

95 Bégon, Ordonnance des principaux habitants du la paroisse de l'Ancienne Lorette concernant les chemins, 24 June 1713, Fonds Intendant, C-13588, pp. 207–9, LAC.

96 See, Bégon, Ordonnance qui porte que le pont du Trou Saint-Patry, 13 April 1722, C-13588, vol. 7, pp. 92–4, LAC; and Bégon, Ordonnance qui enjoint aux habitants de Batsican, 11 January 1723, Fonds Intendant, C-13588, vol. 7, pp. 300–2, LAC.

97 Raudot, 13 December 1709, Fonds Intendant, C-13587, pp. 223–4, LAC.
98 Bégon, Ordonnance a tous les habitants des côtes du gouvernement de Quebec, Trois-Rivières, et Montreal de balisé les chemins, 13 December 1713, Fonds Intendant, C-13588, p. 245, LAC.
99 Bégon, Ordonnance entre le sr. Perot seigneur d'Argentay concernant me procès-verbal pour les chemins, 8 July 1717, Fonds Intendant, C-13588, pp. 260–1, LAC.
100 Bégon, Ordonnance pour les habitants de la seigneurie de la Chenaye, Fonds Intendant, C-13588, p. 391, LAC.
101 Ibid.
102 Ibid.
103 Raudot, Ordonnance qui oblige chaque habitants de toutes les côtes de ce pays de une cloture long du front de son habitation, 12 March 1709, C-13587, vol. 2, pp. 417–19, LAC.
104 Bégon, Ordonnance qui Porte que chaque habitant de la baie Saint-Antoine, 4 June 1723, C-13588, vol., 7, pp. 403–4, LAC; and Bégon, Ordonnance qui enjoin aux habitants de Batiscan, 11 January 1723, C-13588, vol. 7, pp. 300–2, LAC.
105 Becancourt, Pour le grand chemin de la côte et seigneurie de Saint-Anne, 18 May 1710, LAC.
106 Bégon, Ordonnance pour les habitants de la paroisse de St Joseph on la seigneurie de Lauzon, 28 November 1719, Fonds Intendant, C-13588, pp. 386–8, LAC.
107 Bégon, 25 November 1721, Fonds Intendant, C-13588, vol. 5, pp. 445–6, LAC.
108 Bégon, Ordonnance concernant le bois nécessaire pour la construction de ponts sur les chemins, 6 March 1713, Fonds Intendant, vol. 4, p. 185, LAC.
109 Bégon, 28 June 1720, Fonds Intendant, vol. 6, pp. 315–16, LAC. See also Bégon, 7 July 1727, Fonds Intendant, vol. 8, pp. 411–16, LAC.
110 Blais, "La representation en Nouvelle France," 54.
111 Bégon, Ordonnance qui convoque une assemblée des habitants de la paroisse de Saint-Laurent, 10 April 1722, Fonds Intendant, C-13588, vol. 7, pp. 91–2, LAC.
112 Bégon, Ordonnance au sujet des chemins, clôtures et fossés des côtes de la Bouteillerie et de la Grande-Anse, 13 April 1718, Fonds Intendant, C-13588, vol. 5, pp. 291–3, LAC.
113 Bégon, Ordonnance qui convoque une assemblée des habitants de la paroisse de Saint-Laurent, 10 April 1722, Fonds Intendant, C-13588, vol. 7, pp. 91–2, LAC.
114 Bégon, Ordonnance qui Porte que le pont du Trou Saint-Patrice, 13 April 1722, Fonds Intendant, C-13588. vol. 7, pp. 92–4, LAC.
115 Gowas, *Church Architecture in New France*, 70–1.
116 See, Bégon, Ordonnance qui porte que chaque habitant de Boucherville contribuer a reconstruction de l'église, 9 September 1713, Fonds Intendant,

C-13588, vol. 4, pp. 235–7, LAC; and Bégon, Ordonnance qui commet le sieur de Tonnancour au sujet de la construction du prebytère, 7 March 1719, Fonds Intendant, C-13588, vol. 5, pp. 331–2, LAC.

117 Raudot, Ordonnance qui oblige les habitants de la Durantaye a bâtir un presbytère et un pont, 5 February 1709, C-13587, vol. 2, pp. 334–5, LAC.

118 Bégon, Ordonnance qui commet le sieur de Tonnancour au sujet de la construction du prebytère, 7 March 1719, Fonds Intendant, C-13588, vol. 5, pp. 331–2, LAC.

119 Bégon, Ordonnance pour la construction du presbytère de Champlain, 17 June 1720, Fonds Intendant, C-13588, vol. 5, pp. 449–50, LAC.

120 Bégon, Ordonnance qui porte que chaque habitant de Boucherville contribuer a reconstruction de l'église, 9 September 1713, Fonds Intendant, C-13588, vol. 4, pp. 235–7, LAC.

121 Bégon, Ordonnance qui oblige chaque habitants de l'île Dupas a fournir trente-cinq pieds de bois pour la construction du presbytère, 11 February 1716, Fonds Intendant, C-13588, vol. 5, pp. 127–8, LAC.

122 Liste de habitants oblige de fournir chacun une journée pour la eglise, Cap Santé, 15 June 1710, BANQ.

123 For example, see Bégon, Ordonnance au sujet des chemins, clôtures et fossés des côtes de la Bouteillerie et de la Grande-Anse, 13 April 1718, Fonds Intendant, C-13588, vol. 5, pp. 291–3, LAC; and Bégon, Ordonnance pour les chemins des seigneuries de Notre-Dame de Bonsecours, Port-Joly et la Grande-Anse, 22 August 1727, Fonds Intendant, C-13589, vol. 9A, pp. 459–64, LAC.

124 All of these records come from Fonds Intendant. See Raudot, Ordonnance au sujet du chemin, 2 April 1709, vol. 2, LAC; Bégon, 25 July 1717, vol. 5, pp. 263–5: 19 June 1719, vol. 5, pp. 359–61; 17 May 1720, vol. 5, pp. 422–3; 19 June 1721, vol. 6, pp. 298–300; 4 June 1722, vol. 7, pp. 130–1; 20 June 1723, vol. 7, pp. 443–4; 24 March 1725, vol. 8, pp. 309–11; and 21 June 1727, vol. 9A, pp. 377–81.

125 Bégon, Ordonnance qui oblige les habitants de l'Ancienne-Lorette de réparer incessamment le grand chemin, Fonds Intendant, vol. 4, C-13588, 207–9, LAC.

126 Bégon, Ordonnance au sujet des chemins, clôtures et fossés des côtes de la Bouteillerie et de la Grande-Anse, 13 April 1718, Fonds Intendant, C-13588, vol. 5, 291–3, LAC.

127 Bégon, 28 June 1720, Fonds Intendant, vol. 5, C-13588, 465–6, LAC.

128 2 August 1714, Royal Jurisdiction of Montreal, TL4, series 1, D1601, BANQ.

129 Bégon, 13 December 1713, Fonds Intendant, C-13588, 245, LAC.

130 Bégon, 11 January 1723, Ordonnance qui enjoint aux habitants de Batiscan, Fonds Intendant, C-13588, vol. 7, 300–2, LAC.

131 Bégon, 22 August 1727, Fonds Intendant, C-13589, vol. 9A, 459–64, LAC.

132 Chaussegros de Léry to the Minister, 20 October 1732, AC, C11A, vol. 58, 203–7, LAC.

133 Vaudreuil to the Minister, 18 May 1725, AC, C11A, vol. 47, 149–54, LAC.

134 Ibid.

135 Donald J. Horton, "Lanoullier de Boisclerc, Jean-Eustache," in *Dictionary of Canadian Biography*, vol. 3, University of Toronto/Université Laval, http://www.biographi.ca/en/bio/lanoullier_de_boisclerc_jean_eustache_3E.html.

CHAPTER TWO

1 Charles de la Boische, Marquis de Beauharnois, Extrait de Registres Tenus au Bureau du Controle de la Marine a Quebec, 12 August 1745, Archives des Colonies, C11A, vol. 84, 218–21, LAC.

2 While still a form of representation, this assembly was different from the "assembly of habitants," which was a primarily local affair in each individual parish. The assembly mentioned here instead derived from a legal tradition of having the governor and intendant call upon the city's principal residents to consult them on decisions, such as, in this instance, the construction of fortifications. See Blais, "La representation en Nouvelle France," 59–60.

3 Procés-verbal de la première assemblée des principaux officiers, négociants et habitants de Quebec au sujet de l'enceinte, 26 July 1746, AC, C11A, vol. 85, p. 76, LAC.

4 Ibid., pp. 77–8.

5 Chaussegros de Léry to the Minister, 1 October 1747, AC, C11A, vol. 89, pp. 198–203V, LAC.

6 Robichaud, "Le pouvoir, les payans et la voirie au Bas-Canada a la fin du XVIIIe siècle." See also Robichaud, "Relier Québec et Montréal par le Chemin du Roy." Orders for this type of labour began as early as Bégon, 13 April 1718, Ordonnance au sujet des chemins, clôtures et fossés de côtes de la Bouterillere et de la Grande-Anse, Fonds Intendant, C-13588, vol. 5, pp. 291–3, LAC.

7 On the Longueuil-Chambly Road see Gilles Hocquart, Ordonnance qui porte que les habitants de Longueuil travailler au chemin de Chambly, 18 July 1730, Fonds Intendant, vol. 10, C-13589, pp. 285–7, LAC; and, Beauharnois and Hocquart to the Minister, 5 October 1740, vol. 73, pp. 19–20V, LAC. For the Saint Jean-Chambly Road, see La Galissonière and Bigot to the Minister, 26 September 1748, AC, C11A, vol. 91, LAC.

8 Beauharnois to Hocquart, 15 May 1738, AC, C11A, vol. 69, pp. 13–29V, LAC.

9 Louvigny to the Minister, 21 October 1706, Québec, AC, C11A, vol. 25, 25–46, LAC.

10 The most comprehensive study of the Beauharnois and Hocquart administration remains Donald J. Horton, "Gilles Hocquart, Intendant of New France, 1729–48." Other important monographs include Hardy, *Judicial Politics in the Old Régime*; Eccles, *La Société canadienne sous le régime français*.

11 Horton, "Gilles Hocquart," 60.

12 For competition between France, Britain, and Spain, see Pagden, *Lords of All the World*, 66–7.

13 Morrissey, *Empire by Collaboration*, 4.

14 Ibid., 8.

15 White, *Voices of the Enslaved*, 7.

16 Choquette, "Center and Periphery in French North America," 200.

17 Horton, "Gilles Hocquart," 62–5.

18 Ibid., 62.

19 S. Dale Standen, "Charles de la Beauharnois," in the *Dictionary of Canadian Biography*.

20 White, *Middle Ground*, 185.

21 Standen, "Charles de la Beauharnois." On Hocquart's execution of these orders, see Horton, "Gilles Hocquart," 70–2.

22 Horton, "Gilles Hocquart," 169.

23 Hocquart, Commission qui commet et subdélègue le sieur Lanoullier de Boisclerc, 26 February 1734, Fonds Intendant, vol. 12, C-13590, pp. 216–17, LAC.

24 Horton, "Gilles Hocquart," 169.

25 Didier, "Subdélégués et subdélégations dans l'espace atlantique français," 7.

26 Hocquart, Commission qui commet et subdélègue le sieur Lanoullier de Boisclerc, 26 February 1734, Fonds Intendant, vol. 12, C-13590, pp. 216–17, LAC.

27 Didier, "Subdélégués et subdélégations dans l'espace atlantique français," 31.

28 Ibid., 249.

29 Ibid., 248.

30 Brewer, *Sinews of Power*, 69.

31 Wilson, "Rethinking the Colonial State," 1295. For scholarship on early modern European state expansion, see also Tilly, *Coercion, Capital, and European States*; and Ertman, *Birth of Leviathan*.

32 Wilson, "Rethinking the Colonial State," 1,295. See also Sen, "Uncertain Dominance,"392–406.

33 Wilson, "Rethinking the Colonial State," 1,300.

34 Beauharnois and Hocquart to the Minister, 14 October 1733, AC, C11A, vol. 60, pp. 80–4, LAC.

35 Varin to the Minister, 2 November 1748, AC, C11A, vol. 92, pp. 295–6v, LAC.

36 Beauharnois to Hocquart, 15 May 1738, AC, C11A, vol. 69, pp. 13–29v, LAC.

37 Varin to the Minister, 2 November 1748, AC, C11A, vol. 92, pp. 295–6v, LAC.

38 For the Quebec fortifications, see Louvigny to the Minister, 21 October 1706, Québec, AC, C11A, vol. 25, LAC. For the Montreal fortifications, see Gideon, Sub-Engineer, to the Minister, 19 November 1713, AC, C11A, vol. 34, pp. 114–6v, LAC; and Vaudreuil to the Minister, 16 October 1716, AC, C11A, vol. 36, pp. 81–2v, LAC.

39 Levasseur to the Minister, 12 November 1707, Québec, AC, C11A, vol. 27, LAC.

40 Bégon, Ordonnance qui oblige les habitants de l'Ancienne-Lorette de réparer incessamment le grand chemin, Fonds Intendant, vol. 4, C-13588, pp. 207–9, LAC.

41 See Grinberg, *Écrire les coutumes*; Mauclair, *La justice au village*; Thompson, "Custom Law and Common Right."

42 Bégon, Ordonnance des principaux habitants du la paroisse de l'Ancienne Lorette concernant les chemins, 24 June 1713, Fonds Intendant, C-13588, pp. 207–9, LAC.

43 Bégon, 13 April 1718, Ordonnance au sujet des chemins, clôtures et fossés de côtes de la Bouterillere et de la Grande-Anse, Fonds Intendant, C-13588, vol. 5, pp. 291–3, LAC.

44 Bégon, 28 June 1720, Fonds Intendant, vol. 6, pp. 315–6, LAC. See also Bégon, 7 July 1727, Fonds Intendant, vol. 8, pp. 411–16, LAC.

45 Scott, *Domination and the Arts of Resistance*, 45.

46 Ibid., 57.

47 Louvigny to the Minister, 21 October 1706, Québec, AC, C11A, vol. 25, pp. 24–46, LAC.

48 Conchon, *La corvée des grands Chemins au XVIIIe siècle*, 75.

49 Banks, *Chasing Empire across the Sea*, 88.

50 Conchon, *La corvée des grands Chemins au XVIIIe siècle*, 43.

51 Hocquart, Ordonnance qui porte que les habitants de Longueuil travailler au chemin de Chambly, 18 July 1730, Fonds Intendant, vol. 10, C-13589, pp. 285–7, LAC.

52 Vaudreuil to the Council of the Marine, 17 October 1717, Quebec, C11A, vol. 38, pp. 121–4v, LAC.

53 Hocquart, Ordonnance qui porte que les habitants de Longueuil travailler au chemin de Chambly, 18 July 1730, Fonds Intendant, vol. 10, C-13589, pp. 285–7, LAC.

54 Robichaud, "Relier Québec et Montréal par le Chemin du Roy," 4–5.

55 Boisclerc, Procès-verbal pour la réparation des ponts de la seigneurie de Beauport, 26 February 1731, Cahier 2, p. 23; Boisclerc, Procès-verbal au sujet des ponts qui sont sur le grand chemin qui conduit de la ville de Quebec à l'Ancienne-Lorette, 17 March 1731, Cahier 2, p. 33; Boisclerc, Procès-verbal au sujet des ponts qui sont sur le grand chemin qui conduit de la ville de Quebec a Saint-Jean, Sainte-Foy, et a la rivière de Cap-Rogue, 18 March 1731, Cahier 2, p. 19; Boisclerc, Procès-verbal règle et plaque un chemin royal en les seigneuries de Gatineau, de la Grand-Rivière-Yamachiche et de a la Petite-Rivière-Yamachiche, 5 June 1732, Cahier 5, p. 33. All in Fonds Grand Voyer, BANQ.

56 Hocquart, Lettres de provisions par Sa Majesté de la charge de grand voyer

de la Nouvelle-France, 10 April 1731, Cahier 2, Fonds Grand Voyer, Cahier 1, BANQ.

57 On an extensive discussion of the grand voyer, see Robichaud, "Relier Québec et Montréal par le Chemin du Roy," 6–7.

58 Hocquart, Résumé d'une lettre de Hocquart datée du 10 Octobre 1732, 5 January 1733, AC, C11A, vol. 58, pp. 243–7v, LAC.

59 Beauharnois and Hocquart to the Minister, 14 October 1733, AC, C11A, vol. 60, pp. 80–4, LAC.

60 For Charlesbourg, Raudot, 2 April 1709, Fonds Intendant, vol. 2, C-13587, pp. 463–6, LAC; for Cap Rogue, Raudot, 7 July 1713, Fonds Intendant, vol. 4, pp. 212–14, LAC; for Beauport, Bégon, 10 June 1719, Fonds Intendant, vol. 5, C-13588, pp. 361–2, LAC; for l'Ancienne Lorette, Bégon, 11 June 1720, Fonds Intendant, vol. 5, C-13588, pp. 426–30, LAC.

61 For Neuville, Raudot, 7 July 1713, Fonds Intendant, vol. 4, pp. 212–4, LAC; for l'Ange-Gardien, Bégon, 27 March 1727, vol. 9A, C-13589, pp. 138–43, LAC.

62 For La Durantaye, Bégon, 28 June 1721, Fonds Intendant, vol. 6, C-13588, pp. 315–17, LAC; for Lauzon, Bégon, 28 November 1719, Fonds Intendant, vol. 5, C-13588, pp. 386–8, for Saint-Nicolas, Bégon, 25 October 1721, Fonds Intendant, vol. 6, C-13588, pp. 429–31, LAC.

63 For Montreal, Raudot, 10 June 1709, Fonds Intendant, vol. 3, C-13587, pp. 55–7, LAC; for Lachenaie and Longueuil, Bégon, 17 January 1723, Fonds Intendant, vol. 7, C-13588, pp. 313–5 LAC; for Boucherville and Varennes, Bégon, 19 June 1724, Fonds Intendant, vol. 8, C-13588, pp. 171–3, LAC.

64 All statistics derive from "Le Recensement des Gouvernments de Montreal et de Trois-Rivièries," in *Rapport de l'Archiviste de la province de Québec*, 1936–37, 1–200. In addition, see Greer, *Peasant, Lord, and Merchant*, 21.

65 Boisclerc to the Minister, 28 October 1736, AC, C11A, vol. 36, pp. 121–4v, LAC.

66 Hocquart, Résumé d'une lettre de Hocquart datée du 10 Octobre 1732, 5 January 1733, AC, C11A, vol. 58, pp. 243–7v, LAC.

67 Beauharnois and Hocquart to the Minister, 14 October 1733, AC, C11A, vol. 60, pp. 80–4, LAC.

68 Ibid.

69 Hocquart, Résumé d'une lettre de Hocquart datée du 10 Octobre 1732, 5 January 1733, AC, C11A, vol. 58, pp. 243–7v, LAC.

70 Beauharnois and Hocquart to the Minister, 14 October 1733, AC, C11A, vol. 60, pp. 80–4, LAC.

71 Ibid.

72 Boisclerc to the Minister, 28 October 1736, AC, C11A, vol. 36, pp. 121–4v, LAC.

73 Ibid.

74 Beauharnois and Hocquart to the Minister, 14 October 1733, AC, C11A, vol. 60, pp. 80–4, LAC.

75 Boisclerc to the Minister, 28 October 1736, AC, C11A, vol. 36, pp. 121–4v, LAC.

76 Ibid.

77 For reference, see Boisclerc, Procès-verbal de Boisclerc au sujet des ponts de la seigneurie de Boucherville, 1 February 1732; Boisclerc, Procès-verbal tracer un nouveau chemin sur la seigneurie de Verchères, 2 February 1732; Procès-verbal Boisclerc, marque le chemin royal de la seigneurie de Champlain, 30 May 1732. All in Fonds Grand Voyer, BANQ.

78 Boisclerc to the Minister, 28 October 1736, AC, C11A, vol. 36, pp. 121–4v, LAC.

79 Beauharnois and Hocquart to the Minister, 14 October 1733, AC, C11A, vol. 60, pp. 80–4, LAC.

80 Boisclerc to the Minister, 28 October 1736, AC, C11A, vol. 36, pp. 121–4v, LAC.

81 Beauharnois and Hocquart to the Minister, 14 October 1733, AC, C11A, vol. 60, pp. 80–4, LAC.

82 Ibid.

83 Hocquart, Ordonnance qui oblige tous les habitants du gouvernement de Montreal de traviller, Fonds Intendant, vol. 15, C-13590, pp. 369–71, LAC.

84 Beauharnois to Hocquart, 15 May 1738, AC, C11A, vol. 69, pp. 13–29v, LAC.

85 Beauharnois and Hocquart to the Minister, 5 October 1740, AC, C11A, vol. 73, pp. 19–20v, LAC.

86 Hocquart to the Minister, 28 September 1740, AC, C11A, vol. 73, pp. 105–9, LAC.

87 Beauharnois and Hocquart to the Minister, 5 October 1740, AC, C11A, vol. 73, pp. 19–20v, LAC.

88 Beauharnois to Hocquart, 15 May 1738, AC, C11A, vol. 69, pp. 13–29v, LAC.

89 Vallette de Chévigny to the Minister, 12 September 1738, AC, C11A, vol. 72, pp. 248–9v, LAC.

90 Beauharnois and Hocquart to the Minister, 5 October 1738, vol. 69, pp. 39–43, LAC. In addition, see Boisclerc, "Plan des terres des environs du fort Saint-Frédéric," 1739, AC, C11A, vol. 126 and AC, C11B, vol. 39, LAC.

91 Beauharnois to Hocquart, 15 May 1738, AC, C11A, vol. 69, pp. 13–29v, LAC.

92 Ibid.

93 Ibid.

94 Ibid.

95 Vallette de Chévigny to the Minister, 12 September 1738, AC, C11A, vol. 72, pp. 248–9v, LAC.

96 Chaussegros de Léry to the Minister, 7 November 1744, AC, C11A, LAC; on corvée, see La Galissonière and Bigot to the Minister, 26 September 1748, AC, C11A, vol. 91, LAC.

97 Jacques Raudot, Ordonnance qui oblige habitants du gouvernement de Montreal pour la bâtisse en pierre du fort de Chambly, 16 November 1709, Fonds Intendant, vol. 3, C-13587, pp. 196–8, LAC.

98 Beauharnois and Hocquart to the Minister, 5 October 1740, AC, C11A, vol. 73, pp. 19–20v, LAC.

99 Ibid. For the defensive capabilities of the Richelieu, see Varin to the Minister, 2 November 1748, AC, C11A, vol. 92, pp. 295–6v, LAC.

100 Beauharnois and Hocquart to the Minister, 5 October 1740, AC, C11A, vol. 73, pp. 19–20v, LAC.

101 Ibid.

102 Ibid.

103 La Galissonière and Bigot to the Minister, 26 September 1748, AC, C11A, vol. 91, pp. 40–5, LAC.

104 Ibid.

105 Ibid.

106 Boisclerc to the Minister, 5 November 1748, AC, C11A, vol. 89, pp. 220–1v, LAC.

107 Josué Dubois Berthelot de Beaucours, Mémoire de Beaucours concernant les defenses du gouvernement de Montréal, 1744, AC, C11A, vol. 78, pp. 317–7v, LAC.

108 Ibid.

109 Beauharnois and Hocquart to the Minister, September–October 1745, AC, C11A, vol. 83, pp. 3–36v, LAC.

110 Beauharnois, Extrait de Registres Tenus au Bureau du Controle de la Marine a Quebec, 12 August 1745, Archives des Colonies, C11A, vol. 84, pp. 218–21, LAC.

111 Ibid.

112 Ibid.

113 Ibid.

114 Procés-verbal de la première assemblée des principaux officiers, négociants et habitants de Quebec au sujet de l'enceinte, 26 July 1746, AC, C11A, vol. 85, p. 76, LAC.

115 Ibid., pp. 77–8.

116 Procés-verbal de la première assemblée des principaux officiers, négociants et habitants de Quebec au sujet de l'enceinte, 12 August AC, C11A, vol. 85, pp. 77–8, LAC.

117 Chaussegros de Léry to the Minister, 10 October 1747, AC, C11A, vol. 89, pp. 198–203v, LAC.

118 Ibid.

119 "D'espenses a occasional guerre, 1746 et 1747," AC, C11A, vol. 88, p. 206, LAC.

120 "Mémoir pour MM. de Plaine et Cerry," 21 July 1744, Fonds Intendant, vol. 17, C-13591, pp. 379–81, LAC.

121 Ibid.

122 "D'espenses a l'occasion de la guerre, 1746 et 1747," AC, C11A, vol. 88, p. 206, LAC.

123 Information on the function of the cajeux are taken from MacLeod, *Northern Armageddon*, 22–6. References to corvée on cajeux and signal fires initially derives from Dechêne, *Le Peuple*, 337.

124 Habitants were responsible for wood collection and aiding in the transport of materials, not for the sailing of the cajeux, or "brûlots," the fire-ships. Captains and their crews volunteered to sail the cajeux and "brûlots" close to the enemy ships before abandoning them. This information comes from, Chaussegrous de Léry to the Minister, 13 November 1746, AC, C11A, vol. 86, AC, C11A, pp. 250–51v, LAC.

125 Hocquart, "Cajeux d'artifice," 1747, AC, C11A, vol. 88, p. 201, LAC.

126 Ibid.

127 Anderson, *Crucible of War*, 55.

128 Nicolai, "Different Kind of Courage," 60. See also Crouch, *Nobility Lost*, 82.

129 Nerich, "Le system de defense de la Nouvelle-France face a la Guerre de la Conquete,"284.

130 Nicolai, "Different Kind of Courage," 59.

131 Crouch, *Nobility Lost*, 71.

132 Stanley, *Canada's Soldiers*, 23. The role of Canadian militia workers is also supported by Nicolai, "Different Kind of Courage," 63.

133 This included a great many language groups and communities in Canada, British America, and First Nations territory. In particular, Christian Crouch notes the Hurons, Nipissing, Kahnawake, Kanesatake, Odanak, Oswegatchie in addition to the Ottawas, Ojibwas, and Menominees. See Crouch, *Nobility Lost*, 2.

134 Ibid, 74.

135 Procès-verbal de Pierre de Lino, réparer le pont qui est sur la rivière de Portneuf, September, 24 1754, Fonds Grand Voyer, Cahier 6, p. 41, BANQ.

136 Procès-verbal de Pierre de Lino, marque un chemin de sortie pour la quatrième concession de Saint-Michel, 22 December 1755, Cahier 6, p. 42, BANQ; and Procès-verbal de Pierre de Lino, trace un chemin de la sixième concession a la Saint Charles de la Rivière-Boyer, 20 April 1757, Fonds Grand Voyer, Cahier 6, p. 44, BANQ.

137 Procès-verbal de Pierre de Lino, marque un chemin de vignt-quatre pieds de large entre deux fossés pour communiquer, 26 July 1757, Fonds Grand Voyer, Cahier 6, p. 50, BANQ.

138 Procès-verbal de Pierre de Lino, marque un chemin sur le travers des terres dans la seconde concession, 1 August 1757 Fonds Grand Voyer, Cahier 6, p. 52, BANQ.

139 Louis Antoine de Bougainville, Mémoire de Bougainville sur l'Etat de la Nouvelle France a l'époque de la Guerre de Sept Ans 1757 (1790), p. 595, LAC.

140 Crouch, *Nobility Lost*, 71–2.

141 Nerich, "Le system de defense de la Nouvelle-France face a la Guerre de la Conquete," 284.

142 Dechêne, *Le Peuple*, 334.

143 For Carillon, see Dechêne, *Le Peuple*, 372. The bunkers are listed in the document Lévis, Lettre du chevalier de Lévis au maréchal duc de Belle-Isle, Collection des manuscripts du maréchal de Lévis, vol. 12, p. 413, LAC. See also Lévis à Bourlamaque, au sujet des travaux, vol. 3, pp. 257–60, LAC. On habitants contributing to the fortifications on the Ile-aux-Noix, see Lévis, 30 Juin 1759, *Journal des Campagnes*, 182.

144 Rene Chartrand, "La milice Canadienne et la Guerre de Sept Ans," in Fonck and Veyssières, *La Guerre de Sept Ans en Nouvelle France*, 294.

145 Lévis, 18 Octobre 1758, *Journal des Campagnes*, 157.

146 Dechêne, *Le Peuple*, 372.

147 Vaudrueil to the Minister, 4 November 1758, C11A, vol. 103, p. 302, LAC.

148 Dechêne, *Le Peuple*, 373.

149 Memoir on Canada, 1759, C11A, F-104, pp. 462–71, LAC.

CHAPTER THREE

1 Murray, November 1759, James Murray Collection (hereafter JMC), series 3, C-2225, pp. 6–7, LAC. See also Laberge, "Le régime seigneurial après la Conquête," 326.

2 Plans for maintaining or removing French Canadian Catholic priests derive from a comprehensive legal inquiry conducted in 1767. See Elie de Beaumont, Target, and Rouche, "Opinions of three Eminent Lawyers of Paris prepared at the Request of the Canadian Authorities, as to the Legality of certain Clauses and Conditions commonly inserted in Titles to Seigniorial Lands," 14 February 1767, *DST*, 201, 218–26.

3 Adam Mabane, Thomas Dunn, Francis Mounier, and J. Goldstan, Council Chamber, 2 December 1765, Reports of the Councils of Quebec relating to Highways, Roads, and Bridges (hereafter RCQ), submissions to the Highways Committee of the Executive Council by the Grand Voyers, 1765–91, Councils of the Province of Quebec, RG1, E1, vol. 106, LAC.

4 Sir Henry Cavendish, "Examination of Frances Maseres," in Government of Canada, *Debates of the House of Commons in the Year 1774 on the Bill for Making More Provision for the Government of the Province of Quebec* (hereafter *DHC*), 133.

5 Stanwood, *Empire Reformed*, 6.

6 Armitage, *Ideological Origins of the British Empire*, 9.

7 Calloway, *Scratch of a Pen*, 17.

8 Gould, *Persistence of Empire*, 120.

9 Ibid., 133.

10 Brewer, *Sinews of Power*, 91.
11 Ibid., 35–6.
12 Ibid., 69.
13 Ibid., 51.
14 Bollettino, "Black Soldiers and the British Empire," 511.
15 Ward, "Army of Servants," 79.
16 Anderson, *Crucible of War*, 139.
17 Ibid., 308–9.
18 Ibid., 362–5.
19 Murray, November 1759, JMC, series 3, C-2225, pp. 6–7, LAC.
20 Ibid.
21 Ibid.
22 Murray to Hussey, Commanding the Detachment at Lorette, 20 November 1759, JMC, series 3, p. 11, LAC.
23 Ibid.
24 Murray, Instructions to Leslie, November 1759, JMC, series 3, p. 15, LAC.
25 Murray to Hussey, Commanding the Detachment at Lorette, 20 November 1759, JMC, LAC.
26 Murray, Instructions to Walsh, November 1759, JMC, series 3, p. 9, LAC.
27 Dechêne, *Le Peuple*, 259.
28 On Trois Rivières, see Lévis, *Journal des Campagnes*, 242; on the southern parishes of Quebec, see ibid., 238.
29 Lévis, "Instructions concernant l'ordre dans lequel les milices attachées a chaque battaillon seront formées pour camper et server pendant la campagne," in Lévis, *Journal des Campagnes*, 251.
30 Ibid., 248.
31 Eccles, "Lévis, François de, Duc de Lévis," in *Dictionary of Canadian Biography*, vol. 4, University of Toronto/Université Laval, 2003, http://www.biographi.ca/en/bio/levis_francois_de_4E.html.
32 Amherst, article 34, extracts from the Articles of Capitulation of Montreal, 8 September 1760, *DST*, 193.
33 Ibid.
34 Ibid., 194.
35 Return of the Number of Souls in the Several Parishes belonging to the Government of Quebec, 1761, submitted by James Murray to Parliament, Great Britain, Colonial Office Papers of Quebec (hereafter CO), reel 2, 1761–64; and "Le Recensement des Gouvernments de Montreal et de Trois-Rivièries," in *Rapport de l'Archiviste de la province de Québec*, 1936–7, pp. 1–200.
36 Return of the Number of Souls in the Several Parishes belonging to the Government of Quebec, 1761, submitted by James Murray to Parliament, Great Britain, reel 2, 1761–64, Colonial Office, Canada, Original Correspondence, Quebec Co42, p. 6, CO.

37 James Murray to William Pitt, Quebec, 13 May 1761, Great Britain, Colonial Office, Canada, Original Correspondence, Quebec Co42, reel 2, pp. 7–8, CO.
38 The concept of "legibility" derives from Scott, *Seeing Like a State.*
39 Murray, The State of the Government of Quebec, 1762, mss. 21667, reel 4, p. 1, HP.
40 Gage, The State of the Government of Montreal, 1762, mss. 21667, reel 4, p. 43, HP.
41 Haldimand, Return of the Canadian Inhabitants Settled in the Town and Government of Three Rivers in May 1763, reel 10, p. 16, HP.
42 Return of the Number of Souls in the Several Parishes belonging to the Government of Quebec, 1761, submitted by James Murray to Parliament, Great Britain, reel 2, 1761–64, p. 16, CO.
43 Ibid.
44 Murray, The State of the Government of Quebec, 1762, mss. 21667, reel 4, p. 7, HP.
45 Ibid.
46 Ibid.
47 Ibid.
48 Ibid.
49 James Murray, report of General James Murray on the State of Canada under the French Administration, 5 June 1762, *DST*, 199.
50 Ibid.
51 Ibid., 200.
52 Ibid.
53 Gage, The State of the Government of Montreal, 1762, mss. 21667, reel 4, p. 44, HP.
54 Ibid., p. 45.
55 Ibid.
56 Ibid.
57 Ibid.
58 Ibid.
59 Ibid., p. 46.
60 All statistics derive from "Le Recensement des Gouvernments de Montreal et de Trois-Rivières," in Rapport de l'Archiviste de la province de Québec, 1936–37, 1–200.
61 Laberge, "Le régime seigneurial après la Conquête," 329.
62 Jean Baptiste Nicolas Roch de Ramezay, Liste des habitants de Sorel et de leurs redevances en 1761–3, Fonds de la familie de Ramezay, 1532–42, LAC.
63 Amherst, article 34, Extracts from the Articles of Capitulation of Montreal, 8 September 1760, *DST*, 193–4.
64 Haldimand, The Present State of the Government of Three Rivers in Canada, reel 10, pp. 2–17, HP.

65 Ibid.
66 Ibid.
67 Haldimand to the Lords Commissioners for Trade and Plantations, The Present State of the Government of Three Rivers in Canada, in answer to the Heads of Enquiry, relative to the State of Canada, Whitehall, 9 March 1763, 1776, 1758–84, mss. 21682-2, 21681, papers relating to the Government of Three Rivers in Canada, and to the ironworks in that district, reel 10, HP.
68 Haldimand, Return of the Canadian Inhabitants Settled in the Town and Government of Three Rivers in May 1763, reel 10, p. 16, HP.
69 Cooper, *Enslavement of Africans in Canada*, 13.
70 Raudot, Mémorie de Raudot, 1708, Archives des Colonies, series C11G, Correspondence général, F-421, pp. 66–9v, LAC.
71 The translation of this article in the Capitulation derives from Cooper, *Enslavement of Africans in Canada*, 13. The original treaty can be found at "Articles de Capitulation," 8 September 1761, C11A, vol. 105, pp. 155–6, LAC.
72 Greer, *Peasant, Lord, and Merchant*, 23–4.
73 Ibid., 24.
74 Green, *Constitutional Origins of the American Revolution*, 67.
75 Ibid., 65.
76 Ibid., 64.
77 "Instructions to Governor James Murray concerning the Granting of Lands in Canada," 7 December 1763, *DST*, 213,
78 Ibid.
79 Ibid., 214.
80 Ibid., 214–15.
81 Haldimand, The Present State of the Government of Three Rivers in Canada, reel 10, HP; and Haldimand, Return of Wood Received from the Different Parishes, reel 10, HP. Implicit instructions were given by Parliament in "Instructions to Governor James Murray concerning the Granting of Lands in Canada," 7 December 1763, *DST*, 214.
82 Ibid., 213.
83 Ibid.
84 Ibid., 214.
85 Samson, *Forges of Saint-Maurice*, 15.
86 Ibid., 24. Similar draft labour and corvée would also be used by the British after the Conquest. The actual mining of iron ore was done by day labourers hired for that specific purpose, while habitants in the neighbouring parishes provided corvée for logging and the transportation of that timber.
87 Vaudreuil, summary of a letter from Vaudreuil regarding the government of Trois-Rivières, June 1750, C11A, p. 241, LAC.
88 Ibid.
89 In the early 1750s, the British construction of fortifications in the Ohio Coun-

try signalled a move towards challenging French diplomatic supremacy in the region. See Balvay, "Les forts du Pays d'en Haut et de Louisiane pendant la guerre de sept ans," 227.

90 "Instruction to Governor James Murray concerning the Granting of Lands in Canada," 7 December 1763, *DST*, 214–15.

91 Ibid., 214.

92 Haldimand, The Present State of the Government of Three Rivers in Canada, reel 10, pp. 2–19, HP.

93 Ibid.

94 Samson, *Forges du Saint-Maurice.*

95 "Account of the Expences Made at the Forge of St Maurice from the first day of October 1760 to the last day of December 1761," reel 10, mss. 21681, 67, HP. In the eighteenth century, a "batteaux" referred to a flat-bottom wooden vessel used to navigate streams, rivers, and lakes. "Battoe Men" were skilled in the navigation of these vessels on North American rivers. I have maintained the eighteenth-century spelling of "batteaux." In the modern French language, "bateau" translates into "boat."

96 Ibid.

97 This analysis is taken from a number of wage lists submitted to the governor of Quebec. In particular, "Expenses of the Forges of St. Maurice, 1762," 38–40, "The State of Expenses from the Forges, June 1764," and "The Expenses of the Forges of St. Maruice from the 1st of June to the last Day of August 1764," in reel 10, mss. 21681, pp. 131–2, HP.

98 "Expenses of the Forges of St. Maruice from the 12th day of July to the last day of December 1762," reel 10, mss. 21681, p. 97, HP.

99 "Expenses of the Forges of St. Maruice from the 25th day of October 1763 to the last day of May 1764," reel 10, mss. 21681, p. 120, HP.

100 "Etat de la depense faite aux forges of St. Maruice depuis le 22nd Octobre, 1763 jusqu'au premier Juin 1764," reel 10, mss. 21681, p. 123, HP.

101 All information on wage labourers, their tasks, and wages derive from "Etat de la depense faite aux forges St. Maurice depuis le 22nd Octobre, 1763 jusqu'au premier Juin 1764," reel 10, mss. 21681, p. 123, HP.

102 Receipt from Lt Gage, Secretary to the Government of Trois-Rivières, 31 August 1764, reel 10, mss. 21681, p. 130, HP. Expenses for bateaux men were allocated from 1762 to 1765 and are included in the wage lists.

103 "Etat de la depense faite aux forges St. Maurice depuis le 22nd Octobre, 1763 jusqu'au premier Juin 1764," reel 10, mss. 21681, p. 123, HP.

104 Return of Wood Received from the Different Parishes, reel 10, mss. 21681, p. 50, HP.

105 Ibid.

106 Account of the expenses made at the Forge of St. Maurice from the first day of October 1760 to the last day of December 1761, 67, HP.

107 Murray to the Justices of the Peace of the District of Montreal, 9 October 1765, JMC, series 3, p. 199, LAC.

108 The dispute is covered in depth by Scott, "Civil and Military Authority in Canada," 131–3.

109 Murray to the Justices of the Peace of the District of Montreal, 9 October 1765, JMC, series 3, p. 199, LAC. Scott covers the "specific circumstances" in Scott, "Civil and Military Authority in Canada," 132.

110 Murray to Samuel Martin, Quebec, 28 August 1761, JMC, series 3, 107, LAC; Murray to the Barracks Master, 10 February 1765, JMC, p. 210, LAC; Murray to Captain Carden, 2 December 1765, JMC, p. 288, LAC.

111 Murray to Major General Burton, 17 October 1765, JMC, series 3, p. 206, LAC.

112 Ibid.

113 Murray to the Justices of the Peace of the District of Montreal, 9 October 1765, JMC, series 3, p. 201, LAC.

114 Ibid., p. 199.

115 Ibid.

116 Murray to Major General Burton, 17 October 1765, JMC, series 3, p. 205, LAC.

117 Murray to the Justices of the Peace of the District of Montreal, 9 October 1765, JMC, series 3, p. 201, LAC.

118 Ibid.

119 Ibid., p. 202.

120 Ibid.

121 Ibid.

122 The British Office of the Grand Voyer exhibited some of the more unique legacies of the conquest. While it left several offices in place regarding the administration of the colony, the grand voyer was one of the most pervasive and intimate: the appointee gained full authority over the mobilization of rural labour and redirected roads to generate an imperial communication network in the province of Quebec. The routine of mobilizing corvée was also one of the longest-lasting forms of seigneurial obligation, remaining in place, mostly unaltered, until the 1856 abolition of feudal tenure.

123 Adam Mabane, Thomas Dunn, Francis Mounier, and J. Goldstan, Council Chamber, 2 December 1765, Reports of the Councils of Quebec relating to Highways, Roads, and Bridges, submissions to the Highways Committee of the Executive Council by the Grand Voyers, 1765–91, Councils of the Province of Quebec, RG1, E1, vol. 106, LAC.

124 Several documents relate to the discussion of maintaining corvée and the Office of the Grand Voyer. See Adam Mabane, Council Chamber, November 1765, "Consider Representation of the Surveyor of Roads," RCQ, LAC; Observations made by the Surveyors of the Highways, 26 November 1765, RCQ,

LAC; and "Instruction to Governor James Murray concerning the Granting of Lands in Canada," 7 December 1763, *DST*, 207.

125 Observations made by the Surveyors of the Highways, 26 November 1765, RCQ, LAC.

126 "Instruction to Governor James Murray concerning the Granting of Lands in Canada," 7 December 1763, *DST*, 207.

127 Murray, The State of the Government of Quebec, 1762, reel 4, mss. 21667, p. 7, HP.

128 The *Côte Nord* included Quebec City and all immediate environs, giving Cugnet jurisdiction over the largest population centre in the province.

129 François-Joseph Cugnet, Procès-verbal sur l'état du chemin de la Petite-Rivière, 1 May 1762, Fonds Grand Voyer, BANQ.

130 Observations made by the Surveyors of the Highways, 20 November 1765, RCQ, LAC.

131 For Charlesbourg, 15 May 1762, 17 May 1762, and 19 May 1762; for Cap-Rogue, 18 May 1762; for Porte de Saint-Louis, 18 May 1762. All in Fonds Grand Voyer, BANQ.

132 For May 1762, see 14 May La Petite-Rivière; 15 May Charlesbourg; 17 May Bourg-Royal; 18 May Cap-Rogue; 19 May Charlesbourg; 21 May Saint Foy et Saint Jean de Quebec; 23 May, la Petite Rivière; 24 May, General order for Quebec; 26 May, Beauport; 27 May, Charlesbourg; 31 May, Charlesbourg. For June 1762, see 2 June, Charlesbourg; 2 June, La Canardière; 7 June chemin de la Suère; 9 June, Saint Gabriel et Saint Jean; 11 June, Saint Augustin; 15 June, la Peitite-Rivière; 16 June, l'Ancienne-Lorette; 16 June, la Petite-Rivière; 22 June, Portneuf. All in Fonds Grand Voyer, BANQ.

133 Cugnet, Procès-verbal aux capitaines de malice du gouvernement de Quebec, 24 May 1765, Fonds Grand Voyer, BANQ.

134 Jacques Raudot, Mémorie de Raudot, 1708, Archives des Colonies, Series C11G, Correspondance général, F-421, pp. 66–9v, LAC.

135 Cugnet, Procès-verbal a la demande et du consentment des habitants de Saint-Charles, 14 August 1762; Cugnet, Procès-verbal qui a la rèquistion des habitants du village Saint Joseph, 29 August 1762. Both in Fonds Grand Voyer, BANQ.

136 Cugnet, Ordre de Cugnet aux corvées générale de habitants de la Peitite-Rivière, 16 June 1762, Fonds Grand Voyer, BANQ.

137 Observations made by the Surveyors of the Highways, 20 November 1765, RCQ, LAC.

138 Retaining the Grand Voyer and customs of corvée is in line with other French customs that the British maintained at the local level. See Donald Fyson, "The Quebec Act and the Canadiens: The Myth of the Seminal Moment," in Furstenberg and Hubert, *Entangling the Quebec Act*, 83.

139 Observations made by the Surveyors of the Highways, 20 November 1765, RCQ, LAC.
140 Ibid.
141 Adam Mabane, 27 November 1765, RCQ, LAC.
142 Observations made by the Surveyors of the Highways, article 2, Ferries of the Rivers, 20 November, 1765, RCQ, LAC.
143 Ibid.
144 Ibid.
145 See Bégon, Ordonnance qui porte que le pont du Trou Saint-Patry, 13 April 1722, C-13588, vol. 7, pp. 92–4, LAC; and Bégon, Ordonnance qui enjoint aux habitants de Batsican, 11 January 1723, Fonds Intendant, C-13588, vol. 7, pp. 300–2, LAC.
146 Observations made by the Surveyors of the Highways, article 7, Summer-Winter Roads, 20 November 1765, RCQ, LAC.
147 Ibid.
148 Ibid.
149 Ibid.
150 Mabane, Dunn, Mounier, and Goldstan, Council Chamber, 2 December 1765, RCQ, LAC.
151 Ibid.
152 Fyson, *Magistrates, Police, and People*, 10.
153 Ibid.
154 Adam Mabane, 27 November 1765, RCQ, LAC.
155 Ibid.
156 Haldimand, Account of the Expenses made at the forge of St Maurice, reel 10, p. 67, HP.
157 Mabane, Dunn, Mounier, and Goldstan, Council Chamber, 2 December 1765, RG E1, RCQ, LAC.
158 Ibid.
159 Ibid.
160 Ibid.
161 Ibid.
162 Mabane, Dunn, Mounier, and Goldstan, Council Chamber, 2 December 1765, RCQ, LAC.
163 Ibid.
164 Bégon, Ordonnance au sujet des chemins, clôtures et fossés des côtes de la Bouteillerie et de la Grande-Anse, 13 April 1718, Fonds Intendant, C-13588, vol. 5, 291–3; and Bégon, 28 June 1720, Fonds Intendant, vol. 5, C-13588, pp. 465–6, LAC.
165 Mabane, Dunn, Mounier, and Goldstan, Council Chamber, 2 December 1765, RCQ, LAC.
166 Ibid.

167 Petition de seigneurs de St. Michel et Beaumont et de Lauzon et les habitants, 21 November 1767, RG1, E1, vol. 106, p. 252v, RCQ, LAC.

168 Petition submitted by Stephen Moore, John Franks, Peter Faneuil, Inhabitants of the Lower Town, 14 November 1767, RCQ, LAC.

169 Petition de seigneur Michel Chartier de Lotbinière au sujet d'un chemin dans la seigneurie de Vaudreuil, 19 December 1767, vol. 106, RCQ, LAC.

170 Petition de Charles Doyon et Joseph Praux et les habitants de la Nouvelle Beauce, December 1767, vol. 106, RCQ, LAC.

171 Cugnet, Réglement pour le retablissement entretien et reparation des a rues dans les villas et auburns, et des chemins dans les campagnes, 5 December 1767, RG1, E1, vol. 106, 253–8, RCQ, LAC.

172 Cugnet, Réglement pour le retablissement entretien et reparation de sa rues dans les villas, pp. 253–8, RCQ, LAC.

173 Ibid.

174 Ibid.

175 On French civil law, see Carleton's inquiry into French custom, Elie de Beaumont, Target, and Rouchet, "Opinions of three Eminent Lawyers of Paris prepared at the Request of the Canadian Authorities, as to the Legality of certain clauses and Conditions commonly inserted in Titles to Seigniorial Lands, February 14, 1767," *DST*, 218–26. Carleton's thoughts on English common law derive from Guy Carleton, "Despatch of Governor Carleton to the Earl of Shelburne regarding the Administration of English Law in Canada, 24 December 1767," *DST*, 227–3.

176 On the Stamp Act protests and the British Empire, see Greene, *Peripheries and Center*; Gould, *Persistence of Empire*; and Breen, *Marketplace of Revolution.*

CHAPTER FOUR

1 Preamble, "An Act for making more effectual Provision for the Government of the Province of Quebec in North America," 7 October 1774, transcribed by Yale Law School, the Avalon Project: Documents in Law, History, and Diplomacy, Lillian Goldman Law Library.

2 Green, *Constitutional Origins of the American Revolution*, 149.

3 For the imperial crisis in the Anglo-American colonies, see Greene, *Peripheries and Center*; Breen, *Marketplace of Revolution*; McConville, *King's Three Faces*; and Carp, *Rebels Rising*. On the ideological underpinnings of the British Empire and imperial law, see Armitage, *Ideological Origins of the British Empire*, 9. See also Pagden, *Lords of All the World*.

4 On the inter-imperial political consequences, see Calloway, *Scratch of a Pen*. See also Baugh, *Global Seven Years' War*. The economic instability caused by the regime change was detailed in the last chapter. See Samson, *Forges of Saint-Maurice*; Murray to the Justices of the Peace of the District of Montreal,

9 October 1765, JMC, series 3, p. 199, LAC; Murray to Samuel Martin, Quebec, 28 August 1761, JMC, series 3, p. 107, LAC; Murray to the Barracks Master, 10 February 1765, JMC, p. 210, LAC; Murray to Captain Carden, 2 December 1765, JMC, p. 288, LAC.

5 Anderson, *Crucible of War*, 481. Anderson also discusses Parliament's solutions to replenish the treasury in the chapter entitled "Crisis and Reform: An Urgent Search for Order," 564.

6 Pagden, *Lords of All the World*, 130.

7 Carp, *Rebels Rising*, 9.

8 Ibid.

9 Carleton, "A tous les Capitaines et autres Officers commandans les Milices dans la Province de Quebec, &c.," 19 October 1775, *Quebec Gazette*.

10 Articles 34 and 37 in the Capitulation of Montreal secure land ownership under seigneurial law and the feudal obligations that habitants owed their seigneur. In the Treaty of Paris, article 4 passes all "sovereignty, property, possession, and all rights" in French Canada to the king of Britain. Article 4 also granted Canadians the liberty to practise Catholicism. See *The Definitive Treaty of Peace and Friendship between his Britannick Majesty and Most Christian King, and the King of Spain* (Treaty of Paris, 1763), Yale Avalon Project: Documents in Law, History, and Diplomacy, Lillian Goldman Law Library.

11 Elliott, *Empires of the Atlantic World*, 318. Armitage, *Ideological Origins of the British Empire*, 9.

12 Brunsman, *Evil Necessity*, 37–8.

13 Ibid., 38.

14 Gould, *Persistence of Empire*, 124–5.

15 Pagden, *Lords of All the World*, 130–1.

16 "Chapitre VIII, Démembrement de Fief, Article I," in *An Abstract of Those Parts*, 25–6.

17 The English used "alienation of land," or "*res nullius*," to seize property in Ireland, the Caribbean, and North America. On Ireland, see Canny, "Ideology of English Colonization: From Ireland to America." On property in the Americas, Stephen Arons, "Rights in the Woods on the Trans-Appalachian Frontier," and Jane T. Merritt, "Metaphor, Meaning, and Misunderstanding "Language and Power on the Pennsylvania Frontier," in Clayton and Teute, *Contact Point*. For a brief discussion of English land speculation strategies, see Seed, *Ceremonies of Possession*.

18 Beauharnois, Ordonnance qui commet le sieur Levasseur, chef de construction des vaisseaux, 26 January 1740, Fonds Intendant, vol. 15, C-13590, pp. 257–8, LAC; and Beauharnois, Ordonnance entre les habitants de la côte du nord de l'île Jésus, 16 March 1740, Fonds Intendant, vol. 15, C-13590, pp. 287–6, LAC.

19 Murray, Instructions to Walsh, November 1759, JMC, series 3, AC, p. 9 LAC; Murray to Hussey, Commanding the Detachment at Lorette, 20 November 1759, JMC, LAC.

20 James Murray, November 1759, JMC, series 3, C-2225, pp. 6–7, LAC.

21 Murray to Halifax, Quebec, 7 June 1762, reel 2, pp. 27–32, CO. As early as 1762, the Canadian economy experienced a serious deflation in the value of French livres. Even after the Treaty of Paris, the French Crown refused to pay the debt of Canada, which further complicated the matter.

22 Horton, "Gilles Hocquart." Other important monographs on French diplomacy include Hardy, *Judicial Politics in the Old Régime*; and Eccles, *La Société Canadienne sous le régime français*. For the transition to British rule, see White, *Middle Ground*; and Calloway, *Scratch of a Pen*.

23 The disagreements between these factions are well documented, but the grievances laid before Parliament derive from "Charges and Defences of Governor James Murray," JMC, bundle 9, pp. 211–45, LAC.

24 Ibid.

25 Carleton to William Petty, "Despatch of Governor Carleton to the Earl of Shelburne regarding the Administration of English Laws in Canada," 24 December 1767, *DST*, 227.

26 Carleton, "Examination of General Carleton, Governor-General of Canada," *DHC*, 113.

27 Jeffery Amherst, article 34, Extracts from the Articles of Capitulation of Montreal, 8 September 1760, *DHC*, 193.

28 Ibid.

29 Ibid., 194.

30 The maintenance of seigneurial customs after the Conquest is also covered in Fyson, "Quebec Act and the Canadiens," in Furstenberg and Hubert, *Entangling the Quebec Act*, 77–8.

31 Observations made by the surveyors of the highways, 20 November 1765, RCQ, LAC; Mabane, Dunn, Mounier, and Goldstan, Council Chamber, 2 December 1765, RCQ, LAC.

32 Carleton to William Petty, "Despatch of Governor Carleton to the Earl of Shelburne," *DST*, 227.

33 Elie de Beaumont, Target, and Rouche, "Opinions of three Eminent Lawyers of Paris prepared at the Request of the Canadian Authorities, as to the Legality of certain Clauses and Conditions commonly inserted in Titles to Seigniorial Lands," 14 February 1767, *DST*, 218–26.

34 Ibid., 220.

35 Ibid., 219.

36 Ibid.

37 Ibid., 220.

38 Ibid., 221.

39 Ibid.

40 Ibid.

41 Ibid. William Blackstone's *Commentaries on the Laws of England* was originally published in 1765 by the Clarendon Press in Oxford. The Parisian

lawyers used Blackstone's work on English common law as a foundation for their report to Carleton. For a more comprehensive analysis of criminal law reforms and the integration of common law in Quebec, see Fyson, *Magistrates, Police, and People.*

42 Beaumont, Target, and Rouche, "Opinions of three Eminent Lawyers of Paris," DST, 222.

43 Carleton to William Petty, "Despatch of Governor Carleton to the Earl of Shelburne regarding the Administration of English Laws in Canada," 24 December 1767, DST, 227.

44 Ibid.

45 Ibid.

46 Ibid.

47 Ibid.

48 Ibid.

49 Ibid., 228.

50 Ibid., 230.

51 Ibid.

52 Ibid.

53 Ibid.

54 Carleton, "Draft of 'An Ordinance for continuing and confirming the Laws and Customs that prevailed in this Province in the Time of the French Government, concerning the Tenure, Inheritance, and Alienation of Lands,' 24 December 1767, DST, 233.

55 Ibid.

56 Ibid., 234.

57 Willis, "Rethinking Ireland and Assimilation," 174.

58 Many ministers in Parliament also expressed the belief that a unified legal code for the province would ultimately support industry in Quebec. See Burset, "Quebec, Bengal, and Authoritarian Legal Pluralism," 138.

59 Murray, Report of General James Murray on the State of Canada under the French Administration, 5 June 1762, DST, 199. See also Instructions to Governor James Murray, 7 December 1763, DST, 214. This is further discussed in Beaumont, Target, and Rouche, "Opinions of three Eminent Lawyers of Paris," DST, 221.

60 Carleton, "Draft of An Ordinance," DST, 234; and Carleton to William Petty, "Despatch of Governor Carleton to the Earl of Shelburne," DST, 227.

61 Carleton to Charles Townshend, "Despatch of Governor Carleton to the S ecretary of State, giving a Short Outline of the Seigniorial System," 12 April 1768, DST, 236.

62 Ibid.

63 Trudel, *Les débuts du régime seigneurial au Canada*, 175. The French Crown subdivided Canada into three "governments": Quebec, Montreal, and Trois-

Rivières. Each had its own court to oversee parish legal disputes within its jurisdiction.

64 Carleton to Townshend, "Short Outline of the Seigniorial System," 12 April 1768, DST, 236.

65 Ibid.

66 Ibid., 237.

67 Royal Instructions to Governor Carleton permitting the governor-in-council to make further Grants of Land under the Seigniorial Tenure, 2 July 1771, DST, 240.

68 Ibid.

69 On opposition to seigneurial law in Canada, see Thomas Townshend, "Debates in the House of Commons," Thursday, 26 May 1774, DHC, 3. See also Townshend, p. 14; and Mr Dunning, p. 17.

70 Dunning, 26 May 1774, DHC, 17.

71 Townshend, p. 6; Dunning, p. 19; and Edward Thurlow, Attorney General, 26 May 1774, DHC, 28.

72 Lawson, *Imperial Challenge*, ii.

73 Ibid., 25.

74 Townshend, p. 5; Lord North, p. 12; Thurlow, DHC, 27.

75 Fyson, *Magistrates, Police, and People*, 251.

76 Townshend, Thursday, 26 May 1774, DHC, 14.

77 Ibid.

78 Colley, *Britons: Forging the Nation*, 102.

79 Muller, "Redefining Loyal Subjects in 1774," 61.

80 Burset, "Quebec, Bengal, and Authoritarian Legal Pluralism," 137.

81 Carleton, "Examination of General Carleton, Governor-General of Canada," DHC, 113.

82 Ibid., 108.

83 Ibid., 112.

84 Sir Henry Cavendish, "Examination of Frances Maseres," DHC, 133.

85 Ibid.

86 Ibid.

87 Ibid., 135.

88 Cavendish, "Committee Findings, Lord North, Wednesday, June 8," DHC, 244.

89 Scott, *Moral Economy of the Peasant*, 167.

90 Breen, *Marketplace of Revolution*, xv.

91 Green, *Constitutional Origins of the American Revolution*, 160.

92 Ibid., 161.

93 Dickinson, "Aux Habitants de la Province de Québec," 4.

94 Ibid., 5–6.

95 Ibid., 6–7.

96 Ibid., 13–14.

97 Baby et al., *Journal of François Baby*, xxxii.

98 Breen, *American Insurgents*, 275–6.

99 McConville, *King's Three Faces.*

100 Carleton to Dartmouth, 7 June 1775, Great Britain, Colonial Office, Canada, Original Correspondence, Quebec Co42, reel 34, pp. 142–5, the David Library of the American Revolution, Washington's Crossing, PA (hereafter CO).

101 Ibid.

102 Ibid.

103 Ibid.

104 Carleton, "A Proclamation," 15 June 1775, *Québec Gazette.*

105 Carleton, "A tous les Capitaines et autres Officers commandans les Milices dans la Province de Québec, &c.," 19 October 1775, *Québec Gazette.* This appears to be Carleton's first order of corvée of the American Revolution. Both collections of Carleton's correspondence in the Colonial Office Papers and the Haldimand Papers indicate that, prior to this date, Carleton expected the "lower sort," "peasantry," or "habitants" to enrol in the armed militia.

106 Carleton, "A tous les Capitaines et autres Officers commandans les Milices dans la Province de Québec, &c.," 19 October 1775, *Québec Gazette.* Guerets meant to plough the unseeded land.

107 Carleton, "A tous les Capitaines et autres Officers commandans les Milices dans la Province de Québec, &c.," 19 October 1775, *Québec Gazette.* Carleton specifically issues an order to put the "batimens," meaning the community's buildings, in a wintering state.

108 This is supported by a letter written by Carleton to Dartmouth, in which he describes the movements of the Continental Army and the desperation of the combined British and loyal Canadian forces. See Carleton to Dartmouth, 5 November 1775, pp. 222–3, CO.

109 Carleton to Dartmouth, 15 April 1775, CO.

110 Hancock, "Lettre Addressée Aux Habitants Opprimés de la Province de Québec, De la part du Congress General de l'Amerique Septentrionale, tenu a Philadelphie," 29 May 1775, p. 180, CO.

111 Ibid.

112 Serulnikov, *Subverting Colonial Authority*, 137.

113 Ibid., 139.

114 Ibid., 140.

115 Serulnikov, *Revolution in the Andes*, 33.

116 Francis Maséres, "A Contemporary Account of the Disorders," *DST*, 201.

117 Baby, Cap Santé, 15 June 1776, in Baby et al., *Journal of Francois Baby* (hereafter *Baby Journal*), 29.

118 Baby, For St Féréol, Sunday, 26 May 1776, *Baby Journal*, 11.

119 Baby, St Laurent-Ile D'Orléans, Thursday, 20 May 1776, *Baby Journal*, 21.

120 Ibid., 29.

121 Carleton to Dartmouth, 7 June 1775, pp. 142–5, CO.

122 Berthier-en-Haut was a small seigneurie immediately south of Sorel in the district of Three Rivers.

123 Francis Maséres, "A Contemporary Account of the Disorders connected with the Attempt to enforce the Feudal Obligation of Military Service in the Province of Quebec during the American Invasion of 1775," DST, 201.

124 Baby, Pointé aux Trembles, 4 June 1776, 26, and St Vallier, 8 July 1776, *Baby Journal*, 75.

125 The Royal Emigrants were a provincial regiment of British soldiers composed of men who had immigrated to Quebec. Throughout the war, the Emigrants helped Carleton organize militia duty. In 1777, the officers of the Royal Emigrants gained control over the Transport by Corvée at Fort Ticonderoga. See Baby, Pointe aux Trembles, Tuesday, 4 June 1776, *Baby Journal*, 27.

126 Baby, St Pierre-D'Orleans, Thursday, 30 May 1776, *Baby Journal*, 21.

127 Ibid.

128 Baby, St Vallier, 8 July 1776, *Baby Journal*, 75.

129 Ibid.

130 Badeaux, *Invasion of Canada by the Americans*, 25.

131 Ibid., 8–9.

132 Ibid., 9.

133 Ibid.

134 Ibid., 11.

135 Ibid., 12.

136 Maseres, "A Contemporary Account of the Disorders connected with the Attempt to enforce the Feudal Obligation of Military Service in the Province of Quebec during the American Invasion," DST, 244.

137 Ibid., 245.

138 Baby, Gentilly, 15 June 1775, 47; Bécancour, *Baby Journal*, 42.

139 Baby, St Foye, 2 June 1776, 24; Pointe Lévy, 5 July 1776, 65, *Baby Journal*. Fascines are bundles of sticks woven together and used for eighteenth-century military fortifications.

140 Baby, St Henry, 24 to 25 June, *Baby Journal*, 57. A redoubt is a small, earthenwork defensive structure.

141 For wheat, see Baby, St Vallier, 8 July 1776, 75; and St Roch, 13 July 1776, 101. For flour, see St Nicholas, 19 June 1776, 54. For various other provisions, see Cap Santé, 5 June 1776, 29, St Anne, 7 June 34, Batiscant, 7 June 1776, 36; and St Anne, 13 July 1776, 105. All in *Baby Journal*.

142 Several parishes built signal fires for corvée duty, Baby, St Vallier, 8 July 1776, 75; Berthier, 8 July 1776, 79; L'Islet, 12 July 1776, 97; and Rivière Ouelle, 14 July 1776, 109. All in *Baby Journal*.

143 The duration of travel is taken from various entries in the *Baby Journal*, specifically, their first stop in Vielle Lorette on Wednesday, 22 May 1776, 3, and

their last stop at St Michel on 18 July, 116. The biographies of the three commissaries derive from Michael P. Gabriel's edited volume, *Quebec during the American Invasion, 1775–6*, which serves as the introduction to the *Baby Journal*.

144 This represents the majority of the entries in the *Baby Journal*. The commissaries did, however, make several inspections at 3:00 p.m. and 7:00 p.m.

145 Baby, Chateau Riche, Sunday, 26 May 1776, *Baby Journal*, 10.

146 Baby, Ste. Anne, Friday, 7 June 1776, *Baby Journal*, 34.

147 Baby, Les Grondines, Thursday, 6 June 1776, *Baby Journal*, 34.

148 Baby, Return to Chateau Riche, Tuesday, 28 May 1776, *Baby Journal*, 14.

149 Silverblatt, *Modern Inquisitions*, 82.

CHAPTER FIVE

1 Burgoyne, "Memorandum and Observations," 201.

2 Burgoyne to Lord George Germain, Camp upon the River Bouquet, 22 June 1777, in Government of Canada, *A History of the Organization, Development, and Services of the Military and Naval Forces of Canada from the Peace of Paris in 1763 to the Present Time* (hereafter CMD), 224.

3 Ibid.

4 Burgoyne, "Narrative," in Burgoyne, *State of the Expedition*, 7.

5 Ibid. 7. Evidence suggests that eight hundred to one thousand corvée labourers operated in rotations during the campaign. Burgoyne to Carleton, 26 May 1777, CMD, 212; Carleton to Cramahé, Montreal, 9 June 1777, reel 15, p. 124, HP; Phillips to Carleton, St Jean, 17 June 1777, reel 15, p. 127, HP.

6 Brewer, *Sinews of Power*, 176.

7 For the legal tradition of *corvée militaire*, see Desloges, "La corvée militaire à Québec au XVIIIe siècle," 333–56; and Dechêne, *Le Peuple*.

8 The first appearance of this is in Carleton to Cramahé, Quebec, 25 July 1776, reel 15, doc. 98, HP.

9 Carleton to Germain, Chambly, 8 July 1776, CMD, 179. Additionally, Burgoyne issued a general order that the road be "mended." See Burgoyne to Carleton, 18 June 1776, reel 15, HP.

10 E. Foy to Simon Fraser, Montreal, 24 June 1776, reel 15, p. 6, HP.

11 Carleton to Fraser, Varennes, 17 June 1776, reel 15, p. 5, HP.

12 Carleton to Cramahé, Quebec, 25 July 1776, reel 15, doc. 98, HP.

13 Ibid.

14 Ibid.

15 Ibid.

16 Carleton to Monsieur Tonnancour, 3 July 1776, Chambly, p. 15 HP.

17 His request comes from a number of sources, specifically, Carleton to Cramahé, 1 July 1776, 14; Carleton to Tonnancour, 1 July 1776, docs. 45 and 46 in reel 15, p. 14, HP. See also Carleton to Prestre de Lachine, 15 July 1776, reel 15, doc. 65, p. 18, HP.

18 Carleton to Monsieur du Fie, Colonel des Milices, 25 September 1776, Chamblie, reel 15, doc., 175, HP.
19 John Burgoyne, "Memorandum and Observations," 201.
20 Van Buskirk, Generous Enemies, 21–2.
21 Ibid., 201.
22 Ibid.
23 Ibid., 197.
24 Carleton, "Article I," in the *Ordinance of Regulating the Militia of the Province of Quebec, and rendering it of more general utility, towards the preservation and security thereof*, printed in the *Quebec Gazette*, 3 April 1777.
25 Carleton, "Memorandum on the Militia of the Province," *CMD*, 422.
26 Ibid.
27 Ibid.
28 Ibid.
29 Ibid.
30 Carleton, "Ordinance of Regulating the Militia of the Province of Quebec, and rendering it of more general utility, towards the preservation and security thereof," in *Quebec Gazette*, 3 April 1777.
31 Burgoyne to Carleton, May 26, 1777, Colonial Office Records, series Q. vol. 13, p. 212, LAC.
32 Ibid.
33 Burgoyne, "Memorandum and Observations," 201.
34 Burgoyne to Carleton, 26 May 1777, *CMD*, 212.
35 Burgoyne to Carleton, 26 May 1777, Colonial Office Records, series Q. vol. 13, p. 212. LAC.
36 Ibid.
37 Ibid.
38 Carleton to Burgoyne, Quebec, 29 May 1777, *CMD*, 219–20.
39 Ibid., 220.
40 From May 1777 onwards, the groups of labourers were collectively referred to as "the corvée" or "the corvées." Under the French, the squads of habitants fulfilling corvée were never grouped together in such a manner, nor were they referred to as a proper noun. Indeed, this seems unique to the British Army during the American Revolution.
41 Burgoyne to Germain, Camp upon River Bouquet near Lake Champlain, 22 June 1777, *CMD*, 224.
42 Carleton to Cramahé, Montreal, 16 June 1777, reel 15, p. 126 HP; and Phillips to Carleton, St Jean, 17 June 1777, reel 15, p. 127. HP.
43 Carleton, appointment of commissaries of transport, 15 April 1777, reel 15, docs. 350–2, HP.
44 Carleton to Burgoyne, St Jean, 13 June 1777, reel 15, p. 126. HP.
45 Ibid.
46 Carleton to Burgoyne, 2 July 1777, reel 15, doc. 466, HP.

47 Ibid.
48 Carleton to McLean, 10 July 1777, reel 15, p. 138, HP.
49 Carleton, Montreal, 18 June 1777, *CMD*, 223.
50 On destination of the corvée and the number of rations allotted to them, see Carleton to McLean, 10 July 1777, reel 15, p. 138, HP. On the types of food they received, see "A List of Ships with their Armament to carry Provisions to Canada for the Use of His Majesty's Forces under the Command of His Excellency Sir Guy Carleton," mss. 21687-92, 21687, HP.
51 Carleton to Phillips, 12 May 1777, *CMD*, 212.
52 The French method of using the regional parishes for corvée derives from Beauharnois, Extrait de Registres Tenus au Bureau du Controle de la Marine a Québec, 12 August 1745, Archives des Colonies, C11A, vol. 84, pp. 218–21, LAC; Procés-verbal de la première assemblée des principaux officiers, négociants et habitants de Québec au sujet de l'enceinte, 26 July 1746, AC, C11A, vol. 85, p. 76, LAC.
53 Carleton to Burgoyne, St Jean, 13 June 1777, reel 15, p. 126, HP.
54 For Quebec, see Carleton to Cramahé, Montreal, 9 June 1777, reel 15, p. 124, HP; for Montreal, Phillips to Carleton, St Jean, 17 June 1777, reel 15, p. 127, HP; and Trois-Rivières, Carleton to Burgoyne, 16 August 1777, reel 15, doc. 534. HP.
55 Burgoyne to Carleton, 26 June 1777, reel 15, p. 132, HP.
56 Cramahé to Carleton, 16 June 1777, reel 15, p. 126, HP.
57 Carleton to Phillips, 17 June 1777, reel 15, p. 127, HP.
58 *Ordinance of Regulating the Militia of the Province of Quebec, and rendering it of more general utility, towards the preservation and security thereof*, printed in *Quebec Gazette*, 3 April 1777.
59 On horses, see Burgoyne to Carleton, 26 May 1777 *CMD*, 218; and Carleton to Burgoyne, 29 May 1777, *CMD*, 220.
60 Burgoyne, "Memorandum and Observations," 201.
61 Carleton to McLean, 10 July 1777, reel 15, p. 138. HP.
62 Ibid.
63 Ibid.
64 Hadden, *Orderly Book of James Murray Hadden*, 189.
65 Ibid.
66 Under the French, the *corvée de harnois* forced habitants to provide their carriages and horse teams primarily for fortification construction in Montreal and Quebec City.
67 Mackenzy to Carleton, 23 June 1777, reel 15, HP.
68 Carleton to Burgoyne, 26 June 1777, reel 15, doc. 451, HP.
69 McLean, 13 October 1777, reel 15, p. 19, HP.
70 The Memorial of the Merchants and others of the City of Montreal, 20 November 1778, reel 16, pp. 56–60, HP.
71 Hadden, *Journal of Captain James Murray Hadden*.

72 Burgoyne, "Narrative," in Burgoyne, *State of the Expedition*, 7.

73 Carleton, "Article I: An Ordinance for repairing roads and amending the public highways and bridges in the province of Quebec," *Quebec Gazette*, Thursday, 17 April 1777.

74 Carleton, "Article III: An Ordinance for repairing roads," *Quebec Gazette*, Thursday, 17 April 1777.

75 Carleton, "Article VII: An Ordinance for repairing roads," *Quebec Gazette*, Thursday, 17 April 1777.

76 Carleton, "Article V: An Ordinance for repairing roads," *Quebec Gazette*, Thursday, 17 April 1777.

77 Carleton, "Article I" and "Article XII: An Ordinance for repairing roads," *Quebec Gazette*, Thursday, 17 April 1777.

78 Carleton, "Article XVII: An Ordinance for repairing roads," *Quebec Gazette*, Thursday, 17 April 1777.

79 Carleton, "Article VIII: An Ordinance for repairing roads," *Quebec Gazette*, Thursday, 17 April 1777.

80 Ibid.

81 William Phillips to Carleton, St Jean, 17 June 1777, CMD, 222.

82 Kingston, "Examined by Other Members of the Committee and by General Burgoyne occasionally," in Burgoyne, *State of the Expedition*, 113.

83 On the number of men within a batteaux, see General Orders, *Journal of Captain James Murray Hadden*, Thompson Pell Research Center, Fort Ticonderoga, Ticonderoga, New York. On the supplies Burgoyne ordered to be stored in the bateaux, see Orderly Book of the 47th Regiment Grenadier Company, Major Acland's Battalion, Sunday, River Sable Lake Champlain, Brigade Orders; Tuesday, Camp at River Sable, 10 June 1777, Brigade Orders and After Brigade Orders; and Tuesday, Camp at River Bouquet, 17 June 1777, Brigade Orders.

84 Hadden, 17 July 1777, *Journal of Captain James Murray Hadden*, Thompson Pell Research Center, Fort Ticonderoga, Ticonderoga, New York. Even though this entry appears in 1776, there is no documentation that suggests that either format or process of portaging a bateau at St Jean changed within the year.

85 Riedesel mentions that the army constructed "magazines" once it reached Crown Point and that "transport ships" unloaded goods and ammunition from Saint-Jean. Once the army unloaded the supplies, the vessels "returned to St Jean to reload." The dates the army camped at Crown Point match the dates that the corvée would have been at Saint-Jean loading supplies. Riedesel, *Memoirs*, 110.

86 Carleton to Germain, 10 July 1777, reel 15, p. 187, HP.

87 This is the first mention of the Canadians in the orderly book of the 62nd Regiment while garrisoning at Fort Ticonderoga. See Orderly Book of the 62nd Regiment of Foot, transcript by Eric Schnizter, Wesleyan University

Library. The number of labourers at the fort, four hundred men, comes from a later document, Carleton to Tonnancour, 11 August 1777, reel 15, doc. 529, p. 160, HP.

88 On 24 July 1777, Major Phillips requested that St Dupré leave the province of Quebec and manage the corvée with Burgoyne. Carleton declined, stating that Dupré had duties to attend to in Quebec, and suggested that Dambourgess command the Canadian workers. See Carleton to Phillips, 24 July 1777, reel 15, doc. 511, HP.

89 Money, "Captain Money called in and examined by General Burgoyne," in Burgoyne, *State of the Expedition*, 56.

90 Scott, *Weapons of the Weak*, 29.

91 Ibid., 38.

92 Burgoyne to Germain, Camp upon the river Bouquet near Lake Champlain, 22 June 1777, *CMD*, 224.

93 Ibid.

94 Ibid.

95 Phillips to Carleton, St Jean, 17 June 1777, *CMD*, 222.

96 Carleton to Burgoyne, Quebec, 26 June 1777, reel 15, p. 132, HP.

97 Ibid.

98 Ibid.

99 Powell to Carleton, 5 October 1777, *CMD*, 234.

100 Ibid.

101 Of the five hundred labourers who left Quebec, between 150 and 250 corvée ended up with Burgoyne. The number of labourers he had at Saratoga is unknown.

102 Digby, *British Invasion from the North*, 304.

103 Longueuil to Carleton, 26 September 1777, reel 15, doc., 600, HP.

104 Ibid.

105 Ibid.

106 Powel to Carleton, 29 September 1777, reel 15, pp. 11–12, HP.

107 Cramahé to Carleton, St Jean, 3 October 1777, reel 15, p. 16, HP.

108 The number of Canadian corvée men imprisoned comes from Thomas Carleton to Haldimand, 1 August 1780, Chambly, reel 61, pp. 273–5. HP. The recollection of the Acadian bateaux men derives from a return of prisoners dated 7 September 1778, reel 61, pp. 3–4. HP.

109 "A return of prisoners," 7 September 1778, reel 61, pp. 3–4, HP.

110 "Articles of Convention between Lieutenant General Burgoyne and Major General Gates," in O'Callaghan, *Orderly Book of Lieut. Gen. John Burgoyne*, 147.

111 Lutwidge to Carleton, Crown Point, 5 November 1777, *CMD*, 411–12. It is unclear whether any corvée remained at Fort Ticonderoga by this point. The letter, however, specifies that the army abandoned Fort Ticonderoga, thus any corvée that remained would have left with the army as well.

CHAPTER SIX

1 Return of Prisoners, 17 September 1778, reel 61, mss. 21792-3, p. 3, HP.

2 Ibid.

3 Powell to Carleton, 5 October 1777, *CMD*.

4 Hodson, *Acadian Diaspora*. On the Acadian diaspora, see also Plank, *Unsettled Conquest*.

5 The "Return of Prisoners" includes a brief biography of Belliveau and White, including the seigneurie from which they were mustered during the American Revolution. See Return of Prisoners, 17 September 1778, reel 61, mss. 21792-3, p. 3. HP.

6 Carleton to Germain, 10 July 1777, HP.

7 Powell to Carleton, 5 October 1777, *CMD*.

8 Return of Prisoners, 17 September 1778, mss. 21792-3, reel 61, p. 3, HP.

9 Ibid.

10 Ibid.

11 The Memorial of the Merchants and others of the City of Montreal, 20 November 1778, reel 16, pp. 56–60, HP.

12 Haldimand's emphasis on supplying the Upper Posts derives from a number of documents, including Thomas Carleton to Haldimand, 10 December 1778, reel 96, pp. 41–2, HP; Thomas Carleton to Haldimand, 20 December 1778, reel 96, pp. 45–6, HP; and Haldimand to Col. Carleton, 21 April 1779, reel 96, p. 58, HP.

13 No orders for corvée outside of the province of Quebec appear in Haldimand's extensive collection of papers related to the mobilization of French Canadian labour.

14 Longueuil to Carleton, 26 September 1777, reel 15, HP.

15 On Haldimand's job to fortify the province, see Knox to Haldimand, 10 March 1778, reel 16, pp. 21–5, HP. His orders are reiterated one year later in Germain to Haldimand, 19 April 1779, Whitehall, reel 16, pp. 119–23, HP.

16 Germain to Haldimand, 16 April 1778, Whitehall, reel 16, pp. 28–30, HP.

17 Ibid.

18 McDonnell, "Maintaining a Balance of Power," 78. For more on British motivations in the Upper Posts after the Seven Years' War, see Widder "After the Conquest," 45–6.

19 More, "Severity of This Service," 40.

20 Ibid., 39–41.

21 Taylor, *Divided Ground*, 9.

22 Ibid.

23 Haldimand, "Sketch of the Military State of the Military State of the Province of Quebec," 25 July1778, Quebec, reel, 16, mss. 21701, p. 1, HP.

24 Ibid., 2.

25 Ibid.

26 Ibid., 4.

27 Ibid., 6.

28 Knox to Haldimand, 10 March 1778, reel 16, pp. 21–5, HP.

29 Commission for François Baby, Esq. by Frederick Haldimand, General, 23 January 1779, reel 37, p. 74. HP.

30 Ibid.

31 Commission for St George Dupré, by Frederick Haldimand, General, 23 January 1779, reel 37, p. 73, HP; Commission for Godfrey Tonnancour, by Frederick Haldimand, General, 23 January 1779, reel 37, p. 72, HP.

32 A number of documents discuss the mobilization process and the role of the commissary of transport. In particular, see Foy to St George Dupré, Sorel, 1 September 1778, reel 23, p. 22 HP; and Foy to Captain Law, 24 September 1778, reel 23, pp. 41–2. HP.

33 Account of Payment of Corvée for transporting Artillery Stores from Lachine to Carleton Island, 15 July 1779, reel 83, p. 152, HP.

34 Ibid.

35 Captain Edward Foy worked with the captains of the militia and commissaries of transport by corvée until his death in April 1779. Captain Robert Matthews stepped into that role following Foy's death and organized correspondence between those groups and the governor through the remainder of the war.

36 Colonel Thomas Carleton emerged as the point of contact for corvée working with bateaux destined for the Upper Posts. He closely communicated with Haldimand and Matthews on labour policies and the challenges of mobilizing corvée.

37 The Office of the Grand Voyer remained in place but only issued six orders from 1777 and 1780. For Haldimand, the priority of corvée in the district of Montreal was the Upper Posts supply line, and in Trois-Rivières the construction of the Sorel fortifications. This also reflects a shift in transportation as habitants transported most provisions, ammunition, and supplies via bateaux. Road work and maintenance, however, did continue through the war, primarily around Quebec City.

38 Twiss to Haldimand, 27 September 1778, Sorel, reel 76, pp. 61–2, HP.

39 Account of Payment of Corvée for transporting Artillery Stores from Lachine to Carleton Island, 15 July 1779, reel 83, p. 152, HP.

40 Twiss to Haldimand, 22 November 1779, Sorel, reel 76, mss. 21814, p. 165, HP.

41 Germain to Haldimand, 16 April 1778, Whitehall, reel 16, pp. 28–30, HP.

42 Carleton to Powell, 24 August 1776, Chambly, reel 15, p. 28, HP.

43 Twiss to Haldimand, 9 November 1778, reel 76, pp. 85–7, HP.

44 Foy to the Captains of the Militia, or Officers Commanding the Parishes, 8 September 1778, Sorel, reel 23, HP.

45 Ibid.; and E. Foy to the Captains of the Militia, or Officers Commanding the Parishes (Requisition of Corvée de harnois), 11 September 1778, reel 23, pp. 15–16, HP.

46 Foy to the Captains of the Militia, or Officers Commanding the Parishes, 8 September 1778, Sorel, reel 23, HP.
47 Foy to the Captains of the Militia, or Officers Commanding the Parishes (Requisition of Corvée de harnois), 11 September 1778, reel 23, pp. 15–16, HP.
48 Ibid.
49 Twiss to Haldimand, 27 September 1778, Sorel, reel 76, pp. 61–2, HP.
50 Ibid.
51 Ibid.
52 William Twiss to Haldimand, 9 November 1778, reel 76, pp. 85–7, HP.
53 Ibid.
54 Ibid.
55 Ibid.
56 Haldimand to Powell, 3 June 1779, Quebec, reel 35, p. 54, HP.
57 Ibid.
58 Ibid.
59 Ibid.
60 St Leger to Haldimand, 29 July 1779, Sorel, reel 64, pp. 32–3, HP.
61 Matthews to Twiss, Quebec, 6 January 1780, reel 76, p. 187, HP.
62 Thomas Carleton to Haldimand, Montreal, 3 October 1778, reel 96, mss. 21848, p. 15, HP.
63 Ibid., 27.
64 Longueuil to Carleton, 26 September 1777, reel 15, HP.
65 Twiss to Haldimand, 22 November 1779, Sorel, reel 76, mss. 21814, p. 165, HP.
66 Matthews to Gamble, 18 May 1782, reel 96, mss. 21848, p. 231, HP.
67 The grand voyer, Jean-Baptiste Magnan, issued only five orders from 1778 to 1780 on the general upkeep of roads.
68 Carleton, "An Ordinance for repairing roads and amending the public highways and bridges in the province of Quebec," *Quebec Gazette*, Thursday, 17 April 1777.
69 Procès-verbal de Jean-Baptiste Magnan, Trace un chemin de dix-huit pieds largeur dans le seigneurie de Saint-Etienne, 24 August 1778, Cahier 7, Fonds Grand Voyer, p. 170, BANQ.
70 Procès-verbal de Jean-Baptiste Magnan, Fixe le chemin de sortie de la concession de Pintendre, dans la seigneurie de Lauzon, 31 July 1779, Cahier 6, 211, and Procès-verbal de Jean-Baptiste Magnan, Ordonne que le chemin dans la banlieue de Québec, 19 June 1780, Cahier 7, Fonds Grand Voyer, p. 170, BANQ.
71 Carleton to Haldimand, Montreal, 24 September 1778, pp. 9–10, HP.
72 Account of Payment of Corvée for transporting Artillery Stores from Lachine to Carleton Island, 15 July 1779, Reel 83, p. 152, HP.
73 Carleton to Haldimand, 10 December 1778, reel 96, pp. 41–2, HP.
74 Ibid.
75 Ibid.
76 Ibid., 45–6.

77 Ibid., 47–50.

78 Ibid.

79 Haldimand to Carleton, 21 April 1779, reel 96, p. 58, HP.

80 Shaw, Account of Payment of Corvée for transporting Artillery Stores from Lachine to Carleton Island, filed on 15 July 1779, Montreal, reel 77, p. 152, HP. See also Shaw, Account of Cash disbursed for Corvée of Artillery Stores from the 1 March to 31 July 1779, filed on 2 August 1779, reel 77, p. 154, HP.

81 Carleton to Haldimand, 27 December 1778, reel 96, pp. 47–50, HP.

82 Carleton to Haldimand, 27 November 1778, reel 96, p. 29, HP. See also Carleton to Haldimand, 29 April 1779, Montreal, reel 96, p. 60, HP.

83 Carleton to Haldimand, 29 April 1779, Montreal, reel 96, p. 60, HP.

84 Account of Payment of Corvée for transporting Artillery Stores from Lachine to Carleton Island, filed on 15 July 1779, Montreal, reel 77, p. 152, HP.

85 Carleton to Haldimand, 5 November 1778, reel 96, p. 35, HP.

86 Macbean, Account of Items Laden in Five Bateaux, 18 June 1779, Sorel, reel 77, pp. 150–1, HP.

87 Ibid.

88 Ibid.

89 All information comes from Shaw, Account of Payment of Corvée for transporting Artillery Stores from Lachine to Carleton Island, filed on 15 July 1779, Montreal, reel 77, p. 152. HP. See also Alexander Shaw, Account of Cash disbursed for Corvée of Artillery Stores from 1 March to 31 July 1779, filed on 2 August 1779, reel 77, p. 154, HP.

90 Account of Payment of Corvée for transporting Artillery Stores from Lachine to Carleton Island, filed on 15 July 1779, Montreal, reel 77, p. 152, HP.

91 Haldimand to Robinson, Quebec, 1 July 1779, reel 54, mss. 21780, p. 46, HP.

92 In addition to work orders listed in the Fonds Grand Voyer (such as 24 août, Procès verbal de Jean-Baptiste Magnan qui trace un chemin dans la seigneurie de Saint-Etienne; and 16 juillet 1779, Procès verbal de Jean-Baptiste Magnan qui fixe une route dans l'arrière-fief Beaugin) there are several civilian work orders that appear in the Haldimand Papers, including 22 December 1780, Haldimand to Tonnancour, Chemin du Roi, reel 86; and 26 June 1781, Haldimand to Tonnancour, reel 86, HP.

93 Carleton, "Ordinance of Regulating the Militia of the Province of Quebec, and rendering it of more general utility, towards the preservation and security thereof," *Quebec Gazette*, 3 April 1777.

94 Carleton to Haldimand, 27 December 1778, reel 96, pp. 47–50. HP.

95 Maurer to Genevay, 16 April 1781, Montreal, reel 96, pp. 144–5, HP.

96 Powell, 6 January 1781, Montreal, reel 96, p. 134, HP; Maurer to Genevay, 16 April 1781, Montreal, reel 96, pp. 144–5, HP.

97 For example, in 1777, Carleton conscripted 250 habitants into service to replace deserters at Saint-Jean, Carleton to Burgoyne, Quebec, 26 June 1777, p. 225, HP.

98 Haldimand to Thomas Carleton, May 1781, Quebec, reel 96, p. 161, HP.
99 The first case of desertion appears in a letter from Carleton to Haldimand, 17 September 1778, Montreal, reel 96, p. 3, HP.
100 Carleton to Haldimand, 9 November 1778, Montreal, reel 96, p. 37, HP.
101 Carleton to Haldimand, 27 December 1778, reel 96, pp. 47–50, HP.
102 Matthews to MacLean, 27 January 1780, Quebec, reel 60, p. 47, HP.
103 Ibid.
104 The demands for labour outside the environs of Montreal can be found in Haldimand to Powell, 12 November 1778, Quebec, reel 35, mss. 21740, pp. 48–9, HP.
105 MacLean to Matthews, 3 January Montreal, reel 59, mss. 21789, p. 30, HP.
106 Haldimand to Powell, 3 June 1779, Quebec, reel 63, mss. 21795, p. 81, HP.
107 Ibid., 79.
108 Matthews to MacLean, 27 January 1780, Quebec, reel 60, p. 47, HP.
109 Haldimand to Carleton, May 1781, Quebec, reel 96, p. 1611, HP.
110 Ibid.
111 Fyson, *Magistrates, Police, and People*, 216.
112 Ibid.
113 Haldimand to Powell, 3 June 1779, Quebec, reel 63, mss. 21795: p. 79, HP.
114 Ibid.
115 St Leger to Haldimand, 29 July 1779, Sorel, reel 64, mss. 21796, pp. 32–3, HP.
116 Powell to Haldimand, 6 January 1781, Montreal, reel 96, p. 134. HP.
117 Haldimand to Carleton, May 1781, Quebec, reel 96, p. 161, HP.
118 Ibid.
119 Maurer to Matthews, 3 June 1782, Montreal, reel 96, mss. 21848, p. 245, HP.
120 Matthews to James Maurer, 6 June 1782, Quebec, reel 96, p. 247, HP.
121 Ibid.
122 Fyson, *Magistrates, Police, and People*, 241.
123 Ibid.
124 Ibid., 267.
125 Ibid.
126 Matthews to Maurer, 6 June 1782, Quebec, reel 96, p. 247, HP.

EPILOGUE

1 Fyson, *Magistrates, Police, and People*, 333.
2 Ibid., 332–3.
3 Baby, Tableau du Prix des Corvées du la Ville, Faubourg, et Banlieue de Montreal, Collection Louis-François Georges Baby, Université de Montréal, Montreal, Quebec.
4 The table clearly indicates that corvée at Lachine continued into 1785, with a breakdown of wages and rations offered to labourers. See Baby, Tableau du Prix des Corvées du la Ville, Faubourg, et Banlieue de Montreal, Collection Louis-François Georges Baby, Université de Montréal, Montreal, Quebec.

5 Baby, "Remarks," (1777–85), Collection Louis-François Georges Baby, Université de Montréal, Montreal, Quebec.
6 More, "Severity of This Service," 129–31.
7 Jean Renaud's first order of corvée comes from Jean Renaud, 22 December 1782, Fonds Grand Voyer, BANQ.
8 Renaud's road and bridge construction initiative extends to early 1794, with his last order on 8 January 1794, found in the Fonds Grand Voyer, BANQ.
9 Renaud, Saint-Laurent, 11 January 1783, Fonds Grand Voyer, Cahier 7, p. 10, BANQ.
10 Renaud, Saint-Joseph a Notre Dame de Agnes, 7 January 1783, Fonds Grand Voyer, Cahier 7, p. 9, BANQ.
11 Renaud, "Rapport de Jean Renaud a M. Genevay secrétaire du gouverneur Haldimand," 7 June 1783, Procés Verbaux des Grand Voyer, Cahier 7, p. 32, BANQ.
12 Gratien Allaire, "Jean Renaud," *Dictionary of Canadian Biography*, vol. 4 (1771–1800), http://www.biographi.ca/en/bio/renaud_jean_4E.html.
13 Renaud, Kamouraska, 7 June 1783, Fonds Grand Voyer, Cahier 7, p. 30, BANQ; and Renaud, Rivière-Ouelle et Sainte-Anne, 7 June 1783, Fonds Grand Voyer, Cahier 7, p. 31, BANQ.
14 Renaud, Ordre de Jean Renaud au capitaine Dionne, de Kamouraska, 7 June 1783, Fonds Grand Voyer, Cahier 7, p. 31, BANQ.
15 Records indicate that the committee heard at least two petitions: one in 1781 and one in 1783. The first is entitled "Petition de habitants de la Prairie au sujet de chemin dans la paroisse," 18 October 1781, RCQ, LAC; the second is Henry Caldwell, "Petition of Henry Caldwell concerning the new road over his land known as Cadet's Farm," 16 December 1783, RG1 E1, vol. 111, RCQ, p. 98, LAC.
16 Records of the committee include just one petition in 1774. They reappear in the archives in 1781.
17 The location of Caldwell's farm is confirmed in Marcel Caya, "Caldwell, Henry," in *Dictionary of Canadian Biography*, vol. 5, http://www.biographi.ca/en/bio/caldwell_henry_5E.html.
18 Caldwell, "Petition of Henry Caldwell concerning the new road over his land known as Cadet's Farm," 16 December 1783, RG1 E1, vol. 111, RCQ, p. 98, LAC.
19 Greer, *Patriots and the People*, 25–6.
20 Greer, *Peasant, Lord, and Merchant*, 129.
21 Greer, *Patriots and the People*, 24.
22 Directorate of History, "Canadian Militia Prior to Confederation," Report No. 6, p. 43, LAC. Corvée labour during the War of 1812 is also briefly discussed in Auger, "French Canadian Participation in the War of 1812," 24.
23 Greer, *Patriots and the People*, 267.
24 Ibid., 275.

25 Baptism Record of Jean Baptiste Lamoureux, 14 Septembre 1669, Montreal (Notre-Dame, Montreal), PRDH acte #40005. See also: Marriage between Jean Baptiste Lamoureux and Marie Gareau Stonge, Boucherville (Ste-Famille), PRDH acte #3837.

26 Baptism record of Adrien Lamoureux, 7 Mai 1671, Boucherville (Ste-Famille), PRDH acte #1978.

27 Ordonnance qui porte que chaque habitant de Boucherville contribuer a reconstruction de l'église, 9 September 1713, Fonds Intendant, C-13588, pp. 235–7, LAC.

28 Bégon, "Ordonnance pour faire les ouvrages de enceinte de la ville de Montreal par corvées," AC, C11A, vol. 34, pp. 328–9v, LAC.

29 Rolles de Boucherville, 21 January 1715, AC, C11A, vol. 34, pp. 340–3, LAC.

30 Ibid.

31 Ibid.

32 As discussed in chapter 1, the Montreal work stoppages derive from Ramezay and Bégon to the Minister, 7 November 1715, AC, C11A, vol. 35, pp. 15–52v, LAC.

33 A number of orders were distributed to habitants of Boucherville to construct a highway through these ranks. See Procès-verbal de Jean-Eustache Lanoullier de Boisclerc, 3–4 July 1733, Cahier 5, p. 63; 4 July 1733, Cahier 5, p. 63; 6 July 1733, Cahier 5, p. 68; 8 July 1733, Cahier 5, p. 70; 9 July 1733, Cahier 5, p, 72. All in Fonds Grand Voyer, BANQ.

34 Louvigny to the Minister, 21 October 1706, Quebec, AC, C11A, vol. 25, LAC.

35 Account of Payment of Corvée for transporting Artillery Stores from Lachine to Carleton Island, 15 July 1779, reel 83, p. 152, HP.

36 Documents attest to the British compensating corvée labour for wages during the War of 1812. See Directorate of History, "Canadian Militia Prior to Confederation," Report No. 6, p. 43, LAC.

37 Carleton to Haldimand, Montreal, 24 September 1778, pp. 9–10, HP.

Bibliography

BIBLIOTHÉQUE ET ARCHIVES NATIONALES DU QUÉBEC

Fonds Grand Voyer
Jurisdiction Royale de Montréal, TL4, series 1
Quebec Gazette, 1774–83

DAVID LIBRARY OF THE AMERICAN REVOLUTION

Great Britain, Colonial Office, Canada, Original Correspondence, Quebec, CO42
Haldimand Papers, microform (original papers held in British Museum)
Mss. 21682-2, Government Papers on Three Rivers and the Ironworks of St Maurice, 1760–67
Mss. 21683-6, Instructions to the Office of Ordnance of Quebec, 1770
Mss. 21687-92, Correspondence of Guy Carleton, Governor of Quebec, 1772–80
Mss. 21697-700, Official Register of Letters of Guy Carleton, Governor of Quebec, 1776–78.
Mss. 21701-3, Orders from the British Government to Haldimand, 1780–79
Mss. 21832-4, Correspondence with Joseph Godefroy de Tonnancour, 1778–84
Mss. 21880-4, Register of Montreal and Quebec *Foy et Homage*, 1771–84

NATIONAL ARCHIVES (BRITAIN)

Great Britain, War Office and Secretary at War, In Letters to 1783
Great Britain, War Office and Secretary at War, Out Letters to 1783
Great Britain, Parliament, British Sessions Papers, 1731–1800

LIBRARY AND ARCHIVES CANADA

Archives des Colonies, série C11A, Correspondance générale, Canada
Archives des Colonies, série C11G, Correspondance générale, Canada
Colonies, série B, Correspondance générale, Canada
Bougainville, Louis Antoine de. *Mémoire de Bougainville sur l'Etat de la Nouvelle France a l'époque de la Guerre de Sept Ans 1757*
James Murray Collection

Fonds du Conseil Souverain de Québec
Fonds de la Famille Ramezay (The Ramezay Family Papers, 1553–1913)
Fonds Intendants, 1626–1760
Fonds de la Seigneurie de Boucherville
Lévis, Lettre du chevalier de Lévis au maréchal duc de Belle-Isle, Collection des manuscripts du maréchal de Lévis.
Reports of the Councils of Quebec relating to Highways, Roads, and Bridges, Submissions to the Highways Committee of the Executive Council by the Grand Voyers, 1765–91, Councils of the Province of Quebec

THOMPSON PELL RESEARCH CENTER, FORT TICONDEROGA

Hadden, James Murray. Journal of Captain James Murray Hadden, vols. 1–2, ms. 7204-5.
O'Callaghan, E.B. ed. *Orderly Book of Lieut. Gen. John Burgoyne from His Entry into the State of New York Until His Surrender at Saratoga, 16 October 1777*. Albany: J. Munsell, 1860.
Orderly Book of the 47th Regiment Grenadier Company, Major Acland's Grenadier Battalion, 7 June 1777 to 3 July 1777. Early American Orderly Books, film no. 42, reel 4.
Orderly Book of the 62nd Regiment of Foot.
Orderly Book of the Royal Regiment of Artillery, 8 May 1776 to 9 June 1777. Lloyd Smith Collection.

UNIVERSITÉ DE MONTRÉAL

Louis-François George Baby Collection, Université de Montréal, Montreal, Canada.
P0058/B Documents Seigneuriaux
P0058/D Obligations et rentes
P0058/J Archives judiciaires
P0058/O Commissions civilizes
P0058/P Documents militaires

PRINTED PRIMARY SOURCES

An Abstract of Those Parts of the Custom of the Viscounty and Provostship of Paris, which were received and practiced in the Province of Quebec, in the Time of the French Government. London: Charles Eyre and William Strahan, 1772.
An Act for making more effectual Provision for the Government of the Province of Quebec in North America, October 7, 1774. Transcribed by Yale Law School, Lillian Goldman Law Library, the Avalon Project: Documents in Law, History, and Diplomacy.
Anbury, Thomas. *Travels through the Interior Parts of America in a Series of Letters, By an Officer*. Vol. 1. London: William Lane, 1789.
Baby, Francois, Gabriel Taschereau, and Jenkin Williams, St Charles. *The Journal*

of Francois Baby, Gabriel Taschereau, and Jenkin Williams. Ed. Michael P. Gabriel, trans. S. Pascale Vergereau-Dewey. East Lansing: Michigan State University Press, 2005.

Badeaux, Jean-Baptiste. *The Invasion of Canada by the Americans, 1775–76*. Ed. Mark R. Anderson, trans. Teresa L. Meadows. Albany: SUNY Press, 2016.

Burgoyne, John. "Memorandum and Observations relative to the Service of Canada submitted to Lord George Germain." In *The Parliamentary Register*, vol. 7. London: T. Bensley, 1802.

– *A State of the Expedition from Canada as Laid Before the House of Common, by Lieutenant General Burgoyne and Verified by Evidence*. London: John Almon, 1780.

Dickinson, John. *Lettre Addressée Aux Habitants de la Province de Quebec*. Philadelphia: Imprint of Fleury Mesplet, 1774.

Digby, William. *The British Invasion from the North, The Campaigns of General Carleton and Burgoyne from Canada, 1776–7, with the Journal of Liuet. William Digby of the 53rd, or Shropshire Regiment of Foot*. Albany: Joel Munsell's Sons, 1887.

Government of Canada. *Debates of the House of Commons in the Year 1774 on the Bill for Making More Provision for the Government of the Province of Quebec*. London: Ridgeway, 1839.

Hadden, James Murray. *Hadden's Journal and Orderly Books: A Journal Kept in Canada and Upon Burgoyne's Campaign in 1776*. Albany: J. Munsell's Sons, 1884.

Historical Section of the General Staff, ed. *A History of the Organization, Development, and Services of the Military and Naval Forces of Canada from the Peace of Paris in 1763 to the Present Time*. Ottawa: Government Printer, 1919.

Lévis, François Gaston de. *Journal des Campagnes du Chevalier de Lévis en Canada de 1756 à 1760*. Montreal: C.O. Beauchemin and Fils, 1889.

Munro, William Bennet, ed. *Documents Relating to the Seigniorial Tenure in Canada, 1598–1854*. Toronto: The Champlain Society, 1908.

"Le Recensement des Gouvernments de Montreal et de Trois-Rivièries." In Rapport de l'Archiviste de la province de Québec, 1936–1937, pp. 1–200, BANQ.

Riedesel, Frederich. *Memoirs, and Letters and Journals of Major General Riedesel during His Residence in America*. Trans. Max Von Eelking. Albany: J. Munsell, 1868.

DATABASES

Programme de Recherche en Démographie Historique (PRDH)

SECONDARY WORKS

Anderson, Fred. *Crucible of War: The Seven Years' War and the Fate of Empire in British North America, 1754–66*. New York: Vintage, 2000.

– *A People's Army: Massachusetts Soldiers and Society in the Seven Years' War*. Chapel Hill: North Carolina University Press, 1984.

Armitage, David. *The Ideological Origins of the British Empire*. New York: Cambridge University Press, 2000.

Auger, Martin F. "French Canadian Participation in the War of 1812: A Social Study of the Voltigeurs Canadiens." *Canadian Military History* 10, no. 3 (2001): 23–41.

Banks, Kenneth J. *Chasing Empire across the Sea: Communications and the State in the French Atlantic, 1713–63*. Montreal and Kingston: McGill-Queen's University Press, 2002.

Baugh, Daniel. *The Global Seven Years' War, 1754–63*. New York: Routledge, 2011.

Balvay, Arnaud. "Les forts du Pays d'en Haut et de Louisiane pendant la guerre de sept ans." In *La Guerre de Sept Ans en Nouvelle France*, ed. Laurent Veyssiere et Bertrand Fonck, 225–36. Quebec: Septentrion, 2012.

Benton, Lauren. *Law and Colonial Cultures: Legal Regimes in World History, 1400–1900*. New York: Cambridge University Press, 2002.

Berlin, Ira, and Phillip D. Morgan, "Labor and the Shaping of Slave Life." In *Cultivation and Culture: Labor and the Shaping of Slave Life in the Americas*, ed. Ira Berlin and Phillip D. Morgan, 1–45. Charlottesville: University of Virginia Press, 1993.

Bessière, Arnaud. "La Domesticité dans la colonie Laurentienne au XVIIe siècle et au début du XVIIIe sièclue (1640–1710)." PhD diss., Université du Québec à Montréal, 2007.

Blais, Christian. "La representation en Nouvelle France." *Bulletin d'histoire politique* 18, no. 1 (2009): 51–75.

Bollettino, Maria Alessandra. "'Of Equal or of More Service': Black Soldiers and the British Empire in the Mid-Eighteenth Century Caribbean." *Slavery and Abolition* 38, no. 3 (2017): 510–33.

Breen, T.H. *American Insurgents, American Patriots: The Revolution of the People*. New York: Hill and Wang, 2010.

– *The Marketplace of Revolution: How Consumer Politics Shaped American Independence*. New York: Oxford University Press, 2004.

Brewer, John. *The Sinews of Power: War, Money, and the English State, 1688–1783*. Cambridge: Harvard University Press, 1988.

Brown, Kathleen. *Good Wives, Nasty Wenches, and Anxious Patriarchs: Gender, Race, and Power in Colonial Virginia*. Chapel Hill: University of North Carolina Press, 1996.

Brunsman, Denver. *The Evil Necessity: British Naval Impressment in the Eighteenth-Century Atlantic World*. Charlottesville: University of Virginia Press, 2013.

Burset, Christian R. "Quebec, Bengal, and the Rise of Authoritarian Legal Pluralism." In *Entangling the Quebec Act: Transnational Contexts, Meanings, and Legacies in North America and the British Empire*, ed. Ollivier Hubert and François Furstenberg, 131–62. Montreal and Kingston: McGill-Queen's University Press, 2020.

Calloway, Colin G. *The Scratch of a Pen: 1763 and the Transformation of North American History*. New York: Oxford University Press, 2007.

Canny, Nicholas. "Atlantic History and Global History." In *Atlantic History: A Critical Appraisal*, ed. Jack P. Greene and Phillip D. Morgan, 317–36. New York: Oxford University Press, 2009.

– The Ideology of Colonization: From Ireland to America." *William and Mary Quarterly* 30, no. 4 (1973): 575–98.

Carp, Benjamin L. *Rebels Rising: Cities and the American Revolution*. New York: Oxford University Press, 2007.

Charbonneau, André, Yvon Desloges, and Marc LaFranc. *Québec the Fortified City: From the 17th to the 19th Century*. Ottawa: Parks Canada, 1982.

Choquette, Leslie. "Center and Periphery in French North America." In *Negotiated Empires: Centers and Peripheries in the Americas*, ed. Christine Daniels and Michael V. Kennedy, 193–206. New York: Routledge, 2002.

– *De Français à paysans: Modernité et tradition dans le peuplement du Canada français*. Paris: Presses de l'Université Paris-Sorbonne, 1997.

Clayton, Andrew R.L., and Frederika J. Teute, *Contact Points: American Frontiers from the Mohawk Valley to the Mississippi, 1750–1830*. Chapel Hill: University of North Carolina Press, 1998.

Colley, Linda. *Britons: Forging the Nation, 1707–1837*. New Haven: Yale University Press, 1992.

Conchon, Anne. *La corvée des grands Chemins au XVIIIe siècle: Économie d'une institution*. Rennes: Presses Universitaires de Rennes, 2016.

Cooper, Afua. *The Enslavement of Africans in Canada*. Ottawa: The Canadian Historical Association, 2022.

Crouch, Christian Ayne. *Nobility Lost: French and Canadian Martial Cultures, Indians, and the End of New France*. Ithaca, NY: Cornell University Press, 2014.

Daniels, Christine, and Michael V. Kennedy, eds. *Negotiated Empires: Centers and Peripheries in the Americas, 1500–1820*. New York: Routledge, 2002.

Dechêne, Louise. *Habitants et marchands de Montréal au XVII siècle*. Paris: Plon, 1974.

– *Le Peuple, l'État et la Guerre au Canada sous le Régime français*. Montreal: Boréal, 2008.

Desloges, Yvon. "La corvée militaire à Québec au XVIIIe siècle." *Social History* 15, no. 30: 333–56.

Dider, Sébastien. "Subdélégués et subdélégations dans l'espace atlantique français: Etude comparative des intendances de Caen, Fort-Royal, Lille, Québec et Rennes (fin XVIIe–fin XVIIIe siècle)." PhD diss., Université de Montréal, 2019.

Dubois, Laurent. "The French Atlantic." In *Atlantic History: A Critical Appraisal*, ed. Jack P. Greene and Phillip Morgan, 137–62. New York: Cambridge University Press, 2009.

Eccles, W.J. *La Société canadienne sous le régime français*. Montreal: Harvest House, 1968.

Elliott, J.H. *Empires of the Atlantic World: Britain and Spain in America, 1492–1830*. New Haven: Yale University Press, 2006.

Ertman, Thomas. *Birth of the Leviathan: Building States and Régimes in Medieval and Early Modern Europe*. New York: Cambridge University Press, 2008.

Fonck, Bertrand, and Laurent Veyssières, eds. *La Guerre de Sept Ans en Nouvelle-France*. Quebec: Septentrion, 2016.

Frégault, Guy. *La civilization de la Nouvelle-France*. Montreal: Pascal, 1944.

Fyson, Donald. *Magistrates, Police, and People: Everyday Criminal Justice in Quebec and Lower Canada, 1764–1837*. Toronto: University of Toronto Press, 2006.

Games, Alison. "Atlantic History: Definitions, Challenges, and Opportunities." *American Historical Review* 111, no. 3 (2006): 741–57.

Genovese, Eugene. *Roll, Jordan, Roll: The World the Slaves Made*. New York: Pantheon, 1974.

Gigi, Arad. "Building an Empire: Slaves, Servants, Soldiers, and the Fortification of the French Caribbean." 8 September 2020, Missouri Southern State University, 51:31. https://www.youtube.com/watch?v=_WXFin2MTEA.

– "The Materiality of Empire: Forts, Labour, and the Colonial States in the French Lesser Antilles, 1661–1776." PhD diss., Florida State University, 2018.

Gould, Eliga. *The Persistence of Empire: British Political Culture in the Age of the American Revolution*. Chapel Hill: North Carolina Press, 2000.

– "Entangled Histories, Entangled Worlds: The English-Speaking Atlantic as a Spanish Periphery." *American Historical Review* 112, no. 3 (2007): 764–86.

Gowas, Alan. *Church Architecture in New France*. Toronto: University of Toronto Press, 1955.

Greene, Jack P. *Peripheries and Center: Constitutional Development in the Extended Policies of the British Empire and the United States, 1607–1788*. New York: W.W. Norton and Company, 1968.

– *The Constitutional Origins of the American Revolution*. New York: Cambridge University Press, 2011.

Greene, Jack P. and Phillip D. Morgan. "The Present State of Atlantic History." In *Atlantic History: A Critical Appraisal*, ed. Jack P. Greene and Phillip D. Morgan, 3–34. New York: Cambridge University Press, 2009.

Greer, Allan. *The Patriots and the People: The Rebellion of 1837 in Rural Lower Canada*. Toronto: University of Toronto Press, 1993.

– *Peasant, Lord, and Merchant: Rural Society in Three Quebec Parishes, 1740–1840*. Toronto: University of Toronto Press, 1985.

– *The People of New France*. Toronto: University of Toronto Press, 1999.

– *Property and Dispossession: Natives, Empires, and Land in Early Modern America*. New York: Cambridge University Press, 2018.

Grenier, Benoît. *Brève histoire du régime seigneurial*. Montreal: Boréal, 2012.

– "Gentilshommes Campagnards de la Nouvelle France, XVIIe–XIXe Siècle: Une Autre Seigneurie Laurentienne?" *French Colonial History* 7 (2006): 21–43.

Grinberg, Martine. *Écrire les coutumes: Les droits seigneuriaux en France.* Paris: Presses Universitaires de France, 2006.

Hamilton, Edward P. *Fort Ticonderoga: Key to a Continent.* Boston: Little, Brown, and Company, 1964.

Hardesty, Jared Ross. *Unfreedom: Slavery and Dependence in Eighteenth-Century Boston.* New York: New York University Press, 2018.

Hardy, J. *Judicial Politics in the Old Régime: The Parlement of Paris during Regency.* Baton Rouge: University of Louisiana Press, 1967.

Hodson, Christopher. *The Acadian Diaspora: An Eighteenth-Century History.* New York: Oxford University Press, 2017.

Horton, Donald J. "Gilles Hocquart, Intendant of New France, 1729–1748." PhD diss., McGill University, 1974.

Hubert, Ollivier, and François Furstenberg, eds. *Entangling the Quebec Act: Transnational Contexts, Meanings, and Legacies in North America and the British Empire.* Montreal and Kingston: McGill-Queen's University Press, 2020.

Imbeault, Sophie, Denis Vaugeois, and Laurent Veyssière, eds. *1763: La traité de Paris bouleverse l'Amérique.* Québec: Septentrion, 2013.

Jetten, Marc. *Enclaves amérindienne, les reductions du Canada, 1637–1701.* Quebec: Septentrion, 1994.

Kruer, Matthew. *Time of Anarchy: Indigenous Power and the Crisis of Colonialism in Early America.* Cambridge: Harvard University Press, 2022.

Laberge, Alain. "Le régime seigneurial après la Conquête: Propriété fonciers à l'époque du traité de Paris (1760–1774)." In *1763: La traité de Paris bouleverse l'Amérique,* ed. Sophie Imbeault, Denis Vaugeois, and Laurent Veyssière, 324–31. Québec: Septentrion, 2013.

Lawson, Phillip. *The Imperial Challenge: Quebec and Britain in the Age of the American Revolution.* Montreal and Kingston: McGill-Queen's University Press, 1994.

Linebaugh, Peter, and Marcus Rediker. *The Many-Headed Hydra: Sailors, Slaves, Commoners and the Hidden History of the Revolutionary Atlantic.* Boston: Beacon Press, 2000.

Little, Ann M. *The Many Captivities of Esther Wheelwright.* New Haven: Yale University Press, 2016.

Lozier, Jean-François. *Flesh Reborn: The Saint Lawrence Valley Mission Settlements through the Seventeenth Century.* Montreal and Kingston: McGill-Queen's University Press, 2018.

MacLeod, Peter D. *Northern Armageddon: The Battle of the Plains of Abraham and the Making of the American Revolution.* New York: Vintage, 2017.

Mauclair, Fabrice. *La justice au village: Justice seigneuriale et société rurale dans le duché-pairie de la Vallière, 1667–1790.* Rennes: Universitaires de Rennes, 2008.

McConville, Brendan. *The King's Three Faces: The Rise and Fall of Royal America, 1688–1776.* Chapel Hill: University of North Carolina Press, 2006.

McDonnell, Michael A. "Maintaining a Balance of Power: Michilimackinac, the Anishinaabe Odawas, and the Anglo-Indian War of 1763." *Early American Studies* vol. 13, no. 1 (2015): 38–79.

McDonough, Katherine L. "Building the Roads: Expertise, Labor, and Politics in Provincial France, 1675–1791." PhD diss., Stanford University, 2013.

Moogk, Peter N. *La Nouvelle France: The Making of French Canada – A Cultural History*. East Lansing: Michigan State University Press, 2000.

More, John David. "'The Severity of This Service: Canadien Inland Mariners in the Early Post-Conquest Era, 1760–1817." PhD diss., Queen's University, 2021.

Morrissey, Robert Michael. *Empire by Collaboration: Indians, Colonists, and Governments in Colonial Illinois Country*. Philadelphia: University of Pennsylvania Press, 2015.

Muller, Hannah Weiss. "'As May Consist with Their Allegiance to His Majesty': Redefining Loyal Subjects in 1774." In *Entangling the Quebec Act: Transnational Contexts, Meanings, and Legacies in North America and the British Empire*, ed. Ollivier Hubert and François Furstenberg, 164–94. Montreal and Kingston: McGill-Queen's University Press, 2020.

Negrin, Hayley. "Native Women Work the Ground: Enslavement and Civility in the Early American Southeast." In *Atlantic Environments and the American South*, ed. Thomas Blake Earl and D. Andrew Johnson, 90–11. Athens: University of Georgia Press, 2020.

Nerich, Laurent. "Le système de défense de la Nouvelle-France à la guerre de la Conquête." In *La Guerre de Sept Ans en Nouvelle-France*, ed. Laurent Veyssière and Bertrand Fonck, 269–90. Quebec: Septentrion, 2012.

Nicolai, Martin L. "A Different Kind of Courage: The French Military and the Canadian Irregular Soldier during the Seven Years' War." *Canadian Historical Review* 70, no. 1 (1989): 53–75.

Pagden, Anthony. *Lords of All the World: Ideologies of Empire in Spain, Britain, and France, 1500–1800*. New Haven: Yale University Press, 1998.

Perrier, Sylvie. *Des enfances protégées: La tutelle des mineurs en France, 17e–18e siècles*. Saint Denis: Universitaires de Vincennes, 1998.

Plank, Geoffrey. *An Unsettled Conquest: The British Campaign against the Peoples of Acadia*. Philadelphia: University of Pennsylvania Press, 2003.

Podruchny, Carolyn. *Making the Voyageur World: Travelers and Traders in the North American Fur Trade*. Lincoln: University of Nebraska Press, 2006.

Rama, Angel. *The Lettered City*. Durham, NC: Duke University Press, 1984.

Robichaud, Léon. "Le pouvoir, les payans et la voirie au Bas-Canada a la fin du XVIIIe siècle." PhD diss., Université McGill, 1989.

– "Relier Québec et Montréal par le Chemin du Roy." *Le revue d'histoire du Québec* (2012): 4–9.

Rockman, Seth. *Scraping By: Wage Labour, Slavery, and Survival in Early Baltimore*. Baltimore: Johns Hopkins University Press, 2008.

Roseberry, William. "Hegemony and the Language of Contention." In *Everyday Forms of State Formation: Revolution and the Negotiation of Rule in Modern Mexico*, ed. Gilbert M. Joseph and Daniel Nugent, 355–66. Durham, NC: Duke University Press.

Rushforth, Brett. "'A Little Flesh We Offer You': The Origins of Indian Slavery in New France." *William and Mary Quarterly* 60, no. 4 (2003): 777–808.

– *Bonds of Alliance: Indigenous and Atlantic Slaveries in New France*. Chapel Hill: University of North Carolina Press, 2014.

Samson, Roch. *The Forges of Saint-Maurice: The Beginnings of the Iron and Steel Industry in Canada, 1730–1883*. Quebec: University of Laval Press, 1998.

Sen, Sudipta. *Uncertain Dominance: The Colonial State and Its Contradictions*. New York: Routledge, 2019.

Scott, James C. *Domination and the Arts of Resistance: Hidden Transcripts*. New Haven: Yale University Press, 1992.

– *The Moral Economy of the Peasant: Rebellion and Subsistence in Southeast Asia*. New Haven: Yale University Press, 1976.

– *Seeing Like a State: How Certain Schemes to Improve the Human Condition Have Failed*. New Haven: Yale University Press, 1999.

– *Weapons of the Weak: Everyday Forms of Peasant Resistance*. New Haven: Yale University Press, 1987.

Scott, S. Morley. "Civil and Military Authority in Canada, 1764–1766." *Canadian Historical Review* 9 (1928): 117–36.

Seed, Patricia. *Ceremonies of Possession in Europe's Conquest of the New World, 1492–1640*. New York: Cambridge University Press, 1995.

Serulnikov, Sergio. *Subverting Colonial Authority: Challenges to Spanish Rule in Eighteenth-Century Southern Andes*. Durham, NC: Duke University, 2003.

– *Revolution in the Andes: The Age of Túpac Amaru*. Durham, NC: Duke University Press, 2013.

Silverblatt, Irene. *Modern Inquisitions: Peru and the Colonial Origins of the Civilized World*. Durham, NC: Duke University Press, 2004.

Spalding, Karen. *Huarochirí: An Andean Society Under Inca and Spanish Rule*. Stanford: Stanford University Press, 1984.

Stanley, George F.G. *Canada's Soldiers: The Military History of an Unmilitary People*. Toronto: Macmillan, 1960.

Stanwood, Owen. *The Empire Reformed: English America in the Age of the Glorious Revolution*. Philadelphia: University of Pennsylvania Press, 2013.

Stone, Lawrence, ed. *An Imperial State at War: Britain from 1689–1815*. New York: Routledge, 1994.

Thompson, E.P. *Customs in Commons*. New York: Penguin Books, 1991.

– "The Moral Economy of the English Crowd in the Eighteenth Century." *Past and Present* 50 (February 1971): 76–136.

Tomczak, Richard. "Corvée Labor and the Habitant 'Spirit of Mutiny' in New France." *Labour/Le Travail* 87 (Spring 2021): 19–48.

– "Corvée Labor and the Politics of Popular Insurrection in Trois-Rivières, 1760–1776." *Journal of Colonialism and Colonial History* 20, no. 1 (2019): 44–54.

Taylor, Alan. *The Divided Ground: Indians, Settlers, and the Northern Borderland of the American Revolution*. New York: Vintage, 2007.

Tilly, Charles. *Coercion, Capital, and European States, AD 990–1992*. Hoboken: Wiley-Blackwell, 1990.

Trudel, Marcel. *Canada's Forgotten Slaves: Two Hundred Years of Bondage*. Trans. George Tombs. Montreal: Véhicule Press, 2013.

– *Les débuts du régime seigneurial au Canada*. Montreal: Corporation des Éditions Fides.

Van Buskirk, Judith L. *Generous Enemies: Patriots and Loyalists in Revolutionary New York*. Philadelphia: University of Pennsylvania Press, 2002.

Ward, Matthew C. "An Army of Servants: The Pennsylvania Regiment during the Seven Years War." *Pennsylvania Magazine of History and Biography* 119, no. 1/2 (1995): 75–93.

White, Richard. *The Middle Ground: Indians, Empires, and Republics in the Great Lakes Region, 1650–1815*. New York: Cambridge University Press.

White, Sophie. *Voices of the Enslaved: Love, Labor, and Longing in French Louisiana*. Chapel Hill: University of North Carolina Press, 2019.

Widder, Keith R. "After the Conquest: Michilimackinac, a Borderland in Transition, 1760–1763." *Michigan Historical Review* vol. 34, no. 1 (2008): 43–61.

Willis, Aaron. "Rethinking Ireland and Assimilation: Quebec, Colonialism, and the Heterogenous Empire." In *Entangling the Quebec Act: Transnational Contexts, Meanings, and Legacies in North America and the British Empire*, ed. Ollivier Hubert and François Furstenberg, 165–94. Montreal and Kingston: McGill-Queen's University Press, 2020.

Wilson, Kathleen. "Introduction: Histories, Empires, Modernities." In *A New Imperial History: Culture, Identity, and Modernity in Britain and the Empire, 1600–1840*. New York: Cambridge University Press, 2004.

– "Rethinking the Colonial State: Gender, Family, and Governmentality in Eighteenth Century British Frontiers." *American Historical Review* 116, no. 5 (2011): 1294–322.

– *The Sense of the People: Politics, Culture, and Imperialism in England, 1715–85*. New York: Cambridge University Press, 1995.

Index